W9-AFQ-715

WINNIPEG'S GREAT WAR

A CITY COMES OF AGE

JIM BLANCHARD

University of Manitoba Press

© Jim Blanchard 2010

University of Manitoba Press
Winnipeg, Manitoba
Canada R3T 2M5

www.umanitoba.ca/uofmpress

Printed in Canada.
Text printed on chlorine-free, 100% post-consumer recycled paper.

All rights reserved. No part of this publication may be reproduced or transmitted in any form or by any means, or stored in a database and retrieval system, without the prior written permission of the University of Manitoba Press, or, in the case of photocopying or any other reprographic copying, a licence from ACCESS COPYRIGHT (Canadian Copyright Licencing Agency) 6 Adelaide Street East, Suite 901, Toronto, Ontario M5C 1H6, www. accesscopyright.ca.

Book and cover design: Doowah Design

Library and Archives Canada Cataloguing in Publication

Blanchard, J. (Jim)
    Winnipeg's Great War : a city comes of age / Jim Blanchard.

Includes index.
ISBN 978-0-88755-721-7

    1. Winnipeg (Man.)—History—20th century. 2. World War, 1914–1918. I. Title.

FC3396.4.B535 2010   971.27'4302   C2010-902854-6

The University of Manitoba Press gratefully acknowledges the financial support for its publication program provided by the Government of Canada through the Canada Book Fund, the Canada Council for the Arts, the Manitoba Department of Culture, Heritage, and Tourism, the Manitoba Arts Council, and the Manitoba Book Publishing Tax Credit.

Mixed Sources
Cert no. SW-COC-001271
© 1996 FSC
FSC

ENVIRONMENTAL BENEFITS STATEMENT
The University of Manitoba Press saved the following resources by printing the pages of this book on chlorine free paper made with 100% post-consumer waste.

TREES	WATER	SOLID WASTE	GREENHOUSE GASES
24 FULLY GROWN	10,781 GALLONS	655 POUNDS	2,238 POUNDS

Calculations based on research by Environmental Defense and the Paper Task Force.
Manufactured at Friesens Corporation

For my children, Pili, Jesse, and Ben

Contents

Chapter 5
1918

Epilogue

Notes

Index

List of Illustrations

Acknowledgements

I am indebted to many people who have helped me during the writing of this book. In Ottawa Deborah Baillie secured a number of documents and photographs for me from the Library and Archives Canada. Many staff at the Archives of Manitoba helped me with my work, and I want to especially thank Chris Kotecki for his guidance in finding sources and Sharon Foley for her generous assistance in finding photos. The staff of the serials department at Winnipeg Public Library brought me many dusty volumes of the *Winnipeg Telegram* to look at and never complained. Louis-Phillipe Bujold of Winnipeg Public Library's Local History Room also provided support, and John Richthammer generously lent me photos and sources from his own collections.

The staff of University of Manitoba Press—Director David Carr, Managing Editor Glenn Bergen, and Marketing Coordinator Cheryl Miki—have been patient and supportive. I am especially indebted to Glenn Bergen for his suggestions and advice.

WINNIPEG'S GREAT WAR

INTRODUCTION

Evidence of war:
— bronze plaques of church
— Rolls of honour, schools
— "Book of the Dead"
— old Photos
— stories?

The Great War, or World War I, as it came to be called once we had a second one, is a time that seems more and more remote as the last veterans—and those who knew their stories—pass away. In the City of Winnipeg evidence that there ever was such a war can be missed in the modern streets. Here and there a war memorial stands largely forgotten. Even on November 11 the ceremonies tend to take place inside in our chilly climate. But, if you look closer, the war is much more in evidence than you might at first have thought. Every church from the period has bronze plaques put up by bereaved parents, there are rolls of honour in the older schools, and in Kelvin High School one can find a little shrine with a book of the dead. Then there are the personal memorabilia preserved by so many families. Old photos, a button or a Sam Brown belt, stories of grandfathers told with shy pride. On the rafters of a building in the Exchange District, renovators find a hand-written memorial created by a man's fellow workers to mark the day and place of his faraway death. In the Wolseley neighbourhood, a family learns that the mysterious iron bars on their basement windows were installed by a man closing up his house before going overseas. So the war is remembered in fragments, not unlike the shells that are still being dug out of farmers' fields in France and Belgium, each one bringing a tiny moment of the conflict to life in the present.

For the people who lived through the war in this city the situation was very different. War was a daily reality, colouring everything,

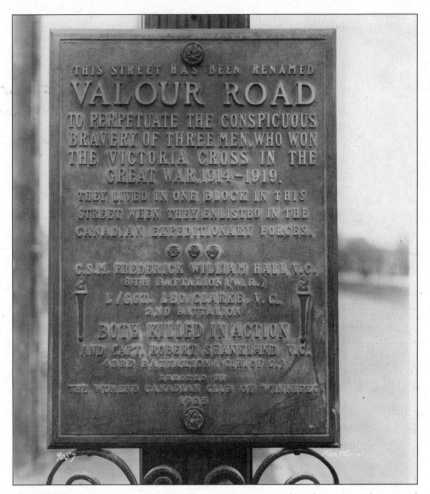

Traces of the Great War can be found across Winnipeg. This plaque on Valour Road recognizes the coincidence of three Victoria Cross winners who grew up on the street.

changing everything, derailing the bouncy confidence that had been the ethos of the place until then. Winnipeggers learned resignation and grim determination from the war, and many were worn down by grief and worry. The young men who marched off to the Great War, cheerful as boys on a summer holiday, either did not come back or returned changed, physically and mentally, by their experiences.

Winnipeg and western Canada responded to the call to arms at the beginning of the war with remarkable enthusiasm. It was a city and a region with more unmarried young men than other parts of the country and, in 1914, many of these men were recent immigrants from Britain. They went home to defend the mother country and their families. Many young Canadian-born men as well as recruits born in other parts of the world joined them.

The people who stayed in Winnipeg also fought, in ways that were essential to the final victory won by the Canadian Corps. They supported the troops overseas, responding to crises with action and donations of vast amounts of money. The city's women donated their time and labour strategically and had a direct impact on the success of the men at the front. The flow of the essential woolen socks, bandages, and "comforts" like cigarettes and newspapers connected the front to the home front in a very immediate way. Many people made real and profound sacrifices, and when victory came they could legitimately feel they had helped to bring it about.

As the war began Winnipeg was the third-largest city in the Dominion, brash and ambitious because of its underdog status in relation to Toronto and Montreal. The City of Winnipeg in 1914 had a population of between 136,000, the number recorded in the 1911 census, and 163,000, the number given in the special western Canadian census of 1916. In that period, Winnipeg was dominated by its Anglo-Canadian elite, who were very much in control of the city. Although their offices and businesses were still located downtown, they had begun to move further away from the centre of the city in the years around 1914, and many lived in homes on the south side of the Assiniboine River or on Armstrong's Point, a secluded suburb enclosed by the river on three sides. More modest middle-class districts existed between Portage and Broadway avenues, and stretched west of Colony Street along both sides of Portage and along the streets that lay on the edges of the more expensive districts south of the river. North of the Canadian Pacific Railway (CPR) yards lay a mixed area of very poor streets with crowded neighborhoods of recent immigrants and, close to the Red River, streets with comfortable middle-class homes.

The city centre was a densely packed retail and commercial district. Dozens of stores crowded Portage Avenue and Main Street competing for customers with large establishments owned by Eaton's and the

Hudson's Bay Company. Office buildings housed real estate, insurance, and trust and loan companies, along with the lawyers and other professionals who supported Winnipeg's huge financial industry.

The area around the Grain Exchange on Lombard Avenue was home to the western headquarters of many national banks, the most palatial being the Bank of Montreal and the Bank of Commerce, modelled on the St. James Street branches of those banks in Montreal. Winnipeg's own national bank, the Union Bank of Canada, occupied the city's first skyscraper across William Avenue from the City Hall.

The entire western Canadian grain crop was marketed on the Grain Exchange trading floor on Lombard, and the banks provided the millions of dollars in loans required to finance the trade and shipment of the crop to the eastern ports and then overseas to Great Britain.

The enormous stations and offices of Canada's three transcontinental railways lay on the outskirts of the central business district, the CPR at Higgins and Main and the Canadian Northern and Grand Trunk Pacific at Broadway and Main. The western headquarters of all three were in Winnipeg, and the grand hotels associated with the two terminals were the finest in western Canada.

The large new limestone and terra cotta business buildings on the main thoroughfares testified to the ambitions of the western metropolis. The old Winnipeg could still be seen in the narrow streets behind this magnificent front, reminding one of city's humbler frontier past with their wooden livery stables and warehouses and small hotels with beer parlors and pool rooms. In small rooms above street level lived an army of clerks, railroad workers, waiters, labourers, and the unemployed. They went out early to their work and ate their meals in small cafés on the side streets.

The depression of 1913 and the collapse of the western real estate boom had arrested the explosive growth that had fed the city's prosperity, and there was still a good deal of unemployment in the city in 1914. But some of the optimism of the preceding years still survived. Certainly the city had suffered a setback, but Winnipeg's remarkable progress had been temporarily interrupted before, in the 1890s and in 1907, so there was no reason to believe it would not resume before long. The first half of 1914 had showed some promising signs of recovery with an increase in the amount of construction and greater

A war memorial for a young Winnipeg soldier, uncovered during renovations in an Exchange District building.

availability of money for loans both in London and locally. The big projects, such as the new Hudson's Bay Company store at Portage and Colony and the new City Hall, both of which had been postponed in 1913, were expected to commence in 1914.[1] As it turned out, both projects were delayed again: the store until the 1920s and the City Hall until the 1960s.

The war halted the recovery of the first months of 1914 and proceeded to deal the city a number of blows that helped put an end to her hopes of overtaking her eastern rivals. Unlike the industrial cities of the east, Winnipeg would not benefit to any great extent from the business of supplying the Canadian and British armies. In addition, government intervention in the grain trade would mean that the Grain Exchange, one of the city's main economic engines, did not profit from the huge exports of grain during the war.

At the same time, the explosion of western development that had enriched the city for ten years before the war was almost completely shut down because of the fighting in Europe. The flow of British capital was cut off and the flow of immigrants slowed, leaving the city's banking and wholesale supply sectors high and dry.

Winnipeg was, in many ways, unique in Canada in 1914. There were many aspects that set the city apart from other Canadian urban centres, but the factor that probably had the most impact was its ethnic variety. The 1911 census showed that Winnipeg was home to more people born outside the British Empire than any other Canadian city. While 90 percent of people in Montreal and 91 percent in Toronto were "British born," that is, born in some part of the British Empire, including Canada, in Winnipeg the figure was only 75 percent. The 1916 census of western Canada reported that Winnipeg had a population that was 67 percent British in origin. In other western cities the proportion was much higher, ranging from 75 percent in Regina to 80 percent in Brandon and 84.4 percent in Calgary. So while the Anglo-Canadian population was firmly in control of Winnipeg, they lived with a much larger population of Germans, Austro-Hungarians, Ukrainians, Poles, and Jews than their counterparts in other cities. The Anglo-Canadian majority's attitude toward and interaction with their "non-British" neighbours was often marked by intolerance and tension that was to have lasting effects on the city, its response to the war, and its internal cohesion during the years of the conflict.

Every Canadian city lost a great many of its young men during the Great War, and Winnipeg was no exception. Given its relatively small size and its isolation, these losses had a greater impact upon Winnipeg than on eastern cities. The effect of the departure of these individuals from the business and political life of the city is difficult to measure, but there is no doubt that it was substantial in Winnipeg. Many of the city's leading families lost sons who might have built upon their fathers' successes after the war, and skilled tradesmen and others with an unknown amount of unrealized potential were lost to the city. The men who did return were often traumatized by the war and many had injuries that shortened their lives, and this too had an effect on their families as well as the city's development.

This book is the story of Winnipeg during the First World War, of some of the men who went to fight, as well as the people and the city they left behind, of the sacrifices they all made, the role they played in winning the war, and the profound impact the war had upon them and their city.

1914

In the summer of 1914 those middle-class families that could afford it left Winnipeg, boarding trains headed for "the lake." Charles Gordon, the minister of St. Stephen's Presbyterian Church and an internationally known novelist under his pen name of Ralph Connor, migrated with his family to their island Birkencraig at Lake of the Woods. In his autobiography, he recorded his memories of the fateful summer of 1914. About the time the Gordons left the city, the newspapers began reporting the assassination of the Austrian heir to the throne in Sarajevo. But the family, like most Canadians, did not pay much attention: "It was glorious weather. With our canoes and boats, with our swimming and tennis, our campfires and singsongs our life was full of rest and happy peace."[1]

The governor general, the Duke of Connaught, and his daughter Princess Patricia, visited the Lake of the Woods in July on their way to a summer vacation in Banff. They stayed at the summer home of Robert Rogers, minister of the interior. At one point, the stern of the duke's boat was damaged and he had to be rescued as it sank under him. The duke's party proceeded to the mountains to enjoy the rest of their holiday on dry land.

Early in the summer the international news on the front pages of the Winnipeg papers was not from Europe but Ireland, where disagreements over the Home Rule Bill passing through Parliament seemed to be leading the country toward civil war. The struggle between Irish

Catholics and Protestants was riveting for Canadians, many of whom had strong feelings about the issues.

Then, Gordon records, "on Thursday, July 30th, our boat returning with supplies brought back a newspaper with red headlines splashed across the page. Austria had declared war on Serbia." Suddenly the peaceful lake community was talking of nothing but the situation in Europe. When the Gordons went to church on Sunday they stopped to chat with a group of fellow cottagers on the wharf in Kenora, Ontario, about how the war had spread to Germany and Russia. Then on August 4, the headlines shouted about the impending declaration of war by the British. "I remember taking the newspaper from my son King and going into the woods to look at the thing and to consider what it had to do with me," he writes.

Gordon was a man in his sixties but he was also the chaplain of the 69th Cameron Highlanders, one of Winnipeg's new militia regiments. He eventually did go to the trenches with the Camerons, but on that day in the woods his first worry was how safe his family would be. He and his son boated over to the wharf in Kenora to talk about the news with their lake neighbours. Gordon remembers speaking to James Ashdown, the owner of the J.H. Ashdown Hardware Company, who, as he rushed to catch the Winnipeg train, said, "everything has changed. We must accommodate ourselves to the change." Over the next four years, Ashdown's concise summary of the situation could have served as the city's wartime motto as its people struggled to adapt to the many changes the war would bring.

Irene Evans, the wife of former Winnipeg mayor Sanford Evans, was also at the lake, with their two children, Gurney and Katherine, and her maid, Molly Barbone, at the family's summer camp, Idyllcrag, on Lake of the Woods at Keewatin. Sanford Evans was working in Ottawa at the time, and his wife's letters, written to him as war broke out, give us another picture of those last sunny days of summer.

Irene and her children had all the tranquil moments normally provided by holidays at the lake. They went with their neighbour Mr. "W" by ferry to the dam on the Winnipeg River and had a "perfect picnic." They caught some pickerel and they cooked and ate the fish with bacon and gathered a "marvelous bunch of flowers."

On the eve of the war, many Winnipeggers were still enjoying time on the shores of Winnipeg Beach.

But there was no ignoring the war news that crept in to poison the calm and beauty of the lake. "It is a somber awesome air we breathe— Fanny writes that two Morton Morse boys, John Galt Jr., three Dennistouns went this week and even our little Reverend Diamond of Keewatin has gone as Strathcona Horse Chaplain."[2] Young men like these, from the middle-class families that, with the Evanses, composed the Anglo-Canadian establishment of Winnipeg, were joining the army in large numbers and boarding trains for the east. Douglas Waugh, the son of Richard Waugh, then mayor of Winnipeg, spent part of July at Minaki and visiting friends at Lake of the Woods. Mere weeks later, he passed Minaki on a troop train taking him and other newly recruited members of the Lord Strathcona's Horse to war. He would return a little over a year later, permanently disabled by wounds received at the Battle of Festubert.

Irene Evans wrote to her husband at the end of August that it was "sickeningly lonely and depressing without you just now, and I dread the return to the city.... The moon almost full—such heavenly peace—the world beyond in a nightmare." She nevertheless wanted the latest information and at the end of the month she asked him to get a couple of copies of the Blue Book issued by the federal government, *Documents Relative to the European War*. It contained all the cables, Orders-in-Council, and speeches connected to the declaration of war, and she wanted him to send one to her father in Toronto. One of their neighbours at the lake had lent her a copy.

She reported to her husband that the economic effects of the war were already disrupting their lives. Many people had had their wages cut, as employers tried to reduce costs. She had decided to cut her own washerwoman's wages from twenty to fifteen dollars. She was also about to lose her maid, who had decided to quit so she could marry her "sojer boy" and thus keep him from enlisting. In the early months of the war, volunteers whose wives objected to their going were rejected by the army. The policy was soon abandoned as the need for troops was too great.

The author Nellie McClung also spent August at the family cottage at Matlock on Lake Winnipeg. The news that war had actually broken out seemed unreal to her: "When the news of war came, we did not really believe it! War! That was over! There had been war of course, but that had been long ago, in the dark ages, before the days of free schools and peace conferences and missionary conventions and labor unions!"[3]

McClung described how war news gradually invaded the calm of life at the beach. The men coming out from the city "brought back stories of the great crowds that surged through the streets blocking traffic in front of the newspaper offices reading the bulletins, while the bands played patriotic airs." War quickly made its way into the games of the children: "Now they made forts of sand, and bored holes in the ends of stove-wood to represent gaping cannon's mouths, and played that half the company were Germans; but before many days that game languished, for there were none who would take the German part."

As the family drove away from the boarded-up cottage at the end of their vacation, she wrote that "instinctively we felt that we had come to the end of a very pleasant chapter in our life as a family; something had disturbed the peaceful quiet of our lives; somewhere a drum was beating and a fife was calling! Not a word was spoken but Jack put it all into words, for he turned to me and asked quickly, 'Mother, when will I be eighteen?'"[4]

Not all Winnipeggers were on holiday that summer. Hugh Sutherland, a Winnipeg pioneer and businessman, by this time a vice-president of the Canadian Northern Railway, was on business in Vienna when war broke out. With all the trains in Europe being commandeered by the military as part of the mobilization, it took Sutherland three days to make his way to England. He had to walk four miles at one point to catch a train bound for Belgium. As he was climbing aboard, a German officer grabbed him by the arm and tried to pull him off the steps. In what may have been the first act of war by a Canadian, the *Winnipeg Telegram* reported that Sutherland hit him hard in the face and "felled him." Near the Austrian border, Sutherland witnessed the execution of four Serbians who had not reported when called up by the Austro-Hungarian Army.[5]

The Coming of War

For Canada, the war began at midnight, London time, Tuesday, August 4, 1914. At that moment, the ultimatum the British had given Germany, demanding that it withdraw from Belgian territory, expired and a state of war existed between the British and German empires. As a dominion with no independent foreign policy, Canada was then automatically at war.

This momentous news arrived in Winnipeg, 3900 miles away, two hours later at around 8 p.m. local time. People had been milling in front of the city's newspaper offices for days, and since late afternoon the crowds had been growing larger, anxiously awaiting information from the centres of the crisis in Europe. Everyone was trying to calculate what time it would be in Winnipeg when it was midnight in London. Bulletins were rushed outside and posted on boards on the wall of the *Telegram* newspaper office at Albert and McDermot. Later in the war the *Telegram* would mount an electric tickertape to get the latest news out more quickly. At the *Winnipeg Free Press* building on Carlton Street a man armed with a megaphone stood on a wooden platform in front of the building and shouted the news to the crowd as it came in over the telegraph wires.

When he announced that war had been declared, the crowds of people filling the street broke into patriotic song. "Rule, Britannia!," "God Save the King," "The Old Red, White and Blue," "The Maple Leaf Forever," and "La Marseillaise" were heard. The *Free Press* reported that "strong voices took up the strain with a will and a volume of glorious sound roared forth and set the blood of the British crowd racing at top speed."[6]

There was another outbreak of enthusiasm when the megaphone man announced that the British fleet had been ordered to "capture or destroy the enemy." "The effect was electric," the *Free Press* reported. "The roar that followed resembled what takes place when a match is touched to a powder magazine. Then, stirred to white heat by patriotic sentiment, the great throng burst forth spontaneously into the National Anthem. The vigor of the outburst was thrilling beyond description." After reading for many years about the race between the European powers to build ever larger and more sophisticated battle ships, the public naturally expected the war to be won or lost at sea. In the end, as usual, it was the long-suffering infantrymen who decided the issue four bitter years later.

The police had blocked traffic on Carlton between Portage and Ellice avenues because of the dense crowd in front of the *Free Press* building. A frustrated motorist, driving a large seven-passenger touring car, forced his way through and injured several people, one of whom was taken away in the police ambulance. The crowd stormed down the street to the corner of Portage Avenue where another car had stopped. Mistaking the driver for the man who had just driven through the crowd, they charged his car shouting "kill him, mob him." He was able to convince them he was not the guilty party before any damage was done. It was as if the coming of the war had released deep-seated aggressive feelings in the citizens of Winnipeg.

Both the Conservative *Telegram* and the Liberal *Free Press*, rivals in politics and in business, claimed that they were the best source for war news. In reality, they received their news from the same sources, telegraphed from Europe over one of several transatlantic cables. Because of the high cost of sending these messages, agencies like the

Associated Press handled the transmission and then distributed the information to subscribers like the Winnipeg papers.

It was no easy matter to obtain news in the early hours of the war. The *Free Press* complained that the cables were being commandeered for government and military use. Very soon the British would cut the German transatlantic cable and North America thenceforth received little or no news with a German point of view.

The *Telegram* informed its readers that they would also be printing dispatches from their special correspondent, "Windemere," in London, and all the papers published letters from troops and others who were overseas to give some background for anxious readers at home. Beginning in 1915 readers could count on the Canadian "Eye Witness," Lord Beaverbrook, whose staff produced a steady stream of positive stories about the exploits of the Canadian Army.

The first of many military parades took to the Winnipeg streets at 8 p.m. With the conflict only two hours old, the members of the 90th Winnipeg Rifles regiment had been summoned to the drill hall at the corner of Broadway and Osborne. They crossed to the university grounds on the north side of Broadway, formed ranks, and marched up Kennedy Street to Portage Avenue. Their band played the regimental march, "Old Solomon Levi" and "Soldiers of the King," and the crowds cheered all along the way, many rushing into the street to march beside the militiamen. Street parades were an important propaganda tool for reaching large numbers of people at a time before radio and when a good portion of the population could not read. They were used extensively to educate the populace about war aims, to show that all elements of society supported the war effort, and to impress the public with the quality of the troops Canada was sending to fight.

It was natural that the 90th Regiment should parade first. It was the oldest militia unit in Winnipeg, formed in 1885 at the time of the Métis resistance in Saskatchewan. Named the "Little Black Devils" by a Métis fighter, referring to their black uniforms, the regiment was a favourite with the people of the city. Many members had volunteered to fight in South Africa, and during World War I the unit, in the form of the 8th Battalion, would be recognized for the bravery and toughness of its men.

At Portage and Main the regiment turned north and marched to city hall, and then headed back toward the drill hall again. When they passed McDermot Avenue a man in the crowd grabbed a flag and shouted for people to follow him. The crowd swept along McDermot and turned right at Albert, running north to Market Square, cheering and singing, replacing the orderly marching of the troops with the unrestrained enthusiasm of the crowd.

In front of the *Free Press* building a young man, William Farmer, described by the newspaper as a "raw-boned six foot specimen of Canadian manhood," jumped onto the platform and shouted to the crowd to follow him. He and John Blair—they both lived in Aberdeen Court at 230 Carlton—led another spontaneous parade down Portage and up Main to the city hall. The newspaper described a crowd of 6000 people, men and women, surging along five and six abreast in the street: "In the van walked half a dozen young men carrying a great union jack, which for want of a pole, was carried spread out over their shoulders."[7]

Another part of the crowd headed for Government House, carrying a Union Jack and a French tricolour, both nailed to clothesline posts taken from someone's backyard. They poured onto the front lawn of the house, cheering when the lieutenant governor, Douglas Cameron, emerged onto the balcony over the front door. Re-enacting, in a modest fashion, the appearance of the king on a balcony at Buckingham Palace only a short time before, he told the crowd that "Britain will never stop while one drop of blood or one coin of money remains unexpended," adding that France was equally determined to win. The crowd was in a mood to cheer and Cameron's grim words were greeted with wild applause.

A *Free Press* reporter visited the city's two largest hotels, hoping to get some reactions to the war news. He found the corridors full of guests discussing events. At the Fort Garry Hotel, which was crowded with attendees at the Knights of Pythias convention, many of the American delegates said they sympathized with the French and British cause. At the Royal Alexandra, the reporter talked to one of the hotel's chefs who was from Alsace Lorraine. He had five brothers, three of whom were fighting in the kaiser's army and two in the army of France. A guest of Austrian birth, "now a loyal British subject," he said Canada "had been good to me" and he had married a Canadian woman. "Naturally I wish the Empire well," he said, but he could not help but feel a natural sympathy for the land where he was born, "not sympathy for the diplomats and those who brought on the war, but for the people."

Outside on the streets such honest sentiments had suddenly become sufficient cause for a beating. At least one man who admitted to being a German was set upon by a crowd and had to be carried home. The *Free Press* reported "there were several fights as a result of the war spirit.... Everything was English, Canadian and French last night. Not a German dared show his head and proclaim his nationality." In the city's North End, it was noticeably quiet: "The foreigners in the city, many of whom belong to nations now enemies of Great Britain showed good common sense in keeping well out of sight. So far as is known they refrained entirely from tactless demonstrations."

Many who had come to Winnipeg from Austro-Hungarian provinces in what is now Poland or Ukraine may well have hoped an Allied victory would free their homelands. But such subtleties of European politics would have been lost on the crowds, and wisely, at least for the moment, the city's eastern European migrants kept a low profile.

The hotel bars throughout the downtown were packed with men toasting the beginning of the war. One of them amused the crowds by marching along the sidewalk on Main Street with a broomstick for a rifle. "Every once in a while he would stop and mark time. Then he would give himself the order 'forward march' and would start off again. He created many a laugh along the street," said the *Free Press* report. Another drinker strutted along behind the parade of Winnipeg Rifles, "and strove valiantly to imitate the military bearing of the officer before him."

The *Free Press* reported that not everyone in the crowd was celebrating. The veterans, who knew better what war meant, fell in with the military bands, but their faces were grim and their jaws "thrust forward." Of course, on August 4 no one could know the extent to which the war just beginning would surpass previous wars in horror and casualties. Very soon, however, the newspapers would begin to carry stories of the first great battles between French and German

Winnipeg veterans of the Boer War celebrated Decoration Day shortly before the outbreak of war in 1914.

troops with their enormous losses on both sides, and most thoughtful people quickly realized what kind of war this was going to be.

When the men of the 90th Regiment marched back to the drill hall, Major W.A. Munro addressed them, saying that their colonel, the sixty-year-old bank manager John de Courcey O'Grady, who was sick in bed, had offered the regiment for service. He said the regiment's office would be open in the morning for recruiting, but ten men pushed forward and handed in their names, the first of many thousands of Winnipeggers who would volunteer to fight in World War I.

Prime Minister Robert Borden had offered the British government a force of 22,000 Canadian men, and on that evening of August 4 militia officials in Winnipeg and the staff of the Military District Number 10 headquarters, housed in Fort Osborne Barracks at Broadway and Osborne, probably thought they were about to start putting the militia's official mobilization plan into action. The plan, devised by Canada's small corps of mostly British staff officers in Ottawa, called for the commanders of the country's military divisions and districts to organize companies of men and send them off to Camp Petawawa near the capital where they would be trained and equipped to go overseas.

Sam Hughes, the minister of militia and defence, had other ideas. A militiaman all his life—he had risen from the rank of bugler to be colonel of the 45th Victoria Regiment of Lindsay, Ontario—he was confident that he and his fellow militia colonels could get an army in the field faster than the professional staff officers in Ottawa with their red tape and procedures. He knew that most of the militia commanders were, like him, businessmen and successful men of affairs who knew how to get things done. They were eager to get into the fight.

Hughes had a low opinion of professional soldiers. A teetotaller, he saw them as womanizing drunkards. His prejudices sprang in part from his experiences during the South African War. He had gone to South Africa eager to see action. After a good deal of lobbying he was given a job as a staff officer with one of the British formations and he seems to have done a competent job. But he soon objected to the tradition-bound British commanders and what he saw as their incompetence. When he took his criticisms, well founded though they were in the early stages of the war, to the press, he was asked to go home and his short career as a wartime officer came to an end. Not for the last time, Hughes's lack of judgement and tact reduced his effectiveness.

Now Hughes, as a Cabinet minister, was in a position to overrule his professional staff officers, and on August 6 he sent express telegrams directly to 276 militia commanders across Canada asking for lists of milita personnel, their stature, marital status, and abilities as marksmen. A week later the militia colonels were asked to dispatch 125 officers and men from each regiment to Valcartier, near Quebec City, where a new army camp was under construction.[8] In less than a month, under Hughes's constant and personal supervision, the more than 30,000 men of the First Contingent were organized into the rough approximation of an army. The process was flawed and chaotic, but dispatching the Canadian Expeditionary Force to England less than two months after the declaration of war was nevertheless an amazing feat.

In Winnipeg the militia units wasted no time in drawing young volunteers in with parades, martial music, and flags. On Wednesday,

August 5, 460 members of the 100th Winnipeg Grenadiers regiment turned out at their headquarters on Main Street just north of York Avenue, and many signed up for active service. The Grenadiers, founded in April 1910, were one of the new regiments created in recent years as part of a wide-ranging reform of the militia. The regiment recruited men for a number of World War I battalions and in 1915 would send a Grenadiers battalion, the 78th, to the front. Most militia regiments wanted to have a battalion identified with their unit, and some of the Winnipeg regiments were successful in achieving that goal. Other battalions from Winnipeg were composite units with companies from different regiments.

Accompanied by their band, the Grenadiers marched through the streets, and crowds marched along with them. As they returned to their barracks they were joined by a column of French and Belgian reservists from St. Boniface, carrying their nations' flags. The regimental band played the Marseillaise and there was more cheering. Colonel J.B. Mitchell, the commanding officer, spoke to the crowds. Many young men listened eagerly and pushed forward to volunteer. Mitchell, the Winnipeg School Board architect who had designed most of the schools attended by the young men before him, was close to sixty-five years old in 1914. He was a veteran of the North West Mounted Police and had been a major in the Winnipeg Grenadiers, but his only fighting experience had been in Ontario during the Fenian Raids in the 1860s. Too old to go to the front, he would spend the war doing administrative work and recruiting and organizing units going overseas.

On August 7, 50,000 citizens lined the streets to see a parade of the 79th Cameron Highlanders. Winnipeg had a long history of Scots settlement, so the Camerons were always a favourite. The regiment, 500-strong and led by Colonel James A. Cantlie, Major Hugh Osler, and Major McKay on horseback, marched along Main Street and over to St. Boniface, where they too were joined by a contingent carrying the French flag. The *Telegram* enthusiastically reported that "nothing has done so much to cement the feeling between the citizens of French and English descent during the past week than the sight of the two flags flying in front of the parade of one of Winnipeg's favorite regiments."

The Camerons, joined by the Highland Cadets at the Industrial Bureau building at Main and Water, continued their march up Main Street to city hall and then back to their barracks at Main and York. When the parade was over, more than 1000 men crowded around to hear Colonel Cantlie. He announced they would parade again on Saturday and Monday so that he could "get in touch with you and let you get in touch with me." This was recruiting the way it had always been done, and anyone brought up on the novels of G.A. Henty and publications like the *Boy's Own Paper* would recognize the scene: the band, the flag, a stirring speech from the colonel, and young men, carried away by the excitement of the moment, rushing forward to join up. About forty volunteered that night.

During the next four and a half years, the regiment would send 3891 men overseas, one-third of whom would be killed in the war.[9] The Camerons' first contribution was one company for the 16th Canadian Scottish Battalion composed of companies from Scots regiments in Halifax, Toronto, Winnipeg, and Vancouver. Later, the Camerons would raise their own battalion, the 43rd.

There was a roster for volunteers in the club rooms of the Army and Navy Veterans' Association above the Home Bank on Main Street, and many men signed their names there. Among them was seventy-two-year-old J.M. Ferres, who had also served in the militia in the 1860s. Ferres "declared that...his experience, knowledge and his life" were at the service of the Empire.

Far into the night that Friday restless crowds of men and boys paraded, halting at every street corner to sing "Rule, Britannia!" or "God Save the King." Cars decorated with flags roared around the downtown streets. The city's well-developed boosterism was in evidence when the *Winnipeg Telegram* stated, "Undoubtedly Winnipeg has reached the acme of patriotism and no matter what the reason, the enthusiasm of its citizens will not be outdone in any part of the British Empire."

The patriotic demonstrations of the first week climaxed on Saturday when the city's veterans turned out to support the cause. Gathering at Market Square, they marched to the 90th Regiment's drill hall on Broadway. Those too old to march rode in cars provided by Eaton's and the Ford Motor Company. There were veterans of the South African

War, as well as men who had fought the Métis resistance in 1885 and others who had served in the British Army and Navy. Several bands played, and at the drill hall the crowd was addressed by Lieutenant Governor Cameron and Premier Roblin. Roblin put the situation succinctly: "Great Britain is at war and when the Motherland is at war, Canada is at war." Cameron added that it was "the duty of every man in the Empire to rally to the call that is before the Motherland." Hugh John Macdonald, a veteran of 1885, had marched in the parade. As a former premier and son of Sir John A. Macdonald, he often played a symbolic role at such times and, after some coaxing from the crowd, he too spoke, saying "it is time for the sons of Britain over the seas to show they are true sons of the race." He said that all the veterans were ready to fight but the men who had served in South Africa would make the best recruits: "They have the youth and experience and none could be better coming from a fighting race as they do."[10] As it would turn out, experience fighting irregular Boer troops on the open veldt would prove to be of little value in the muddy chaos of World War I.

By "race," Macdonald was referring to the people of the British Isles and their relatives in the British Empire around the world. The "Anglo Saxon race" was supposed to have a fighting spirit superior to that of other races. This idea carried with it the corollary that other groups were not sufficiently martial in spirit to make good soldiers. According to the "Great Chain of Race" idea popular at the time, people were valued according to how closely they were related to the Anglo-Celtic population of the British Isles. White Americans, Scandinavians, and, until the war, Germans, were considered to be almost the equals of the Anglo-Saxon. Others, such as southern Europeans, Africans, Asians, and the Aboriginal people of Canada were at the bottom of the chain and hardly worth considering.

These biases informed Canadian recruiting in the first years of the war. Sam Hughes set out to create an army of sober, upright Protestant volunteers. The Canadian Expeditionary Force eventually had over 50,000 members of the Orange Lodge in its ranks, although that figure is not surprising given the lodge's large membership at the time. With the exception of the 22nd Battalion, French volunteers usually found themselves serving in English-language units and French militia of-

ficers were not given commands at the front. The long traditions of
Quebec militia regiments were ignored and discounted by Hughes.

Jewish soldiers/Mobilizing Civilian Pop.

In spite of the prejudices of Canadians like Sam Hughes, the members of ethnic groups other than the British quickly responded to
the call for volunteers and demonstrated their willingness to die for
their new country. Both people from the visible minorities such as
Aboriginal, Japanese, Chinese, and Black men as well as members of
ethnic groups such as Jewish, Ukrainian, and Polish men were anxious to join the Canadian Expeditionary Force in 1914. The choice of
recruits was left to the battalion commanders and while the Militia
Department claimed there was no discrimination against these groups
there is a large amount of evidence that racist attitudes blocked their
enlistment. It was sometimes claimed that they were not accepted into
the army because the Germans would mistreat them if they were captured. A more accurate reason was also often given—white Canadian
soldiers did not want to serve beside these men. Various special
units were created, such as the 114th Battalion in Ontario and the
107th in Manitoba, with the intention that they would be exclusively
manned by Aboriginal recruits. But none of the minority groups was
able to produce enough recruits to fully man the units or to supply
replacements once they were in action.[11] People living in Winnipeg
and the rest of Manitoba experienced the same racist reactions to
their attempts to serve as did those in other parts of the country. The
population of Winnipeg was more diverse than that of other Canadian
cities, with relatively large groups of people with German and Austro-
Hungarian origins. There was a large Jewish community, which at
the time of the 1916 census numbered close to 14,000 people. There
were many ethnic Ukrainian immigrants in the city. Ukrainians born
in Russia were often referred to as "Russian," while those born in
the Austro-Hungarian Empire, in the provinces of Galicia, Bukovina,
and Transcarpathia, were sometimes called "Ruthenians," the term
used by the Austrian government to describe this particular group
of subjects of the emperor. "Galician" was another name assigned to

all the western Canadian Ukrainians, not just to the many who came from that province. It also became a pejorative term used to describe any immigrant from eastern Europe. During the First World War, Ukrainians were commonly called "Austrians," a name that tended to make them seem like the potentially dangerous subjects of an enemy monarch.

The multiplicity of homelands caused divisions within the Ukrainian community in Canada and elsewhere. Some people happily identified with Russia and considered themselves Russians. Ukrainian nationalists who wanted to re-establish a Ukrainian state fiercely opposed these Russophiles, but they themselves were divided into factions based on political philosophy and religion. Because the Austrians had dealt less brutally with Ukrainians than the Russians, some people were pro-Austrian and looked to the Austrian emperor to grant them some form of autonomy or statehood.

Ukrainians began to be recognized as a distinct group in Canada during the war years. Ukrainian was listed as a language for the first time in the 1916 western Canadian census—Canadian-born Ukrainian speakers numbered 200 in Winnipeg and Ukrainian speakers born outside Canada numbered 12,086—but they were not counted in any other way. The census did record people born in Galicia, and other Austro-Hungarian provinces whose populations were largely Ukrainian. There were 3385 people from Galicia in Winnipeg who were naturalized Canadians and 3003 who were not naturalized.

Some of these 3003 would likely have been men who came to Canada not as immigrants but as temporary workers and were stranded here by the war. In the years before the war many young men came to the west to work with the intention of saving money and going home to buy land. Many of these men were interned during the first years of the war.

The status of foreign-born people became an important issue once war broke out. Matters such as who was and was not a Canadian and who should be classified as an "enemy alien" were not clearly defined in Canada in 1914. Canada's status as a dominion in the British Empire meant that it did not have control over the granting of citizenship; British law defined a British subject as anyone born anywhere in the Empire, including dominions like Canada. All others could only

Some young members of the Camerons battalion in full dress. Many Winnipeggers' had Scottish roots, and the kilted Camerons were always a favourite with city crowds.

become British subjects by living in Great Britain for five years and swearing allegiance to the king. An immigrant who came to Canada directly from his or her homeland, therefore, could not become a British subject.[12]

If they wished to become a naturalized Canadian, however, they had to live in the country for three years and show themselves to be of good character. Then they went before a court to swear allegiance. By 1914 about 50 percent of the Ukrainians who had immigrated to western Canada in the previous twenty years had done so under the *Canadian Naturalization Act* (1906) and *Immigration Act* (1910). The differences between them and their neighbours who were British subjects became a problem for them after the outbreak of war.

Many "foreign-born" young men were swept up, like others, in the excitement of the first days of the war. Many Ukrainians and Poles who had lived under the Austro-Hungarian crown saw the war as an opportunity for their peoples to have an independent homeland and decided to fight on the side of the Allies to help bring that about. Many members of minority groups believed that service in the Canadian army would win them acceptance as full-fledged Canadians.

This was understood by some Canadians. The editor of the *Canadian Finance* newspaper, published in Winnipeg, wrote sympathetically about the labourers from Austria, now out of work, who would have already returned to Europe if not for the war. He wrote "that so many are enemy aliens has little bearing on the problem—the Austrian Slav has little affection for Hapsburg or Hohenzollern."[13]

On the evening of Sunday, August 9, at the Industrial Bureau, there was a meeting of 3000 "Ruthenians." The assembly voted to reject Austria-Hungary and pledge allegiance to Canada, where they had found "true liberty." They passed a resolution "that we hereby express our loyalty to the British flag and declare our readiness to stand by the colours whenever called upon."[14] This resolution was sent to the governor general in Ottawa. One of the speakers, J. Arsenycz, a young university student, said that Ruthenians had established themselves as useful citizens and were ready to serve their adopted country in any way asked.

By voting for these resolutions these men were severing their ties with their homeland and offering themselves to serve Canada. But the *War Measures Act*, passed in August 1914, classed people born in the Austro-Hungarian Empire as enemy aliens, not eligible to serve. About 85,000 people registered as enemy aliens across the country, turning in any firearms they had in their homes. Of these, about 7700 were eventually imprisoned in one of the camps set up across the country to hold them and prisoners of war. About 1100 of the internees were German reservists and the rest were Austro-Hungarian in origin, largely Ukrainians.

A lot of the young Ukrainian men were interned not because they were reservists who would go home to fight but because they were unemployed and the municipalities where they were living were unwilling or unable to feed them. Of course other unemployed men were not imprisoned; that was a solution reserved for the "foreign born." The camps were places where heavy work, poor food and discomfort had to be endured. There were suicides amongst the men and a few were killed while trying to escape. In Manitoba, the Brandon city arena was turned into an internment camp. In 1916 and 1917, when the economy began to pick up and their labour was needed, some of the internees were released.

On the same day as the Ruthenian meeting, about 400 Poles gathered at Holy Ghost School on Selkirk Avenue and passed a resolution "that the Polish men of Winnipeg give their aid as far as possible to England as soldiers and especially as fulfilling our duties as good citizens."

Canada was more supportive of the Poles. There were plans to form Polish units to fight on the Western Front, and by 1918 several thousand Poles, mostly men resident in the U.S., had been trained in camps in Ontario and dispatched to England. While these men and others from different parts of Europe did form part of the new Polish army when the Polish Republic was established, they were prevented by émigré politics and the politics of the Allied powers from actually fighting as a unit on the front.[15]

All the European nations except Britain had adopted conscription by 1914. In most cases this meant that, after serving a mandatory number of years in the army, a man would spend another period of years as a reservist, who, in time of war, was expected to report for duty. There were estimated to be about 1000 Austro-Hungarian reservists in Winnipeg, and a smaller number obligated to serve in the German army. In the first days of the war these men were encouraged to go home to report for duty. The Austro-Hungarian consul in Winnipeg, George Reininghaus, announced at the beginning of August that all reservists must do so and that they would be reimbursed for the cost of the trip or given passage money if they did not have it. If they did not go, they would be charged with desertion, a capital offence. At Sunday Mass on August 2, Father Kowalski of Holy Ghost Polish Catholic Church read out a message from Consul Reininghaus about the call to arms issued by the Austro-Hungarian government.

Bishop Nykyta Budka, the Ukrainian Catholic Bishop of Canada, wrote a pastoral letter that was printed in the *Canadian Ruthenian* newspaper on August 1 and read out in churches the next morning. Bishop Budka covered a number of topics in his letter, and exhorted his people to pray and do penance in this dark time. He passed on the message that those who were liable for service in the Austrian army were expected to go home at once. The bishop's letter was to

Bishop Budka, shortly after becoming the first bishop of the Ukrainian Catholic Church in Canada in 1912. His pastoral letter in 1914 encouraging Ukrainian-Canadians to fight for Austria-Hungary caused intense controversy.

haunt him for the next four years, and in spite of the fact that after Canada entered the war Budka consistently advised his people to support the Allied cause, buy war bonds, and contribute money to the Patriotic Fund, he was to be the focus of repeated attacks. He was the accused in two trials, during which no evidence of disloyalty was ever produced. One study attributes the persecution of the bishop to the animosity of his political enemies, including the *Manitoba Free Press* and secular Ruthenian leaders who wanted to reduce the power of the Church.[16]

Some Austro-Hungarian reservists did go home. Two men—Stefan Bertnak and Tphemius Lupul—told the *Telegram* newspaper they were going home early so they would have a chance to visit their families before they were called up. They took very little with them from their time in Canada, each carrying only a small grip for their possessions. They explained that they had to go or they would never be able to return home again.

The names of the young men from Winnipeg who fought for Austria or Germany are not recorded on any monument in the city. There is no doubt that many of them did not survive. It is not uncommon to read of British or Canadian soldiers encountering German troops who had worked in Britain or Canada before the war. For example, during the fighting in August 1918 some German prisoners were passing men of the 44th Battalion, largely a Winnipeg unit. "Is there anybody here from Winnipeg?" shouted one of the Germans. A 44th man nodded, and the German said that he used to work in one of the big Winnipeg hotels. "That so," grins the Canadian. "Well you ain't the only guy that lost a good job through this here war!"[17]

Once Canada and Austria-Hungary and Germany were officially at war the status of the reservists changed. On August 5, Lieutenant Governor Cameron asked the German and Austrian consuls to leave the city, and by August 7 a proclamation had been issued saying that any enemy reservists trying to return home would be arrested.

In spite of the barriers put in their way, an unknown number of men of Ukrainian origin would eventually serve in the Canadian Army. Because of prejudice and language problems, some of these men were placed in labour battalions and employed cutting timber or building rail lines. This was essential work because the front lines consumed vast amounts of lumber in the construction of trenches, and rail lines made supplying the front and evacuating the wounded easier. But many would also fight as members of Canadian units. In 1916 and after, the shortage of new volunteers meant that the army was more interested in men from minority communities and there were active efforts to recruit them.

Ukrainian men born in Russian territory were accepted as the subjects of an Allied power. Many, like Victoria Cross—winner Philip Konowal, distinguished themselves fighting for Canada. Konowal had been a bayonet instructor in the Russian army and he was a corporal in the 47th Battalion when, over a two-day period in the fall of 1917, he knocked out two machine gun positions, killing sixteen Germans. He survived the war and worked for many years in the Parliament Buildings in Ottawa.

Men from the Austrian side of the border were to be rejected as enemy aliens, but some at least lied about their place of birth to recruiting sergeants not always up on geography. We know that one Edmonton man, Michael Hamaluk, gave his birthplace as Czernowitz, Russia, when he filled out his attestation papers. No one caught the fact that Czernowitz was the capital of Austrian Galicia.

The first Ukrainian recruits went overseas with the First Contingent in October 1914, many of them in the 9th Battalion. Ukrainian Winnipeggers served with the battalions associated with the city, such as the 43rd Cameron Highlanders, the 44th, and the 27th City of Winnipeg Battalion. Many were recruited in the years from 1916 to 1918 when there was a manpower shortage. Roman Demisik, who had worked as a labourer and lived at 101 Barber Street before the war, enlisted in April 1916. He was in France with the 78th Winnipeg Grenadiers in July 1917 when he was killed. Several other men, including Mike Parazinski, John Ponomareff, Peter Sergeenko, Metro Krosty, Benjamin Kuryk, and Joseph Kuzyk, were killed in the Battle of Vimy Ridge in spring 1917. At least thirty-one Ukrainian Winnipeggers gave their lives during the war, and the actual number was probably much larger. Because of the confusion over place of birth and the difficulty of identifying people simply by whether their name "sounds" Ukrainian, the real numbers of ethnically Ukrainian men in the Canadian Army is now unknown.[18]

It is estimated that about 25 percent of Canadian Jews of military age volunteered to serve in the Canadian Army, including many young men from Winnipeg. It is difficult to establish exactly how many Jews fought because they may not have given their religion on their attestation papers and the army did not record their numbers. Half the sixty-five members of the Winnipeg Montefiore Club enlisted. One local Jewish man, William Cowan, joined the Fort Garry Horse as a sergeant and during the war rose to the rank of captain. He was wounded five times, won the Military Cross, and was a prisoner of

war. Alex Lyone enlisted in the 27th Battalion as a private and rose
to the rank of lieutenant before his death in the Battle of the Somme.
Jewish soldiers sometimes faced discrimination in Canadian units.

It was difficult for many families who had come from eastern
Europe and Russia to see their sons go into the army. In Russia, Jewish
conscripts had been treated with notorious brutality and forced to
convert to Christianity. Joseph Wilder recalls his mother's reaction
when he told her he was going to enlist: "Memories of the old country
shook her. The pogroms she had witnessed, the raiding of her village
by rowdy soldiers...all the reasons for our leaving Romania came to
her mind.... 'We have a nice life in Canada,' I told her, 'and it is up to
one of us five boys to show our appreciation of this freedom.'" When
she answered that "every child is a piece of a mother's heart, and if
one piece is broken, the whole heart is forever damaged," he decided
not to enlist. He did join the 76th Artillery Battery as a sergeant later
in the war and when, during training, he and his batman rode up to
her house on Alfred Avenue on horseback, she proudly "turned to her
neighbours and said 'That's my son!'"[19]

Aboriginal men were another group of Manitobans that had an am-
biguous position at the outbreak of the war. There were fifteen "Indian"
Winnipeggers, according to the 1916 census and 14,000 "Indians" in
Manitoba. Winnipeg undoubtedly had a large Métis population, but
even if they had declared themselves, that category was not included
in the census.

In Canada as a whole, one in three Aboriginal men of military age
eventually volunteered to go to war, one of the highest percentages of
any Canadian group. As with other groups they were actively discour-
aged from joining up in 1914 and 1915, although some were taken into
the battalions of the first contingents. After 1916 they were actively
recruited and the Department of Indian Affairs was active in recruiting men from the reserves. This pattern held true in Manitoba. Twenty
men, or 16 percent of the total male population, of the Peguis Reserve
joined the Canadian Army; eleven of these were killed and eight were
wounded or taken prisoner. From St. Peter's Reserve, thirty-three
men, or 25 percent of the male population, joined up; seven of these
men were killed and nine wounded. The Pas sent nineteen men, 20

percent of the men on the reserve. The Griswold Reserve sent twenty men, or 23 percent of the male population.[20]

There is no doubt that these men had the same motivations as anyone else who joined the army—a search for adventure, a desire to see the world outside their communities, and the pressure of wanting to go to war with their friends and relatives. They also wanted to be accepted as men like any other Canadian man, to prove that they could perform with as much courage and skill as any white man. Private Philip McDonald, a Mohawk from St. Regis, Quebec, was a member of the 8th Battalion, Winnipeg Rifles. In 1914, writing to his mother from England, he proudly told her that his battalion's men were "made a fuss of by the British" and that he was "supposed to be a good specimen of a Canadian and we are welcomed everywhere."[21] The acceptance that MacDonald experienced must have been exhilarating for a young Aboriginal man who had grown up amidst the racism and restrictions of the Canadian reserve system. Unfortunately the contribution made by these young soldiers did little to improve their living conditions or status after the war was over.

Canadian Aboriginal men were often placed in pioneer units where they worked cutting timber or doing construction work. But there were many who fought bravely in the trenches. Some Aboriginal men were used as snipers, probably because they were often more skilled with a rifle than other troops. Philip McDonald killed forty of the enemy before he was killed in action. Another sniper of the 8th Battalion was Private Philip Riel, Louis Riel's nephew. He killed thirty of the enemy before he was killed by a shell near Messines, south of Ypres, in January 1916. For part of the year his rifle was on display in the window of British Columbia House in London, with a plaque informing passers by that it had belonged to "Pte. P. Riel, nephew of Louis Riel of the Riel Rebellion."[22]

In April 1917, the *Telegram* carried a feature on "What the Indians of Canada are Doing." In addition to acknowledging the numbers of Aboriginal men who had gone to the front from Manitoba, the piece noted that money had been donated to the Patriotic Fund from Indian reserves. As well, donations had been made to the Red Cross and a great deal of sewing and knitting was done for the troops by women volunteers on reserves. The total contributions from Canadian reserves to war causes would eventually total over $44,000, a staggering amount when the poverty of most of the communities is taken into account.

The *Telegram* story focussed on one of the Manitoba men from Norway House. Alex Saunders, who was fighting in the trenches in 1917, had been a fire ranger at home and had written a letter to the Chief Ranger, J.T. Blackford. He told how he crawled through no man's land, badly wounded: "But after I was wounded I didn't leave my rifle and bayonet behind. While I was coming back I saw 3 Germans. I was going to shoot them but they put their hands up. Well I can't tell you much but I'll tell you they don't like the bayonet." Sanders took the three men prisoner and brought them back to the Canadian trench. He asked Blackford to tell his father that he was okay. He was wounded in the thigh during an attack. There were men falling all around him but he was not afraid. "I don't know why," he said.[23]

Half of the soldiers in the 107th Battalion were Aboriginal men. A "Pioneer" or engineering battalion, the 107th was commanded by Colonel Glen Campbell of Winnipeg. Campbell had been chief inspector of Indian agencies before the war and spoke some Aboriginal languages. The battalion included two famous runners, Tom Longboat and Joe Keeper. Longboat, from the Six Nations Reserve on the Grand River, was a well-known professional runner in Canada and the U.S. He served as a messenger in the army and was wounded twice. Joe Keeper, from Norway House, Manitoba, had competed at the 1912 Olympics in Stockholm where he came fourth in the men's 10,000-metre race and he too served as a messenger in the 107th. Both Keeper and Longboat won many races at army sports days during the war.

During the war Aboriginal soldiers won the respect of their comrades and much positive attention from the press. Once the war ended the men often found that their war service was forgotten and they were once more the victims of racism in their own country. The Soldier Settlement program, which gave veterans loans to buy farms, was not successful for many returned soldiers, Native or white, but Aboriginal men in particular were treated as second-class veterans. They were given much smaller initial loans than non-Natives and received less support from the government during the bad years of the Depression.[24] By the 1940s, most of the Aboriginal veterans supported by the program had defaulted on their loans and lost their farms.

The first troops left the city bound for the battlefields of France and Belgium on the afternoon of August 15, 1914. The platform of the CPR station on Higgins Avenue was packed with new recruits and their family and friends while the railroad police struggled to keep everyone else off the platform. Some city dwellers pushed through to board trains that would take them to cottages on Lake Winnipeg and at Kenora, determined to experience a little more normalcy before it was all swept away by troop trains and war. About 200 men from Winnipeg and 100 from Saskatchewan were climbing aboard the eighteen-coach train waiting to take them east. The men were recruits for Canada's newest regiment, the Princess Patricia's Light Infantry. The Patricias had been raised and outfitted with money given by Hamilton Gault, a Montreal millionaire who had fought in South Africa. Unlike most of the wealthy men who made such donations, Gault actually went to France with the regiment. Wounded four times, he survived to become commanding officer in 1918.

Newspaper advertisements for the Princess Patricias had stated that preference would be given to former regulars in the Canadian or Imperial armies, and to men who had fought in South Africa. Many of the men were veterans of British regiments like the Black Watch, the Scots Guards, and the Royal Irish Fusiliers. There had been no shortage of men eager to join the new "crack corps" and the regiment was now complete. Count de Bury, the lieutenant governor's aide-de-camp, had been in charge of recruiting in the west, and he had carefully chosen the most experienced and fittest men from the many who presented themselves. The newspapers commented on the healthy, tanned faces that crowded the train windows. Their civilian clothes showed that they came from every level of society—farm hands and labourers, office workers, and professional men. The men among these recruits with previous military experience were the closest thing that Canada had to the millions of reservists that the systems of conscription produced in European countries.

Winnipeg had given the departing men a send-off to remember. On the previous night there had been a boozy celebration at the Army

The Winnipeg Rifles Drill Hall at Broadway and Osborne was the centre for many of the city's recruiting and training activities during the war.

and Navy Club. The *Telegram* reported that "calling each other comrade, the seasoned fighters in a bluff off hand way that concealed a deep feeling, clasped hands, patted shoulders and demonstrated in the manner of shy old soldiers, their mutual fellowship." Several veterans were moved to make speeches.

The newly recruited Patricias were headed for Ottawa, where, on August 23 at Lansdowne Park, Princess Patricia herself, the governor general's daughter and the regiment's honorary colonel, presented them with their regimental colours. She had embroidered the flag herself and it would be present on all the battlefields where they fought for the next four years. The Princess Patricias were ready to depart for France on August 28, but various delays resulted in their sailing with the rest of the Canadian Expeditionary Force at the end of September. Because many of their number were already experienced soldiers, they went to France earlier than the other Canadian units and were to fight as part of British formations until November 1915, when they became part of the Canadian Corps.

On August 16 another 550 Patricias and 120 men of the Lord Strathcona's Horse, the regular army regiment stationed at Fort Osborne Barracks, left the city. The Strathcona's commanding officer was Colonel A.C. Macdonnell, a graduate of the Royal Military College in Kingston, where he would be principal after the war. He was a veteran of the North West Mounted Police and the South African War. Macdonnell, at this time in his mid-forties, was a rarity in the Canadian Expeditionary Force—a Canadian professional, many of the permanent force officers being British. He was a tough disciplinarian, but he was popular with his men and he would have what would be termed a "good war," returning to Winnipeg in 1918 as General Sir A.C. Macdonnell.

That afternoon, the Strathcona's Horse and the volunteers gathered at the drill hall on Broadway and prepared to leave. Then they assembled across the street on the open grass of the university grounds, now the site of Memorial Park. The formation, with Winnipeg men on the north side, were inspected by Colonel Sam Steele, the commander of Military District 10, and other dignitaries including Hugh John Macdonald. Steele addressed the men, saying he hoped they would "return in good health and spirits...shoot well and be men all the time." He drew a sharp contrast between them and the troops they would be facing, saying that, as volunteers, "you will go into the fight with the proper spirit different from the pressed men of some nations." They were soldiers who were not only shedding blood but who wanted to fight to bring peace and put the kaiser in a position where he could no longer cause trouble. The portrayal of the Canadian troops as volunteers rather than "pressed men" was an often-repeated message in the early years of the war.

The scene that followed, a march to the CPR station, was described by the *Free Press* the next day: "All along the line of march large crowds were standing while autos and pedestrians followed the march right to the depot...Again and again that strange 'lump in the throat' feeling came to the one who followed them, as some pathetic incident was observed...now and again some friend of one of the departing men would rush into the ranks and grasp his friend's hand convulsively and say huskily 'Goodbye old fellow, good luck.' ... In front of the CPR Depot itself a great crowd had gathered and it was with the utmost difficulty that the contingent passed through the press of people." The paper continued, "Military officers that were present said the troops were as fine a body of men as they had ever looked over. One glance was sufficient to see that they were seasoned, toughened men, men of stout hearts and the right temper for war, men whom western Canada will be proud of in the months to come." The *Telegram* used the same magniloquent tone: "Resolute, determined and knowing what it meant, they again responded to the Empire's call, showing to the world the quality of the material the Dominion of Canada is able to supply when the tap of the war drum is heard in London."

Finally the roll was called and the men boarded the train. It pulled out shortly after 6 p.m. with a huge crowd cheering and waving farewell. It was not, said the *Free Press*, a sad departure. A few women wept unnoticed in the crowd but most people were cheerful and positive as the train began to move. Reports of the fighting in France had begun to appear in the papers, but the dangers the men would face were still not uppermost in people's minds.

These first troop trains leaving Winnipeg—professional soldiers of the Strathconas and the experienced veterans of the Princess Patricias—were not typical of the men who would soon be gathering at Valcartier Camp to be organized into the battalions of the Canadian Expeditionary Force. The majority of the contingents from the Cameron Highlanders and the Winnipeg Rifles who left the city for Valcartier the following week like most of the Canadian troops in the first contingent were untested in battle and only partly trained.

These were the first recruits for Sam Hughes's volunteer Canadian army, a force that would number close to 600,000 by the end of the war. The process of building this army was not a simple one. The *Militia Act* gave the government clear authority to raise an army for the defence of the country, but it was not at all clear whether sending men overseas to fight fell within the definition of "defending the country." Canada and Great Britain, almost alone amongst the combatant nations, did not have conscription and therefore had no trained reserves to call on. The Canadian government also had to keep in mind that public opinion in Quebec was normally against fighting abroad in Britain's wars. When, for example, Canada was preparing to send troops to South Africa, Prime Minister Wilfrid Laurier proceeded very carefully. At one point he stated that he wished to avoid "an agitation which according to all human probability would have ended in a line of cleavage in this country upon racial lines. A greater calamity could never take place in this country."[25]

In the end he was able to steer a course between Orange Ontario, anxious to go to the aid of the Queen, and Quebec, where many felt that the South African War was none of Canada's affair. Several militia commanders, including Colonel Sam Hughes, a Tory member of Parliament, were offering to raise units to fight and the colonial secretary, Joseph Chamberlain, informed the governor general, Lord Minto, that Britain would be glad to have four Canadian companies of 250 men each to reinforce British units.

In response, Laurier and the Liberal Cabinet sent 1000 volunteers, equipped and transported by Canada, but not officially Canadian militiamen. Laurier claimed that by not simply acceding to the British request for troops, he had preserved Canada's independence "to judge whether or not there is cause for her to act."[26]

In the decade after the South African War, Laurier's minister of militia, Sir Frederick Borden, made a series of reforms that by the time of the outbreak of the Great War had increased Canadian autonomy from the British military, always with the recognition that Canada was a Dominion without an independent foreign policy. The commander-in-chief of the Canadian army was now a Canadian and not a British officer seconded for the purpose. The militia had many new regiments and more money was being spent on them. During the coming war Hughes and others worked hard to keep the Canadians together as a separate corps with at least some autonomy from the British.

In 1914, public opinion was solidly behind sending Canadian troops to Europe and enthusiasm for the war was widespread in Quebec as well as in the rest of the country. Yet, when, in August, Minister Sam Hughes was asked if the militia would be sent to war as a body once the 20,000 men of the first contingent had gone, he replied, "So far as my own personal views are concerned, I am absolutely opposed to anything that is not voluntary in every sense, and I do not read in the law that I have any authority to ask Parliament to allow troops other than volunteers to leave the country."[27]

This policy was emphasized again and again in the early months of the war. On December 18, Prime Minister Borden told the Halifax Canadian Club that "under the laws of Canada, our citizens may be called out to defend our own territory, but cannot be required to go beyond the seas except for the defense of Canada itself. There has not been, there will not be compulsion or conscription."[28]

The first contingent that sailed for England in October 1914 was the largest military formation to leave Canada's shores up to that time. It consisted of 36,267 men. The contingent included the men who crowded into Valcartier Camp near Quebec City in August and September 1914 in response to Hughes's call. They were subjected to a rather chaotic process of being organized, largely by Hughes himself, into four infantry brigades, each with four battalions of 1000 men, three brigades of artillery, each with eighteen 18-pounder guns and a cavalry brigade.

Fully 23,211 of the new soldiers were born in the United Kingdom and had immigrated to Canada. Only 10,880 had been born in Canada, including 1245 French-speaking Canadians. The regional origin of volunteers (as a percentage of the 1911 male population, ages fifteen to forty-four) was 15.5 percent from western Canada; 14.4 percent from Ontario; 4.6 percent from Quebec, and 9.9 percent from the Maritimes. The west's large contribution was a reflection of the large population of young, single men—fully a quarter of all Canadian males eighteen to forty-five years old—living in the west.

The four infantry brigades were commanded by generals chosen by Hughes from among the officers of the militia: M.S. Mercer, a Toronto lawyer and since 1885 a member of the Queen's Own Rifles; R.T.W. Turner, a Quebec City grocery wholesaler who had fought in South Africa and won the Victoria Cross; J.E. Cohoe, long-time militia officer from Niagara region, and Arthur Currie, a Victoria real estate man who was a friend of Garnet Hughes, the son of the minister. With some exceptions—there were Canadian career officers like Colonel Macdonnell of the Strathconas and some seconded British officers like Colonel Louis Lipsett commanding the 8th Battalion Winnipeg Rifles—the battalion commanders and their officers were

A bugler salutes the 43rd Battalion as it departs from the CPR Yards, May 1915.

also militiamen. Although Hughes denied that politics played any role in appointments, many officers had some personal or political connection to the minister. Once appointed, however, these men had to prove themselves in the brutal testing ground of the front. Some, like Currie, succeeded brilliantly and developed into excellent commanders. Others failed and were transferred to jobs away from the fighting. A few, like General Mercer, died alongside their men in battle.

In Winnipeg, relations between the Anglo-Canadian elite of the city and the regular army troops stationed among them, the Lord Strathcona's Horse, had always been positive. The Fort Osborne Barracks were located close to the city's "best" neighbourhoods, and the inhabitants socialized with the officers of the regiment. The daughter of Lieutenant Governor Douglas Cameron had married one of the Strathcona's officers, Captain Thomas Homer-Dixon. Another professional soldier, Captain Huntley Ketchen, had settled with his wife and children into middle-class Winnipeg, and after the war, from which he emerged as a general, he would be elected as a Conservative member for South Winnipeg in the provincial legislature.

The local militia regiments attracted many middle-class English Canadians, and regimental dinners and balls formed part of the social life of the community. Militia officers were drawn from the Winnipeg middle-classes and the units had connections to prominent men: Lieutenant Governor Cameron was the honorary colonel of the Camerons, and his successor in Government House, James Akins, filled the same role for the Winnipeg Rifles, and Premier Roblin was the honorary colonel of the Winnipeg Grenadiers.

As soon as war broke out Manitoba's leaders moved quickly to support the cause. Premier Roblin returned from vacation at Minaki on August 3 and met with Lieutenant Governor Cameron and Colonel Sam Steele, commander of the Tenth Military District. He then made an official announcement that Manitoba would immediately raise and equip an infantry battalion of 1000 men and offer it to Canada "as a slight evidence of Manitoba's appreciation of being part of the British Empire."[29] Sir James Aikins, at the time the Conservative member of Parliament for Brandon, would soon offer to raise a force of 7000 troops, 4000 infantry, 2000 artillery, and 1000 other arms, for western Canada. Although some units were raised and financed by individuals in the first year of the war—Hamilton Gault's gift helped create the Princess Patricia's Light Infantry and Dr. A. Mignault gave $50,000 to support Quebec's famous 22nd Battalion—Roblin's and Aikins's offers were declined. On August 14, Roblin was in Ottawa to discuss the matter, and on August 19 the *Free Press* noted that special volunteer forces would not be required because sufficient troops had been raised by the minister's call to the country's existing militia regiments. The enormous costs of equipping modern troops no doubt played a role in discouraging donors.

It is difficult now to know why many of the Winnipeg volunteers joined up. In January 1915, a Canadian officer offered some possible answers. In his words, men joined "because they thought they would like it, because they were out of work, because they were drunk, because they were militia men and had to save face...but being in they have quit themselves like men."[30] A look at the dates on the attestation papers signed by many men in Winnipeg in the first days of the war suggests that they went with their friends to volunteer.

Captain S.H. Williams, who joined the Fort Garry Horse in August 1914, described the scene when members of the regiment were asked who wanted to have the various shots necessary before going overseas. "Greatly to my surprise there were quite a few who sidestepped the inoculations, and declared themselves for 'home defense' service only. That of course was their business and it was not for the others of us to criticize. We fellows who had taken the inoculations felt nevertheless a bit of a self-righteous feeling."[31]

Saving face became more important as the war progressed, and those who had not immediately enlisted came under increasing pressure. The attitude of men already in the service is clear from a letter Alec Waugh wrote to his mother in December 1915 when he was still training at Shorncliffe Camp in England: "Why hasn't Chick Sharp enlisted, or Wally? From all accounts there is a streak of yellow in both and there is absolutely nothing to justify them staying away much longer.... Charlie Sharp is henceforth an acquaintance"—and, presumably, no longer a friend.[32]

Poor Women + the Patriotic Fund / Manitoba Red Cross

With the exception of the first of Canada's military nurses, those who joined the army were overwhelmingly young men. But women and those who did not volunteer were called upon emphatically to match the patriotism of their sons and husbands by giving their time and money to support the fighting men.

World War I was a total war in that the whole populations of the combatant nations were exhorted to become involved in the fight. Unlike women in some other countries, Canadian women did not participate in the actual fighting during the war. But Canadian nurses, the tens of thousands of volunteers who made bandages and a myriad of other supplies used by the troops and the women who worked in factories, shops, and offices all played an essential role in securing the Allied victory. Many men who did not join the armed forces also participated in the war effort on the home front in crucial ways.

As always happens, many innocent people's lives were disrupted and marred by the war. With the departure of their husbands and fathers in the fall of 1914, the women and children who depended upon them often faced serious problems. Few married women worked and there was very little child care outside the home, so getting a job was not always an option. Unmarried men might be leaving behind a mother or sisters who had looked to them for financial support. How would these women survive while their sons and husbands were away at the war?

In Winnipeg in 1914 such questions were as much the business of private individuals as they were the responsibility of the government. As in other large Canadian cities, the managers and owners of businesses, the lawyers and judges and government officials and their wives took the lead in organizing the Patriotic Fund and the other organizations that would ensure the vulnerable were taken care of. In all these efforts women played an essential role, providing leadership, thousands of hours of free labour, and donations of money.

Winnipeg women organized one of their first large fundraising events of the war on August 18 when a parade of women's groups collected for St. John Ambulance. The parade was organized by Mrs. E.D. Martin, the wife of a local wholesale merchant and civic politician. Three hundred women moved through the streets and circulated collection boxes among the crowd. Several militia bands took part, along with a long line of 160 cars carrying the members of various women's organizations. One woman, Grace Stapleton, stood on a float dressed as Britannia. There were many nurses in the parade, including seventy volunteers being trained by Dr. Ellen Douglass for service overseas.

For the rest of the week the Imperial Order Daughters of the Empire (IODE) produced a review, performed twice a day at the Walker Theatre. Called "The War," it included a "Patriotic Tableau," songs and readings, some motion pictures of military scenes, and talks by local people, such as Hugh John Macdonald, about the war and what it meant. Men in uniform were admitted free and the money raised was donated to war causes. Activities intended to bolster feelings of patriotism were a regular part of the IODE's mission, and the war gave the members great scope for this work.

Another charitable organization, the Manitoba Patriotic Fund, was born when the Board of Trade and its agency the Industrial Bureau resolved on August 10, six days after the declaration of war, to organize a committee which would "formulate such plans as were necessary to cope with the situation created by the mobilization of British Reservists and others for overseas service."[33] A week later the Industrial Bureau committee met together with other charitable groups such as the Associated Charities, the City Relief Department, and the Salvation Army and came up with a detailed plan of action. Adopting an idea that had been used in the past by the city's Protestant churches for charitable campaigns, they divided Winnipeg into 100 districts. In each district money would be raised and distributed to families in need, but no assistance would be given "without personal investigation of the applicant at home."

By August 31 the Winnipeg Patriotic Fund had a complete organization in place. Banker Augustus Nanton served as chair, with Judge Robson, grocery wholesaler John Galt, and printer W.J. Bulman as members, and Charles Roland, the manager of the Industrial Bureau, as secretary. The Winnipeg Patriotic Fund opted to be a province-wide organization independent of the "Canadian Patriotic Fund in the way of raising and administering funds...although quite willing to cooperate with the national organization in general work and policy." The main reason for this separate organization was that in Manitoba the organizers had decided they would look after "relatives and dependents of soldiers on active service, but they aimed also to relieve all distress and unemployment caused by the war."[34] Unemployment was a huge problem in Winnipeg and western Canada, and during the first year of the war the Manitoba Patriotic Fund paid out $70,000 to support unemployed civilians.

This decision was also characteristic of the Winnipeg elite's desire to be independent of their counterparts in Toronto and Montreal and maintain control of their own organizations and funds. Much of the work of administering the fund was done personally by the executive. During the early months of the war, Nanton, Robson, Bulman, and Galt met personally every day with men thinking of going overseas. The prospective recruits wished to be assured "that their wives and children would be taken care of while they were absent." The assurances of the committee and the knowledge that large amounts were being raised made it possible for many men to enlist with some peace of mind.

Nanton continued to be the chair of the Manitoba Patriotic Fund and was the only westerner to serve on the national executive. He donated large amounts to the fund but he also took personal responsibility for the families of soldiers. One story included in his biography is of a mother, the wife of a soldier, whose child had taken ill on a stormy winter night. A phone call was made to Nanton's house, and he in turn called a doctor who said he would go but that he could not get his car out because of the snow. Nanton got dressed and drove his own car, taking the doctor to look after the sick child.[35]

The large women's committee of 300, under Lady Nanton, did much of the actual work of the Patriotic Fund, such as visiting the homes of recipients to ensure the money was needed, and collecting and distributing thousands of items of clothing. Some were resented by the recipients for their superior attitudes, but they worked for free and without their labour the fund could not have functioned. In the end, the fund did not always live up to the promises Nanton and the others made to the departing soldiers. There was never enough money for all the needs and many wives and families knew real hardship, especially those who had no other means of support.

By April 1, 1915, the Winnipeg and Manitoba Patriotic Fund had raised $909,000. Of this $485,000 was paid out to 1839 soldiers' families. Nanton and her group had distributed 15,000 items of clothing. The fund had also given unemployment relief money to 2329 cases. One of its initiatives was a wood camp, set up and supervised by hardware merchant James Ashdown and Mayor Richard Waugh. It provided paid work for 357 unemployed men at a cost of $15,000.

Because of a small file of papers belonging to Edith Rogers, the first woman elected to the Manitoba legislature, which still survives in Archives of Manitoba, we can follow the lives of a few poor women who depended upon the Patriotic Fund for their income during the war. From their cases it is clear that the fund was not enough, by itself, to keep the women from real hardship. Although part of every soldier's pay was assigned to his dependent wife or mother at home, and the Patriotic Fund was intended to support the wives and families of soldiers, these sources alone did not provide enough for them to live with dignity and without want.

One such woman was May E., twenty-six years old in 1914 when her husband Charles went off to join the army. She had one son, an infant at the time, and her father living with her. Her fifty-two-dollar monthly income consisted of a twenty-dollar Separation Allowance, a sum paid to her by the army, seventeen dollars in assigned pay, her share of her husband's pay, and fifteen dollars from the Patriotic Fund.

At first, however, the Patriotic Fund portion of her income was not paid because her husband had been confused with another Charles E. who had gone to Valcartier but had been rejected as unfit and sent home again. May had to engage a lawyer, C.S.A. Rogers, who wrote to the Patriotic Fund office in Winnipeg to explain the situation. Rogers also asked Charles's commanding officer in his battalion to write a letter saying he was "capable, honest and sober." Those who administered the Patriotic Fund insisted that recipients be people of "good character," something which could lead to humiliating inquiries into people's personal lives.

Malicious gossip could also play a role in the lives of poor women. May E.'s payments were further delayed when two donors to the Patriotic Fund wrote a letter to Charles Roland, the administrator of the fund, complaining that their money was going to support May E. She was, they said, capable of working and refused to do so. They added that her father was also able to work but spent his days drinking in hotels. They summed up by saying, "We think they are both capable of working as there is only one child to provide for there is many cases need looking after more than this family."

Although the letter was anonymous, Roland was obliged to investigate and he asked the city's Unemployment Department to visit Mrs. E. After five visits the visitor had still found no one home. Her neighbours reported that she was out helping a sick friend. Roland wrote to her and asked her to visit him on September 15. By spring 1916, a year and half after her husband joined up, the matter was settled and she was receiving ten dollars a month from the fund.

In the fall of 1916 her two-year-old son was ill and had to be admitted to hospital. She had doctors' bills of twenty-four dollars and wrote to the Patriotic Fund to ask if they could help pay them. The fund replied that they were not responsible for doctors' bills. Months later, in the spring of 1917, she still owed four dollars to a Dr. Hill, who

These Cree soldiers from outside of The Pas, Manitoba, were among the many Aboriginal enlistees.

sent a bill with a note on it which said, "I think you are unreasonable in expecting me to allow this account to remain unpaid indefinitely. Would like to hear from you regarding same."

Like poor people everywhere, May moved a good deal from place to place: from an apartment at Aikins Street and Mountain Avenue to the Rosa Linda Apartments at 33 Evanson Street and then to 93 Harriett Street, 314 Magnus Avenue, and 399 Galloway Street. In spring 1918, when she was living at 33 Evanson, her husband wrote a letter asking that the assigned pay going to May be stopped because he had not heard from his wife for two years. Her support was still coming a year later when she was receiving a thirty-dollar separation allowance, twenty dollars in assigned pay, and nineteen dollars from the Patriotic Fund. In Winnipeg in 1919 an income of sixty-nine dollars a month for three people was inadequate to meet expenses. The cost of living had risen steadily during the war and was a concern to everyone in the city, but people like May E. had little recourse beyond cutting down on expenses. It is likely, with that meagre income, she and her father and son were malnourished.

But she would soon lose even this support. Her husband did not return to her when he left the army but deserted her for another woman. She received a small pension of fifteen dollars as a "desertion case." In 1923 May received a letter from the government informing her that this program was being phased out and she would now get only five dollars a month for one year and then nothing. The letter ended, "Will you please note this and govern yourself accordingly."

In 1928 May's son was old enough that she was working part-time as a cleaning lady at the Customs House. Her father was now bed-ridden and her son, fourteen, was not very strong. The little family was living on fifty-five dollars a month that she earned plus her father's small pension. She had not heard from her husband for six years, and although she had taken him to court twice she had not been successful in getting any help from him.

May E. was not alone among the poor women who were receiving help from the Patriotic Fund. Mrs. Rogers's file contains many examples of women requesting special funds for doctor bills, hospital bills, and advances on the next month's payments. Another case was Mrs. Margaret H., whose husband joined up in February 1916. Margaret had worked as a maid for Hugh Sutherland, a prominent Winnipeg railroad developer, and he gave her the required character reference.

In summer 1917 Margaret was struck by a car and had to have two operations. With two boys, seven and nine, to look after, Margaret told the Patriotic Fund that she had had "severe nervous attacks due to the worry." She asked that they send her husband back to her. The Patriotic Fund suggested she apply directly to Colonel Gray at 256 Main Street, the headquarters of her husband's battalion. The army did not send her husband back, but the fund did help Mrs. H. by paying for a nurse for three days after her accident and sending her some one-time relief payments. They also got in touch with R.R. Glube, who had hit her with his car, but there is no indication that he paid her any money.

Mrs. H.'s monthly budget in February 1918 depicts a situation fairly common for working-class women whose husbands were away.

With expenses exceeding income by ten dollars every month, it was a recipe for constant worry and hardship:

Income

Separation allowance.............	$25.00
Assigned pay....................	$20.00
Patriotic Fund...................	$24.00
Total	$69.00

Expenses

Rent	$20.00
Groceries......................	$25.00
Fuel...........................	$25.00
Gas and light...................	$4.50
Water	$2.50
(every three months)	
Insurance......................	$4.00
Total	$79.00

Mrs. H.'s husband came home in March 1918 on a ten-week leave, but the visit did not help her. Instead, she gave him twenty-five dollars to pay his way back to the front. The Patriotic Fund sent her a special cheque to reimburse her for this. When her husband came home for good a year later he deserted his family to live with another woman.

Mrs. H. was diagnosed with epilepsy in 1918 and then she and her sons all fell ill with the flu during the epidemic. She required more special funding to pay for nursing. Her husband did offer to pay her $100 a month on the condition that she give up the house. She refused the money, not wanting to lose her home. Her husband disappeared in 1922 and was not heard from again.

The Patriotic Fund continued to help her with small amounts of money until 1928, when her boys were able to go out and work. The community in Winnipeg had promised men in 1914 that their families would be cared for if they joined the army, and large amounts of money were donated to the Manitoba Patriotic Fund to do so. But for many women already living in poverty and unable to work to support themselves and their families, the Patriotic Fund fell short of protecting them from severe hardship while their husbands were overseas.

The provincial Red Cross organization was also launched in August 1914. The Red Cross had first been active in Canada at the Battle of Batoche in 1885 and in 1907 it was given its own Royal Charter. The Canadian group was nevertheless classified as a branch of the British Red Cross, since Canada was not seen as an independent nation by the International Red Cross in Switzerland. The first Manitoba Red Cross executive committee was led by George Galt, a wealthy grocery wholesaler and nephew of Alexander Galt, one of the Fathers of Confederation. The committee included Augustus Nanton, R.T. Riley, Lady Aikins, the wife of Sir James Aikins, Mrs. Annie Bond, and Mrs. J.H.T. Moodey. The executives of Red Cross branches in other cities did not include women in these early days, but in Winnipeg women played a central role from the beginning. Mrs. Bond, who had been a nurse with the British Army during the Zulu War, and in Egypt and the Sudan, had a good deal of useful expertise. She was one of the founders of Winnipeg's Children's Hospital.

The first months of the life of the Manitoba chapter were busy with meetings, fundraising, and organizing. By November 1914 there were forty-nine branches in communities all over Manitoba, the fundraising total was $27,000, and over half of that amount had already been disbursed to purchase blankets for the troops and to make a $10,000 donation to Red Cross headquarters in London. A member of the national executive in Toronto commented, perhaps a little condescendingly, "if a little city like Winnipeg can do that, what might we not expect from Toronto."[36]

Winnipeggers and other Manitobans rose to the challenge of funding the new organization beginning in August and their support never faltered all through the war. George Galt had donated $5000 to the cause and his cousin and business partner John Galt had done likewise. Edward Drewery, the brewer, had given $1000, and hundreds of others had given smaller amounts. The Chinese community in Winnipeg raised $453, the largest amount donated in the early weeks by any organization. From outside the city came donations of $400 and $500 from communities like Melita and Gretna. A group of Ukrainian men working in the stone quarries at Stony Mountain sent fifty dollars. Special collections were taken up in churches, and dances, concerts, and lectures were put on to raise funds for the Red Cross. In

Winnipeg, booths were set up in large stores and in the major office buildings to sell memberships.

Nellie McClung, in her book *The Next of Kin*, wrote about Red Cross fundraising in western Canada. She described one well-off woman who was making sacrifices and giving the money saved to the Red Cross: "'I will not even give a present to the boy who brings the paper,' she declared with conviction. Whether or not the boy's present ever reached the Red Cross I do not know. But ninety-five per cent of the giving was real, honest, hard, sacrificing giving. Elevator boys, maids, stenographers gave a percentage of their earnings, and gave it joyfully...one enthusiastic young citizen, who had been operated on for appendicitis, proudly exhibited his separated appendix, preserved in alcohol, at so much per look, and presented the proceeds to the Red Cross."[37]

The Manitoba St. John Ambulance Association had already sent twenty-one shipments with nearly three and a half tons of blankets, wool socks, and other such items when the Red Cross began working with them in the fall of 1914. The two organizations were officially kept separate because of the Red Cross's need to maintain its strictly neutral status. In Canada it was established that the Red Cross would fundraise both for its own projects and for the St. John Ambulance. For the next four years the Red Cross coordinated the efforts of women volunteers all over the province as they produced bandages and hospital supplies for the troops, and packed and shipped material to England.

There were occasional tensions as the independently minded Winnipeg executive questioned the policies and decisions of Red Cross headquarters in Toronto and London. One example of this occurred in the spring of 1915. C.N. Bell, secretary of the Grain Exchange, visited a meeting of the Red Cross executive with the news that donations from Winnipeg were not reaching "their destination as promptly as they should."[38] Bell, whose son was an army doctor and was likely well-informed, suggested that the Manitoba Red Cross should have a western Canada representative to liaise with the British Red Cross in London.

The exact problem Bell was reporting on is obscure but it may have been partly related to the chaotic conditions in the Toronto Red Cross headquarters. In the first months of the war, the offices, located on King Street in a room in the Anglican Church's offices, were disorganized. One volunteer described the scene: "the chaos continued for many months, the work was done with typewriters clicking, passersby enquiring, telephone bells ringing, packers in the rear hammering, with very imperfect lighting and very little ventilation."[39] The headquarters struggled to manage the large amount of money flowing in, and it was not until 1916 that the office adopted the type of modern accounting system that was standard in business offices at the time.

Such a scene might have shaken the confidence of visiting westerners, always ready to criticize the faraway headquarters in Toronto and London. The Manitoba executive responded to Bell's report by sending a telegram to the organization's president, George Galt, who was in the east doing other war-related work. He was asked to clarify the relationship of the Canadian Red Cross with the British organization. Was, they asked, "the Canadian Society looked on purely as a subsidiary to take instructions in a semi-military manner without perhaps understanding particular ends in view?... or, is the Canadian Red Cross considered a practically independent body?"

Galt explained that in fact the Canadian Red Cross was not independent of the British organization for the reasons mentioned above. Red Cross workers were indeed under the semi-military control of the British War Office: "everything we do is subject to military requisition and restriction.... Therefore, when a woman feels that she can provide a better garment or additional supplies she is forgetting the fact that the requirements have come from the War Office, and no one at the Red Cross has the right or authority to deviate from that to any material extent." That said, members of the national executive often pointed out the special advantages enjoyed by the Canadian Red Cross. Organized under its own legislation and reporting directly to the minister of militia, it had a special status, which was often helpful in getting things done.

The Winnipeg executive nevertheless reminded Galt that rumours of problems that were circulating "among the donating public" could lead to a decline in donations. Galt quickly tried to reassure the Winnipeg group that donations to the Red Cross were the best way for people to support the war effort.

Probably at his request, a letter was sent to the Winnipeg group by Adelaide Plumptre, the superintendent of supplies at the Red Cross headquarters in Toronto. Plumptre, an Oxford graduate, had taught in Toronto and would be an important volunteer and organizer for the YWCA, the Red Cross, and other organizations during both world wars. Her letter was published in the society column of the *Free Press*. Plumptre's message was that the system was working and donors and volunteers need not be concerned. The Canadian Red Cross existed, she said, to supply the Canadian hospitals in England and France. She emphasized that supplies sent by the Red Cross had a better chance of making it through to the places they were needed than items sent by other groups or individuals. Red Cross shipments were given special treatment and would be moved by army truck, while supplies sent by individuals went by the French railways, which were overwhelmed by the demands of the war. She closed by saying, "I should be extremely glad if you would make these facts known to your western branches, and try to convince them that we exist to help Canadian hospitals, and are just as anxious as they are that the Canadian Red Cross goods should make it there."[40] The Winnipeggers were not so easily silenced and there would be more friction.

Women's Volunteer Reserve Corps/IODE

Although women did not fight in the Canadian Army, the first women's military units were organized during World War I. Some women's units originated with local volunteer groups like the Winnipeg Women's Rifle Association, which held its first target practice on January 30, 1915, at its new rifle range in the basement of the Industrial Bureau building at Main and Water. The first shot was fired by Dr. Ellen Douglass, the group's president. She scored a bull's eye, just as, according to the newspapers, she had scored a bull's eye in organizing the group. Dr. Douglass, a local medical practitioner, announced that the purpose of the association was to allow interested women to gather twice a week and improve their shooting. Sergeant Broadhurst, a regular army instructor, was in charge of training. One of the city's leading women, Minnie Campbell, the widow of the former attorney general and a key figure in many organizations, had agreed to be the honorary president of the association.

The Rifle Association had proven to be a popular idea when it was founded in 1915 and over fifty women signed up and paid the fifty-cent fee to help defray expenses. The rifle range had to be kept open until quite late in the evening to accommodate everyone and very soon a second range was built. These women, many of whose brothers and friends were volunteering for the army, may have joined the association as an act of solidarity. At least some would have joined in the hope that they too would eventually be called on to defend their country as their male friends and relatives were doing.

In July 1915, Douglass provided the women of the city a chance to participate in the war in a more committed way by joining the Women's Volunteer Reserve Corps. She presided over a meeting of the Rifle Association at which this group was founded. The newspaper accounts seem to suggest that not all the members of the Rifle Association supported this action and care was taken to make the Reserve Corps a separate organization, even as Ellen Douglass led both groups.

Douglass had received encouragement and advice from another medical doctor, Dr. Ella Scarlett-Synge of Vancouver, who had visited her in Winnipeg in early 1915. Scarlett-Synge was the daughter of Lord Abinger and her family included many military men. She was the leader of a movement to establish women's regiments in Canadian communities, to do "home guard" work or even to act as auxiliary units at the front. The object of these units was, as the *British Journal of Nursing* explained in 1915, to prepare women "to relieve the men in such work as signaling, dispatch riding, telegraphing, motor-car driving and camp cooking."[41] These groups were the forerunners of the Women's Royal Canadian Naval Service, the Canadian Women's Army Corps, and the Canadian Women's Auxiliary of the Royal Canadian Air Force in World War II. The *Journal* went on to report that "many of the women who have joined the different corps are already crack shots and good horsewomen."

Not everyone supported the idea. Indeed, some seemed to see the units as a sort of insult to the noble mission of the fighting troops. The *Canadian Annual Review* for 1915 reported that, in Toronto and

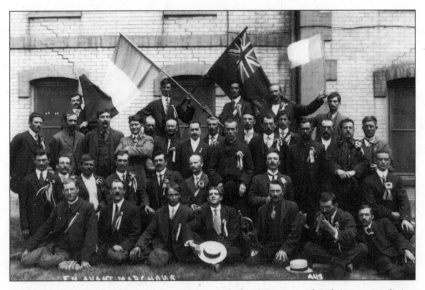

Reservists from several European nations, including France and Belgium, were living in Winnipeg at the outbreak of the war and many went home to join the army.

Montreal, these types of corps had an "ephemeral existence during the year with a tendency in the public mind to look upon them as zealous but mistaken travesties of a serious subject." The *Toronto Star* expressed the opinion on August 31 that "the grim business of enlisting to bear a hand in the life and death struggle convulsing Europe and the world ought not to be mimicked by a toy movement."[42]

Douglass does not appear to have been much worried by such attitudes as she prepared the Reserve Corps to be active and useful in the fight. The July 28, 1915, *Free Press* quoted her: "there was already a splendid nucleus for such a corps for 250 girls had their first aid and home nursing certificates, there were six squads of stretcher bearers as well as a number of expert markswomen in the Rifle Association."

The members of the Winnipeg corps were taught to march and shoot as well as to drive ambulances and operate field telephones. In the summer the members spent time at Gimli where they were drilled by Sergeant Carroll and took swimming lessons. The corps was involved in a variety of activities in Winnipeg, including the same sorts of volunteer work as other women. They raised funds and put on a Christmas party for the children of servicemen at the Royal

Alexandra Hotel, and they maintained a driving school for returned soldiers wanting to get a chauffeur's licence. The corps also operated a registration bureau for women who were willing to take the places of men who wanted to volunteer to go overseas. They raised funds for these activities in a variety of ways, including putting on a play at the Walker Theatre and selling sheet music for a popular song they had published called "Boys, Our Hearts Are With You." The women of the corps also participated in military parades and helped with recruiting. In 1917, eighty-five members marched in the Decoration Day parade, led by Dr. Douglass, by then a lieutenant colonel.

Douglass's other main focus during the war was the St. John Ambulance Society, of which she was acting deputy commissioner. She worked hard to recruit volunteer nurses and in January 1918 took a contingent of nurses to France. She was to stay there for over a year, serving as a major in the British Army Medical Corps in Calais.

Minnie Julia Beatrice Campbell was Douglass's colleague in the St. John Ambulance as well as being involved in many other organizations that fought the war on the home front. But it was as regent of the Fort Garry chapter and Manitoba provincial president of the IODE that Campbell made her greatest contribution.

The IODE was founded in 1900 by Margaret Polson Murray of Montreal to provide support for the Canadian volunteers who were going to fight in South Africa. Murray, a native of Scotland, was the wife of a philosophy professor at McGill University and had been active in many charitable organizations in the city. The IODE was intended to be an organization that would promote patriotism, service to others, and loyalty to the Crown.

The IODE enjoyed a quasi-official status, and from the beginning had the patronage of the governors general and their wives. For the IODE at this time, patriotism meant loyalty to Canada as a part of the British Empire, with an emphasis on personal loyalty to the monarch. They attempted to instill these feelings of loyalty in school children by giving prizes for essays on patriotic topics and distributing such things as cards with a short history of the Union Jack to schools. The pre-war IODE supported other campaigns, and had chosen the fight against tuberculosis as a special cause. In Manitoba various chapters had raised funds to help build a sanitorium at Ninette. In one four-day period, a committee chaired by Mrs. Campbell raised $12,000 toward the construction of a pavilion at the Ninette hospital. Roughly equivalent to $300,000 in today's money, the total would be considered an amazing accomplishment for any fundraiser.

When World War I began, the IODE devoted itself to the war effort, and members certainly saw themselves as being very much in the fight. National president Mrs. A.E. Gooderham of Toronto defined the order's wartime role: "to provide every possible necessity and comfort for the brave men volunteering to serve their country, through the Red Cross for sick and wounded, and field comforts for the fighting man and to make things better for the wives and children and all dependents left at home."[43] A Manitoba IODE publication, reporting on the organization's successes, expanded on these aims: "we sincerely hope that when this souvenir is received by husbands, sons, brothers and friends of the members they will feel that while they have been in the thick of the fight their women-folk have tried, with all their heart and soul, to do their part at home."[44]

Minnie Campbell was probably the most influential leader of the IODE in the west. She travelled widely to help local groups set up chapters and became well-known from Manitoba to British Columbia. In an organization dominated by women from Toronto and Montreal, she provided western members with a strong and determined leader. She was certainly one of the most important women in Winnipeg at the outbreak of the war. She was a well-organized and determined activist whose forceful personality gave her a lot of influence over events. Her position also derived in part from her wealth—when her husband, Colin Campbell, died in October 1914, he left the equivalent of $2.7 million in 2010 dollars. Much of this bequest was invested in real estate and solid investments in companies like the CPR, Great-West Life, and the Bank of Hamilton. As a wealthy woman she was able to employ servants to care for her children and to run her house, thus securing free time for herself to pursue her activities.

A second source of influence was her husband, who, until he suffered a stroke in the spring of 1913, was Premier Roblin's closest collaborator, his attorney general, and his likely successor as Conservative leader. Her connections to the Conservative Party, provincially and federally, were useful in her work. She had married Colin Campbell in the early 1880s in Ontario before they emigrated to Manitoba. As the wife of a rising young lawyer in Winnipeg she became involved in various organizations and was one of the group of women who helped turn Winnipeg from a rough frontier town into a major centre with the services and charities of a growing city.

In 1912 Campbell had written to his wife that he was "tired and feel I need a rest...I have worked long enough. It is now 40 years since I started." But he did not rest. He kept up a killing pace as the minister of public works and the man responsible for party patronage, a job that entailed dealing with a huge correspondence from people wanting favours from the Conservative government. When he fell ill, his wife bent every effort to help him recover. He was in New York when he suffered his stroke and she asked their friend Robert Rogers to lend them his private railway car so she could bring Colin home. Together they spent the next year and a half travelling to various spas in Jamaica, Egypt, France, and the U.S. in an effort to speed his recovery, but nothing worked. He died in October 1914, leaving his wife a relatively young widow at fifty-two with two school-aged children.

While her husband's death profoundly changed her life and put an end to many of her ambitions, she was not content to retreat into her house, dressed in mourning. On the contrary, she made the war her cause and let her fellow IODE members know in November that she "meant to take up her work immediately. There is so much that we women can do now for King and Empire and the world in this time of war."[45]

In the 1915–16 *Canadian Who's Who*, Campbell was one of the few Canadian women with her own entry. Two pages were devoted to her accomplishments and there was a large portrait photo showing a formidable woman swathed in furs. The entry tells us that Minnie Campbell had studied at the Western Female College in Hamilton in the 1870s and then taught at the Presbyterian Ottawa Ladies' College in 1881 and 1882. Her work for the YWCA, the IODE, and in other areas was described.

Campbell had always pursued conservative imperialist political goals, working to foster close ties with Britain and the Empire. She frequently spoke of the United Empire Loyalist origin of both her parents and of the importance of loyalty to the crown. She was proud

of having been a guest at the coronations of both Edward VII and
George V, and had been presented at court. She often mentioned these
details in speeches she gave in Winnipeg and elsewhere. She worked
to bring former British servicemen to western Canada as homesteaders to strengthen the British population base.

As president of the Manitoba IODE and regent of the Fort Garry
chapter she was one of the main leaders of the group's war efforts in
the province. Her work had actually begun in 1913 when she became
chair of a War Aid Committee for the St. John Ambulance. When the
war began, this group was ready to begin immediately the work of
sending "comforts"—small luxuries like cigarettes, reading material,
writing paper, and warm socks—to the troops.

But the IODE would be her main focus. At a meeting of the Fort
Garry chapter held in her house on September 8, she reported on
the national IODE's aim of raising funds for a hospital ship. Minnie
Campbell had proposed a national goal to raise $100,000 in one week
for the project, and back home the Manitoba chapters would take just
one week to raise close to $7000. By the end of September 1914, the
25,000 IODE members across Canada had raised a quarter of a million
dollars. Ultimately, the money would not be needed for a ship and instead was used at the Royal Navy Hospital at Haslar near Portsmouth
and for the purchase of forty motor ambulances for use at the front.[46]

The IODE worked with other organizations like the Women's
Christian Temperance Union, the Women's Institutes, and the Council
of Women branches, and many women held memberships in more
than one of these national organizations. Besides fundraising, the
women visited the families of soldiers who had gone overseas, sewed
and knitted, usually working in groups in private homes or church
or community halls, put on entertainments for troops billeted in their
communities, and provided canteens and reading rooms.

In the first months of the war, Campbell involved herself directly in
supporting the troops. She was chair of an IODE committee that aimed
to provide 100 nightshirts for wounded soldiers. The order provided
the money, and unemployed seamstresses were hired to do the work
in the sewing room of the YWCA in Winnipeg. Chapter members also
donated money to have 100 grey flannel shirts made for the army in a
local garment factory.

The women of Imperial Order Daughters of the Empire worked along with many other women's groups throughout the war to provide Canadian troops with essential supplies such as warm socks.

At this time Campbell was writing five or six letters a day, asking for donations to various campaigns. She organized teas in her home to raise money for "comforts" for Canadian soldiers. By the end of March 1915, the Fort Garry chapter had produced 1056 pairs of socks, thirteen scarves, five pairs of mitts, and fifty-four cholera belts for the army. When the 32nd Battalion left the city in February, Campbell was at the station to hand out a pair of socks to each man. Such small contributions, multiplied by the thousands of Canadian women who made them, combined to form an essential support system for the army in Europe.

On October 8, 1914, Campbell published a column in the *Free Press* passing on information for volunteer knitters and sewers. Addressed to "the women of Manitoba" and beginning "Dear Compatriots," the column outlines the specifications for socks: "use number thirteen needles and fourply wool. Some socks sent in are knitted on too coarse needles for comfort, warmth and durability. We want an authorized standard of work." She was glad that the "good old-time art" of knitting was enjoying a revival now because of the need for good socks for the infantry. And she took the opportunity to remind her readers of the good example of Queen Mary, who knit constantly for the soldiers and who expected ladies visiting her to do the same. She reported that pillows were no longer needed as the first contingent of Canadians had enough, but that nightshirts, bed jackets, and dressing gowns were now needed in great numbers for the inevitable wounded.

Campbell described the work of the St. John Ambulance volunteers who purchased the first supplies of material, cut out the pieces for the garments, and mailed them on to volunteer sewing groups around the province. When the items returned, the volunteers at the St. John Ambulance rooms in the Industrial Bureau packed them up and sent them on their way to England.

There was now a great need for blankets as there was a shortage of these in England. Winnipeg housewives were asked to respond to this "call to the colours" and send their own blankets for the troops and the Red Cross hospitals. To inspire them, Campbell wrote, "Were you not touched by the loyalty and generosity of the German women living in Italy, who sent two car loads of linen bandages and ravellings from their house wife stores to the German soldiers?" She closed her column by telling her readers that Lord Roberts had put out a call for donations of binoculars for the army. She said she was sure that Winnipeg men would "freely offer their field glasses for service." Campbell delivered similar exhortations to her provincial executive members, encouraging them to be strong minded, wear out their old clothes, trim their old hats, and "cultivate talents growing dormant," like knitting. Winnipeg women were to live their lives, in all ways, to support the war effort.[47]

A year later, in the fall of 1915, the provincial IODE chapter in Manitoba was shaken by a quarrel. Minnie Campbell had been away in Cape Breton for the summer, resting and avoiding the, for her, humiliating fall of her dead husband's colleagues from power. In her absence, Mrs. Coombes, wife of the dean of St. John's Cathedral, had been acting president. A cheque had been received and Coombes had refused to endorse it. The treasurer, Mrs. George Hughes, then sent the cheque on to Campbell in Nova Scotia and she signed it and it was deposited.

The acting president saw this as improper, stopped the cheque, and returned it. Then the executive voted to remove Hughes and install another treasurer. The quarrel attracted the attention of the IODE's national executive, which sent a detailed letter directing the Manitoba chapter to hold a special meeting and listing what should be discussed. There was clearly concern that scandal might affect the flow of donations for IODE causes and the situation had to be examined.

Campbell, now back from her vacation on Cape Breton, called a meeting for October 23 and distributed copies of the letter to all who would be present. Anticipating trouble, she asked a lawyer, W.J. Wright, to attend the meeting to interpret the constitution, and arranged for a court reporter to make a verbatim record of the discussions. While it was not explicitly stated, there is no doubt that the disastrous collapse of the Conservative government, of which her dead husband had been such a prominent member, influenced some IODE members. If her husband was suspected of having been involved in illegal activities involving taxpayers' money, then Minnie Campbell might not be the best spokeswoman for the order. She moved decisively to safeguard her reputation and her career as a community leader.

The meeting took place at the Industrial Bureau on Main Street and lasted for six hours. There was a lively discussion of matters such as the duties of the treasurer. The *Telegram* reported that "Mrs. Campbell conducted the meeting in a business-like manner. Repeated efforts were made to stampede her but she steadfastly stuck to the agenda...and ruled excited members out of order when they did not do the same." The former treasurer, Hughes, defended her actions and pointed out that she had been invited to serve a second term a month before being asked to leave by Coombes. All her accounts had been audited and found in order.

Finally, Coombes and fourteen other officers and councillors who had been seated together near the front of the hall rose together and laid their resignations on the table: "as a protest against the unconstitutional methods of the President and Treasurer. Mrs. Campbell asked the meeting 'Do you accept them?' and there was loud applause." A formal vote then confirmed the acceptance of the resignations and another vote, 124 to 54, confirmed the reinstatement of Hughes. This was followed by a vote of confidence in Campbell and a confirmation

of new members of the executive selected to fill the places of those
who had resigned.

This meeting shows Minnie Campbell at her fighting best, challeng-
ing her opponents head-on and winning. The following February the
national executive confirmed Campbell's actions, and when Coombes
and her supporters protested they were told to behave themselves.
Campbell had her summary of the events in the controversy printed
along with Coombes's rebuttal and distributed it to the entire IODE
membership in Manitoba.

City Politics in 1914/1914 election

In the ornate council chamber at city hall on Main Street, the war
years were a time of change. From being dominated by businessmen
in 1914, the council became more representative, by 1918, to include
enough pro-labour aldermen to establish the principle of collective
bargaining for city workers. There was also a change in the city's long-
standing bad relations with Sir William Mackenzie and the Winnipeg
Electric Railway. Both as president of the Canadian Northern Railway
and of the street railway, Mackenzie had been in conflict with the city
over the location of railway lines and aspects of the administration
of the streetcar company. During the years from 1915 to 1918, competition from jitneys (privately operated taxis) brought the electric
railway close to bankruptcy and made it much more responsive to the
city's demands.

During World War I, Winnipeg municipal government was based
on a Board of Control model. The mayor and four controllers were
elected annually, and the board acted as a sort of executive, dealing
with money matters and controlling all the city departments. Fourteen
aldermen were elected for two-year terms, seven at each annual municipal election. All male British subjects over twenty-one could vote
in provincial elections, and women won the right to vote in 1916, but
city voting rules were much more restrictive. Property ownership or
tenancy at specific dollar levels were required for both candidates
and voters, and many property owners had not one but several votes
based on the location of their holdings. Corporations with property in

the city could assign their votes to people designated by the owners. Women who owned property were able to vote in city elections. These rules gave Winnipeg's business elite firm control of the municipal government.[48]

Civic politics in Winnipeg during the war years were focussed on problems created by the war. The cost of living rose steadily from 1914 to 1918 and although wages also rose, after an initial period of depression, they never kept pace with the rise in prices. The increasing pressure forced wage earners to become increasingly militant in demanding higher wages and a more just distribution of the wealth that was being created by the war.

In the early months of 1914, western Canada was still suffering through the economic depression that had begun in 1913. Winnipeg, the city that had arguably benefitted most from the boom of the previous decade, now faced the lion's share of the effects of its collapse. As would happen again in the 1930s, Winnipeg became home to large numbers of unemployed men because it was the great labour clearing house for western Canada to which men unable to find work on the railroad-building crews or in the bush, cutting trees for lumber, returned, looking for a job. When they ran out of money they turned to the city to provide them with relief.

On May 26, 1914, around 2000 of these men had gathered in Market Square behind city hall to listen to speakers and to protest their hopeless condition. The men were preparing to march through the downtown, asking for work or bread, when the police intervened. Fighting broke out, and the police used their nightsticks on the unemployed men, causing many injuries. Some witnesses claimed that when the police attempted to arrest one of the speakers they were attacked by men carrying shovels.

Shortly afterwards the council received a letter from the Social Democratic Party, accusing the police of starting the riot. Most of the crowd, the letter contended, were men with families to look after who had met together to try and decide what to do about their difficult situation. The police had been too free with the use of their sticks, in the opinion of the Social Democrats.[49] There is no doubt that in Winnipeg, still a brawling frontier city in many ways, with a large population of young single men, the police were often free with the use of their billy clubs.

The city council's reaction to the unemployment problem was similar to that of many other bodies in Canada—they sought to stop or slow down immigration while at the same time providing work for the unemployed on public projects. Pro-labour aldermen Richard Rigg and R.J. Shore asked Council to send a letter to Prime Minister Robert Borden "requesting that more rigorous regulation be applied to immigrants coming to western Canada until the labour market improves and recommending that the Dominion government push forward public works as a means of relieving distress."

W.J. Roche, minister of immigration, responded that notification had already been placed in the British papers and notification had been sent several times so far in 1914 to steamship agents, government officers, and booking agents in Europe and Great Britain to discourage immigration of "the artisan or laborer skilled or unskilled." Only those who wanted to homestead or work as domestic servants were encouraged. Immigrant labourers had been absolutely prohibited from entering British Columbia by Order in Council until September 30. Immigration had fallen 50 percent as a result, and Roche wrote, "We think therefore that the government are doing everything in their power to prevent a further influx of the labor element."[50]

The control of immigration into British Columbia was a particularly hot topic in the spring of 1914 because of the *Komagata Maru* incident. A Sikh businessman in Hong Kong had decided to challenge Canada's laws restricting the immigration of British subjects from India. He chartered a Japanese vessel, the SS *Komagata Maru* and sold tickets to people of Sikh background living in Hong Kong and wishing to move to Canada. The ship arrived in Vancouver on May 23, 1914. Two months later, when it sailed away again, only a few of the passengers had been allowed to land in spite of the efforts of lawyers and supporters to get permission for the immigration of all on board. Public opinion in British Columbia and elsewhere was firmly opposed to allowing unrestricted non-white immigration, and the doors remained firmly closed to all but a carefully controlled quota of Asians wanting to settle in Canada. The infamous head tax made life particularly hard for Chinese men who settled in Canada, and Chinese women were generally not allowed into the country at all. Japanese immigration was strictly controlled.

Not everyone wanted to see immigration slowed down. Alderman Altar Skaletar presented a letter and resolution to council from a large meeting of Jewish citizens of Winnipeg, which said in part, "after listening to the arguments against the suppression of immigration to Western Canada and the arguments advanced by the Trades and Labor Council and their representative Alderman Rigg, we the Jewish citizens of Winnipeg unanimously disapprove of the action taken by the Trades and Labor Council in regard to the suspension of immigration to Western Canada."[51] Most Jewish families in Winnipeg had relatives in Russia and eastern Europe who they were anxious to bring to Canada. The war would soon cut off hope of further immigration and leave many stranded.

This was the case with the Wolodarsky family. Joseph Wolodarsky had come to Winnipeg before the war to earn money and prepare a home for the mother and sister he left behind in Russia. The outbreak of war caught the two women in transit to Canada and they were forced to return and wait several more years before finally joining Joseph in Winnipeg.[52]

Another woman, Chasie Karpachevsky, decided she was coming to Canada in spite of the complications placed in her path by the war. Together with her two children, she travelled all the way to Winnipeg from Russia to join her husband Moses. Driven from her home village by Cossacks, who beat her and her children with whips and robbed them of their savings, she set out with only a piece of paper with her husband's name on it as a passport. She and her children travelled through Siberia and crossed to Japan. Then she made her way to San Francisco, Prince Rupert, Edmonton, and finally to her husband on Boyd Street in Winnipeg.

There had actually been signs of recovery in some areas of the economy in Winnipeg in early 1914, as money had become a little easier to borrow in the London market, the chief source of capital for western Canada. By August, the value of building permits had already reached $12.1 million, two-thirds of the total for 1913. New apartment blocks and houses were under construction, especially in River Heights and Crescentwood.

Then the war put a final stop to the recovery as the province ceased all expenditures in the capital account, including work on the new legislative building, and many more men were out of work than before. British capital, the lifeblood of western Canadian development, became unavailable at reasonable rates. Local businessmen were forced to postpone or abandon plans like those R.T. Riley was making for a mortgage company that would loan money to farmers in the west. He and his partners had been successful in selling stock in Canada and they opened an office in London in July 1914 to sell debentures to investors there. They closed the office a few weeks later when, Riley writes, "we realized that there was little opportunity of getting 4% money in England, or anywhere else, for some time to come. We never sold any debentures, as we could not afford to pay a higher rate."[53]

Toward the end of September 1914, Mayor Deacon reported to city council on a speech made by British Chancellor of the Exchequer David Lloyd George, in which he made a strong appeal to the people of Great Britain not to permit any money to go out of Great Britain that could be avoided. He strongly expressed the opinion that the present war would be a contest of resources as well as of arms, and urged upon the people of Great Britain not to subscribe for municipal debentures which he particularly mentioned, or other forms of capital expenditure which could be avoided until after the war, using the expression "it would probably be the last few hundreds of millions which would finally turn the scale in favor of the nation possessing them," and urged the people of the British Isles to see that they had money on hand when the time came.

Deacon thought that the British people would do as Lloyd George said, so he could not see where money for further development in the Canadian west would come from. Deacon felt it was unlikely that Canada would be able to borrow in the United States, although that is exactly what would happen later in the war. He continued: "I therefore suggest that it will be the course of prudence on behalf of the city just now to husband its resources and not completely exhaust the credits we have on hand in case some unforeseen emergency or accident should occur before the war is over."[54]

The slowdown in immigration and western growth undermined Winnipeg's economy and its position of dominance in western Canada.

A great deal of the city's prosperity in the past decade had depended upon the regular flow of British capital. Local firms acted as conduits for British funds being invested in western projects, and Winnipeg established itself as a supply centre for the rapid development taking place all over the west and as a marketplace for the growing stream of western products resulting from the investment. An additional factor later in the war was that Winnipeg did not participate to any great extent in the wartime manufacturing boom that enriched eastern cities like Montreal and Toronto.

In addition to the problem of unemployment was the fact that many of those who did keep their jobs at the outbreak of the war were put on reduced salaries. Irene Evans wrote to her husband in late August 1914 that many people were being put on half pay. She herself was reducing the salaries of her servants and "even Judge Robson says he had to because demands were so many and salary no greater. For over 2 weeks I have done nearly all the cooking and its no small undertaking." Many other women fired their maids to save money, and by early 1915 the city relief office was appealing to people to keep their maids so they would not have to go on relief.

The numbers of unemployed in the city continued to be high, although the pressure was alleviated somewhat by the large numbers of men who left the city at the time. Some were among the 12,000 to 14,000 men who joined the army in the first months of the war. In all, it was estimated that 20,000 to 25,000 left the city at the end of 1914 and beginning of 1915. Many people went to search for work elsewhere. For example, about 100 skilled tradesmen were recruited to work in British munitions plants, and another group went all the way to Russia to work on railroad construction.[55]

In November 1914 there was a conference in Regina to discuss the problem of the large number of unemployed men, "chiefly of foreign birth," all over the west, who "had been engaged until recently on construction work in cities and on the railroads." A.J. Crossin went to represent the Winnipeg Board of Trade. On his return he reported on the various ideas that were discussed, including giving unemployed men 150 acres and $1500 for farming equipment. This solution had been rejected on the grounds that the kind of agriculture practised by these men at home in eastern Europe did not exist in Canada and they

An immigrant neighbourhood in North End Winnipeg. The status of foreign-born people became an important issue once war broke out.

might fail. It was unwise, the group decided, to give money to untested men.[56] The attendees may not have been familiar with the many prosperous farms in Ukrainian districts in the western provinces where eastern Europeans had, in some cases, been settled for twenty years. Giving out homesteads as a form of relief was an idea that was often dusted off in the years ahead. Returning soldiers, for example, were given land at the end of the war if they wished to go farming.

Shortly after the Regina meeting, Winnipeg city council voted to put $50,000 into the budget for relief payments to unemployed people. In a speech to council, Premier Roblin promised the province would match what the city appropriated dollar for dollar. Alex Macdonald, a wealthy wholesale grocer and long-time city politician, encouraged council to do even more. Rather than cutting back, he encouraged council to borrow money and embark upon public works to keep the thousands of unemployed men in the city working. He said western Canada should support these men, who were "brought here by us to work and now they have been let go."[57] During 1915, support for the unemployed became better organized, and in the later years of the war there was more work available. Then the focus shifted from unemployment to the rising cost of living, which reduced the buying power of people's wages.

Provincially, 1914 was an election year. The Conservative Party of Rodmond Roblin, which had ruled the province since 1900, won its fourth majority in the July 10 election. Although the years ahead would bring enormous changes in the political landscape of Manitoba, in July it had seemed that things would continue as they had since the turn of the century. While Roblin and his party were showing signs of age, he seemed to be securely in power for another four years. The Conservative Party organization, built by one of the masters of machine politics, Robert Rogers, was still functioning well, although it was now confronted by a determined alliance of reform groups who had allied themselves with the Liberals led by T.C. Norris. Faced with a seemingly unbeatable opponent, Norris had adopted the same strategy used by Robert Borden in 1910 to defeat the Liberals of Wilfrid Laurier: he pulled together a coalition of diverse groups, each opposed to some policy of the government, thus broadening the base of his support and gaining some articulate and skillful allies. The Political Equality League, which campaigned for female suffrage, the various organizations of the temperance movement, the Orange Lodge, and the Social Service Council were the most significant of Norris's allies.

Many of these groups had opposed Roblin throughout his time in office, while some had only recently been his supporters. The main issues they placed before the public in the 1914 election were prohibition, electoral reforms, including votes for women, and education policy. These were peace-time issues, basic questions concerning the type of community that the citizens of the relatively new province wanted. The struggle over these questions would not stop because of the war but the war would certainly influence the depth of people's feelings about many of them.

The temperance movement had long been a powerful influence in English Canadian public life and no politician would willingly antagonize the array of organizations working for the abolition of the liquor trade. Roblin was always quick to describe himself as a temperance man who wanted to ban the bar. But he rejected complete prohibition, preferring to control the trade with licensing rules and the local option, whereby individual municipalities could vote to be "dry." There was a great deal of enmity between Roblin and some of the temperance activists because of his handling of the prohibition law passed by his predecessor, Hugh John Macdonald, in 1900. Roblin, who replaced Macdonald as premier in 1901, wanted Manitobans to confirm their support for the Act in a referendum before proclaiming it. The temperance movement, so close to their long-dreamed-of victory, was outraged and interpreted Roblin's referendum as a plot to kill the Act. They accused the premier of being a pawn of the liquor interests. Many in the movement took the rather illogical position that the vote should be boycotted. Temperance supporters stayed home, with the inevitable result that their opponents won the day.

Roblin then embarked upon a liquor control policy, which, by 1914, had resulted in 80 percent of the province becoming dry through local municipal referenda. Rural French and Ukrainian districts and the cities of St. Boniface and Winnipeg were now the only areas that did not support prohibition. Changes in the licensing rules over the same period abolished the unregulated saloons of Winnipeg's early days and allowed bars only in hotels with a prescribed number of rooms for rent. Bars had to be fully visible from the street and the number of licences granted in each community was strictly limited.

In spite of these and many other measures, Roblin's refusal to introduce a comprehensive liquor ban antagonized temperance activists like the Reverend Charles Gordon, who was also chair of the Social Service Council. Years of friction over the issue had led to the development of a "clear cut and bitter hostility" between such activists and the premier and they campaigned vigorously against him.[58] In early June 1914, Gordon spoke from his pulpit at St. Stephen's Church, encouraging his congregation to defeat the Roblin government and arguing that prohibition "is not a question of party politics but of ethics, patriotism and religion." Another Protestant clergyman, the Baptist F.W. Pugh, told his congregation that "Premier Roblin must be put down and out." At a temperance convention in Winnipeg in March 1914, resolutions were passed supporting the Liberal Party because, if elected, it had undertaken to hold a provincial referendum on total prohibition.

Supporters of women's suffrage, many of whom also supported prohibition, allied themselves with the Liberals, who promised to hold a referendum on this issue as well. On January 27, 1914, a delegation from the suffragist Political Equality League, including novelist

Nellie McClung, went to see Roblin to press their case. The premier was completely opposed to extending the franchise to women, and they left him unmoved as usual. Among other things, McClung argued that boys and girls were educated together and should therefore vote together. Roblin made the same arguments that all opponents of women's suffrage made at the time: if women could vote they would abandon their homes, leaving their children "in the arms of servant girls," a dig at middle-class activists like McClung, who could afford to hire a servant to look after their home. The stability of the family and of society as a whole would be endangered, argued the premier.

The next day the Political Equality League held a public meeting at the Walker Theatre, which included a satirical "Women's Parliament." McClung lampooned Roblin, imitating his style of speaking and, playing the role of a woman politician, argued that if men were allowed to vote, the foundations of the home and family would be shaken. During the six months leading up to the July election she became one of the most persuasive Liberal campaigners, speaking at dozens of meetings throughout the province. The *Canadian Annual Review* stated that it was "the first time in Canadian history a woman was a conspicuous figure in a political fight, a favorite and popular speaker, an eloquent exponent of a cause." She was described as being "gifted with cleverness of speech and unusual powers of logical argument" so that "her attack was interesting and probably effective."

Perhaps the most bitter controversy of a very bitter election campaign was over education. When Manitoba entered Confederation, a school system administered by separate Protestant and Catholic school boards was established. The schools attached to each board were separated by religion but also by language, the Catholic schools being, for the most part, French-language schools. In 1870 the population was evenly divided between Protestant and Catholic, with Catholics slightly in the majority. By 1889, however, the influx of new settlers had changed the makeup of the population such that the Protestant school board was administering 629 school districts while the Catholic board had only ninety, most of them teaching in French.

The newly elected Liberal government of Thomas Greenway passed a new *Schools Act*, replacing the dual school boards with a new secular, state-supported English-language system of schools, a change so extensive and sweeping, and so apparently insensitive to the rights and needs of the French population, that it caused a major crisis in the province.

The changes resulted in a prolonged resistance and protest, with court challenges by both the Catholic and Anglican churches and interventions by the federal government. Finally in 1897 negotiations produced the Laurier-Greenway Agreement incorporated in Section 258 of the *Schools Act*. This section provided that, if there were forty Catholic students in an urban school or ten in a country school, they had to be taught by Catholic teachers and, if ten families requested it, the school had to offer them religious instruction. If ten students in a school came from homes where the mother tongue was not English, the children would be educated in their native language and English "on the bilingual system."

In 1897 it was assumed by many that the French population would continue to decline relative to the English population and Section 258 would not be used very much. This assumption proved to be quite wrong. Between 1897 and 1916 there was enormous growth in the school system in Manitoba. From 1018 school districts and 21,500 students in 1897, the system grew to 1835 districts and 66,561 students. The growth of the population through immigration that produced this expansion also changed the ethnic mix of the province, and the application of Section 258 produced a school system that taught not only in English and French, but also in German, Ukrainian, and Polish. By 1916, 16 percent of the students in the province attended bilingual schools There were 126 French schools with 16,720 students and 234 teachers, 61 German Mennonite schools with 2814 pupils and 73 teachers, and 111 Ukrainian or Polish schools with 6513 students and 114 teachers.

Rodmond Roblin, first elected to the legislature as a Liberal in 1888, broke with the party over the new *Schools Act*, which he opposed. The schools question, so central in the 1890s, remained an important political issue in the years following the compromise. During the first election campaign Roblin fought as premier, in 1903, the Liberals reminded voters that he had voted against the 1890 *Schools Act* and warned that if elected he might turn back the clock and abolish the state school system. Roblin was elected with a healthy majority, based on his success with other issues. Throughout his fifteen years in office, he refused to reopen the schools question, saying he did not want to rekindle the bitter disputes of the 1890s.

During the election campaigns of 1907 and 1910, the Liberals charged that Manitoba students were not learning enough English to succeed in Canada and that many children were not attending school at all. They argued that the bilingual system was a failure, producing graduates who could not understand the value of British liberty and democracy. The Liberals argued that the system had become impossible to administer; they wanted a compulsory education law, an idea popular with the supporters of secular public education in Ontario and Quebec and one which was enjoying growing support in Manitoba among school trustees and groups like the Orange Lodge. Parents who paid for their children to attend parochial schools feared that they would be forced to send their children to the state institutions.

On the other side of the question, Archbishop Langevin credited the Roblin government with lessening the effects of the *Schools Act*, even though they refused to change it. Roblin enjoyed the support of many French and Ukrainian voters because of his support for the existing system and his decision, at Archbishop Langevin's request, to extend it to language groups other than French.

Roblin's party had begun to appeal to Ukrainian voters in 1904 in an attempt to woo them away from the Liberals, who normally had their support. In response to the lobbying of activists like Thomas Jastremsky, who became a Conservative Party organizer, Roblin established a Ukrainian normal school in Brandon in 1905.[59]

The normal school was important in the development of the Ukrainian community in these years. Its graduates, the first Ukrainians to receive higher education, were often farmers' sons born in Manitoba, but some were men who had received their education at home in cities like Lviv and who often had progressive views about society. Many became community leaders, and among their number were Canada's first Ukrainian member of Parliament, Manitoba's first Ukrainian members of the legislative assembly, agronomists, editors, medical doctors, lawyers, and judges.[60]

Roblin's government attempted to steer a course between the various extreme positions on the topic of education. Roblin maintained the bilingual schools were not as inefficient as the Liberals claimed. He said he refused to penalize the "children of parents who speak a language other than English."[61] He said that both parents and children would learn English in good time because it was "in their obvious interest." Conservative Education Minister George Coldwell argued that the government's program to provide more teachers and improve school buildings would improve attendance and that truant officers dealt satisfactorily with those not attending.[62] In 1912 he introduced changes to the *Schools Act*, known as the Coldwell Amendments, which had the effect of making it possible for Catholic students to receive a Catholic education in rooms within a larger state school. It was hoped by some that this would mean school boards would take over Catholic schools and run them as state schools. In 1913 Catholic parents in Winnipeg petitioned the school board to do just that and asked moreover that teachers who were members of religious orders be allowed to wear their habits to teach.[63]

In 1913 the *Free Press* did an extensive survey of bilingual schools and published a long series of articles generally critical of the school system. These articles brought a reaction from Ukrainian activists. Orest Zerebko, editor of the *Ukrainian Voice* newspaper, rebutted the *Free Press* charges and argued that there were actually pedagogical advantages to learning two languages. A protest meeting of Ukrainian farmers at Cook's Creek emphasized the connection between language and identity when they passed a resolution stating, "those who desire to destroy our native language in the schools are destroying us at the same time."

The Orange Lodge, traditionally supportive of the Conservatives, was so outraged by the Coldwell amendments that it expelled George Coldwell from membership and withdrew support from Roblin in the fall of 1913. The lodge campaigned actively for the Liberals in 1914, telling its membership to vote against the party that authored the Coldwell Amendments. Their efforts probably contributed to the Conservative defeat in several southwestern Manitoba ridings.

The heated attacks on the school system were similar to those heard in Ontario against French and Catholic schools there. But in

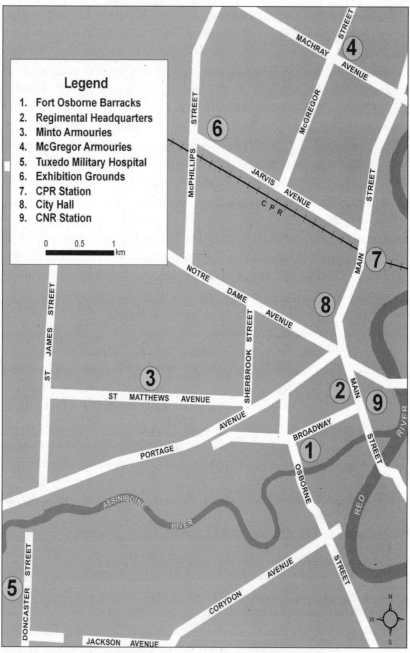

Legend

1. Fort Osborne Barracks
2. Regimental Headquarters
3. Minto Armouries
4. McGregor Armouries
5. Tuxedo Military Hospital
6. Exhibition Grounds
7. CPR Station
8. City Hall
9. CNR Station

0   0.5   1
km

Winnipeg during World War I
Map by Larry Laliberté.

Manitoba there was an added factor—the province's English majority
felt anxiety because of what they saw as a growing population of "foreigners" who in some districts greatly outnumbered English settlers.
As J.E. Rea writes, "The prairie west was not a secure society with
social institutions that would stand the shock of a relatively massive
immigration of people alien in language, religion and culture. The west
was too new, too unformed, too fluid."[64] This insecurity helps to explain the vigour with which the school system was attacked by many
people. One of the characters in Charles Gordon's novel *The Foreigner*
expresses this anxiety when he says, "they must be taught our way or
it will be mighty bad for us here in Western Canada."

The Coldwell amendments did earn Roblin the votes of many
French Manitobans. The St. Boniface paper *La Liberté* stated in 1914
that "both from the religious and the French point of view we have
made notable progress" during the time of the Roblin government.
The duty, therefore, of every Catholic and French Manitoban was to
support the premier. The support of many Ukrainian voters gave the
Conservatives victories in two by-elections in 1913, in Gimli and East
Kildonan. In Gimli the school question was an important issue and
the Conservative candidate, E.L. Taylor, called the *Free Press* series
on bilingual schools a "vicious attack on Ukrainians."[65] After the 1914
general election, the Ukrainian press suggested that Ukrainian votes
in a few key ridings won Roblin his majority.[66] The *Free Press* angrily
agreed, complaining that, in twelve constituencies, Roblin only won
because of Ukrainian support.

This then was the atmosphere in the province when the 1914 election was called on June 16. The campaign, reported the *Canadian
Annual Review*, "was not a satisfactory or pleasant one." Moreover,
Roblin "was not a conciliatory opponent nor a courteous fighter" and
his Liberal opponents "accepted the gauge with true western harti-
ness" in a campaign that was full of "charges of corruption and bitter
personalities."[67]

Election campaigns at this time were exhausting. The best way
to get one's message out was by making speeches to local meetings.
Roblin, in his late fifties and not in good health, spoke at eighteen such
meetings during the first three weeks of the campaign, travelling by
train from one end of the province to the other. Liberal speakers like

Nellie McClung and Tobias Norris kept up a similar schedule, speaking to large audiences without the aid of a microphone.

Conservative speakers reminded voters of the many accomplishments of the Roblin years: a balanced budget, an expanded province, the railroad deal Roblin negotiated with Canadian Northern that had finally broken the CPR monopoly on freight, the introduction of the Manitoba Telephone System, and the many fine public buildings that had gone up or were going up. The Liberals challenged all these accomplishments and spoke about their planned reforms.

By 9 p.m. on election day, July 10, when Roblin mounted the platform before a cheering crowd outside the Conservative *Telegram* newspaper on McDermot Avenue, it was clear that he had won again. In the end he secured twenty-eight seats, the same number he held before the election. But he had lost seats in southwestern Manitoba where his support was normally strong. By winning these ridings and some of the new seats that had been created, the Liberals increased the size of their caucus from thirteen to twenty-one members. Roblin's share of the popular vote fell from 50 to 46 percent, his provincial treasurer was defeated, and some of his ministers held on to their seats with very slim majorities. But the Liberal popular vote also declined, from 44 to 42 percent, with independents and labour candidates taking the rest. As the war began, then, the long rule of the Roblin Conservatives continued although he was clearly being challenged in a more serious way than ever before. Many Liberals, like J.W. Dafoe of the *Free Press*, did not accept the result and simply continued the campaign, and the bitter partisan struggles between the two parties would continue in the months ahead, in spite of the need to focus on the larger wartime issues. Even after the fall of Roblin's government in spring 1915, the Norris government continued for two more years to launch inquiries into the misdeeds of their old adversaries. Given the dedicated manner in which Manitobans and Winnipeggers supported the war effort, this continued political wrangling seems out of place. That it went on so long is a measure of the strength of feeling produced by political conflict at the time.

1915

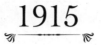

Recruiting the Second Contingent

In the depths of a winter cold snap the governor general, the Duke of Connaught, arrived in Winnipeg on the evening of February 14, 1915, to inspect the city's newest recruits. Four new battalions had been established in the city in the previous months, and their ranks were being filled by thousands of new volunteers. The duke's party was travelling in two private cars, the "Canada" and the "Cornwall," attached to the CPR's Imperial Limited express train. The train was completely encrusted with ice when it pulled into the station. The duke and his party, probably wanting some fresh air, walked through the station, out onto Higgins Avenue, and up the street to the entrance of the Royal Alexandra Hotel. When the duke entered the hotel and climbed the steps to the lobby, the orchestra, which had been giving its regular Sunday-night concert, stopped playing and then struck up "God Save the King," followed by "It's a Long Way to Tipperary."

The next morning the duke inspected the units billeted in the drill hall on Broadway, the new Minto Armoury, the buildings at the Winnipeg Industrial Exhibition grounds, and the old Agricultural College in Tuxedo. As he finished his visit to the 28th Battalion at the Horse Show Amphitheatre, he stopped to speak to Sergeant Major Sissons, a veteran of the British Army, asking him where he had served. When he shook hands with him and told him he had a "fine body of men here," the sergeant major beamed. The duke, a professional soldier for almost half a century, would have understood that

Sam Steele and the Duke of Connaught, the Governor General, inspected new Winnipeg recruits on a very cold February day in 1915.

it was the role of men like Sissons to turn civilians into something resembling fighting men.

After lunch, Connaught, standing in the bitter cold with Sam Steele and Lieutenant Governor Cameron at the corner of Main and McDermot, reviewed the new recruits. In spite of the temperature, there were huge crowds along Main Street. The *Telegram* informed its readers that this was the first time a member of the royal family—the duke was the king's uncle—had reviewed troops in Winnipeg. In all, 7000 men marched past the official party.

On February 18 one of the units the duke had inspected, the 32nd Battalion, became the first of the Second Contingent units to leave Winnipeg. Commanded by Portage la Prairie lawyer Colonel Harry Cowan, the unit would be broken up and used for reinforcements when it arrived in England. Shortly after noon they had received their orders at their quarters in the exhibition grounds. By 6 p.m., the first of the men were marching through the main gate of the grounds led by the battalion band. The cold streets were empty as the men marched past but thousands had gathered inside the Union Station on Main Street. In the great rotunda a lane was kept open by the city police. The band of the 28th Battalion was at the door of the station and began to play as the marching men came into view. "The Girl I Left Behind Me" echoed around the big station lobby, but when the piece was finished the rotunda fell silent and only a few cries of "here they come" were heard from the waiting crowd.

The *Telegram* reporter caught the mood in his description of the scene: "When the order 'Left Turn' rang out and the first troops swung through the front doors of the massive station building, the crowd came to life and the cheers echoed up into the vast dome, drowning out the band's music. Dressed in heavy marching order, each man carrying his pack and full equipment, the lads marched with unfaltering steps down to the subway and up onto the platform."[1]

Sam Steele was there with other senior officers, and he told the men he was proud of them and that he wished that they should come home safely. Minnie Campbell and the IODE handed each man a pair of knitted socks, something now known to be a practical necessity in the water-logged trenches. Some of the men had flags sticking up from the muzzles of their rifles, others had banners of their home cities pinned to them, and one "burly corporal" was inexplicably decorated from head to toe in tinsel. Once they were all on the train, the *Telegram* reported,

the soldiers' wives, mothers, sweethearts and friends were allowed on the platform. Some there were who had come from long distances to see the last of their soldier laddies and these soon picked out their relatives and filled quiet little nooks and unobservantly [sic] wished their loved ones farewell. But the majority of the men gave vent to their long pent up excitement by singing patriotic and popular tunes.... "God isn't it a shame" one lady, the wife of an officer, remarked to her daughter as she turned away after bidding her soldier husband goodbye. It was terrible, 1100 of Canada's finest, their equal perhaps not to be found anywhere in the world, were going away, going away of their own free will, not drafted as the men of European armies and leaving their loved ones behind.

As the train pulled out everyone joined in "Auld Lang Syne," followed by "God Save the King." "One hour later," the report continued, "the second detachment pulled out and only a few weeping women slowly leaving the station gave any indication that another thousand of Canada's sons had answered the call of duty."

Many of the men of the original 32nd Battalion were from rural Manitoba and Saskatchewan, and many likely had no relatives present to say goodbye. Later in the war, a British Columbia mother, Isabella Burkholder of Lillooet, would write to Minnie Campbell with a request about her boy. She was very busy, she wrote, "as it is my Harold boy's last night at home." She told Campbell that he would be travelling across the country by train and asked her, "if they stop at Winnipeg I would like him to see you again."

The men did what they could to master their fears. The *Telegram* carried a story about Lieutenant Gault, a former Eaton's employee in Winnipeg, going overseas with the 5th Artillery Brigade. Gault was carrying a letter from the master of the Emerson Masonic Lodge, where he was a member in good standing. He told the paper he hoped the letter would be of some value in the event that he was captured. It asked for no special treatment, simply certifying that he was a Mason in good standing and leaving it to the Germans to decide how he should be treated.

Thousands of miles away the Canadian Expeditionary Force was about to have its first experience of the brutal reality of the Western Front, where a letter of introduction had no power to save a man's life.

Second Battle of Ypres

On April 14, 1915, the three brigades of the Canadian First Division arrived in the Ypres Salient in Belgium. They occupied, for the first time, front line trenches in the zone where they were to do so much fighting over the next three years. They had played a supporting role to the British at the Battle of Neuve Chapelle in early March, but they had not yet faced the Germans in battle. In the days ahead they would experience their baptism of fire, and for people in Winnipeg and all over Canada the reality of what this war was going to cost hit home with brutal force.

The Ypres Salient was a bulge in the Western Front, protruding into the German line in front of Ypres, the only major Belgian city left in Allied hands. The Germans occupied a semicircle of mostly higher ground around the Salient and tried on several occasions during the war to push the French and British back and straighten the line. The Allies for their part tried to enlarge it, or at least prevent the Germans from eliminating it.

The Canadians took over 4500 yards of front in the Salient from exhausted French soldiers. On their left was the 45th Algerian Division made up of colonial troops, and on their right was the British 28th Division. Men from Winnipeg were spread through many of the Canadian battalions. The 8th Battalion, Winnipeg Rifles, was commanded by Colonel Louis Lipsett, a professional British officer who had been on loan to the Lord Strathcona's Horse in Winnipeg before the war. Lipsett was considered by his men to be tough but fair and he would lead them brilliantly during the fighting ahead. His ability was rewarded and he was soon promoted to the rank of general.

The 16th Battalion, known as the Canadian Scottish, included a company of Winnipeg's Cameron Highlanders under the command of Captain John Geddes, a Winnipeg businessman. The 10th Battalion also contained Winnipeg men from the 106th Winnipeg Light Infantry.

During the week following their arrival, the Canadian First Division worked feverishly to strengthen their trenches. The French Army, with its emphasis on the attack, saw front-line trenches as positions to be lightly held, shallow, and offering little cover. During an attack, they were abandoned and the French retreated, drawing the enemy in toward their artillery and the second line of trenches where they fought. On the other hand, the British, and therefore the Canadians, preferred to fight and hold the front-line trenches at all costs, so they were deepened and strengthened as much as possible.

On April 22, 1915, at 5 p.m., the Germans opposite the French position to the left of the Canadians opened 5730 cylinders, releasing a dense cloud of chlorine gas almost four miles wide. The breeze carried this, the first gas attack in the history of warfare, toward the unsuspecting French. The cynical German code name for the attack was "operation disinfection." The French troops had no gas masks nor any idea of how to protect themselves. Many died in the trenches and many of those who fled died as they stumbled along within the drifting poisonous cloud. A huge hole was created in the Allied line through which the Germans soon began to advance.

Compared to those killed by shrapnel or rifle fire, relatively few men died from gas poisoning during the war. The Allies would soon equip themselves with gas masks and, although gas was used extensively by both sides over the next three years, it would seldom be as effective as it was on April 22 at the second Battle of Ypres. There, surprise and defenceless opponents almost allowed the Germans to achieve a major victory.

Chlorine gas poisoning was a hard way to die. An English medical researcher, J.S. Haldane, visited the Salient a few days after the attack, charged with finding out which gas had been used. He described the effects—men had "acute bronchitis," which caused them to "struggle for breath and turn blue in the face."[2] Haldane declared that the gas was chlorine, something the troops already knew because of the distinctive smell. He would develop an effective gas mask for the troops, as well as introducing the use of oxygen to help soldiers with gas poisoning.[3]

Haldane's medical description "acute bronchitis" failed to capture the terrible reality: if inhaled directly, chlorine destroyed the lining of the lungs. Smaller doses left men handicapped for life; heavy exposure killed them. As Canadian historian Tim Cook writes, "In the end, men drowned in their own searing fluids. It was an ugly death. Victims writhed on the ground, making gagging choking sounds, pulling at their clothes, vomiting 'greenish slime,' propping themselves up to gasp for help, then falling back, exhausted from their struggles."[4]

The road from Ypres to Poelkapelle, once the border between the French and Canadian divisions, now became the front line dividing the Canadians from the advancing Germans. The 13th Battalion, Highlanders from Montreal, spread out down the road, and along with some of the remnants of the French units, fought the Germans from the ditches. About midway along this road between the original front line and Ypres was the village of St. Julien. Canadian artillery and machine-gun units managed to slow down the Germans outside

St. Julien. Here, Canada's first Victoria Cross winner of the war, Corporal Fred Fisher, fired his machine gun, even after all his men had been killed, allowing the Canadian artillery to pull back and save their guns. Like many Victoria Cross winners, Fisher received his medal posthumously; he was killed the next day.

On the night of April 22, Kitchener's Wood, just to the west of St. Julien, became the point of furthest German penetration. After midnight, through the early hours of April 23, the 16th Canadian Scottish Battalion and the 10th Battalion from Calgary were sent forward to drive the Germans out of the wood in the first attack carried out by Canadian troops in the war. About 1600 men of these two battalions advanced, keeping close together so they would not lose contact in the dark. They had gotten only partway to the objective when the Germans heard them coming, sent up flares, and began mowing down the tightly packed troops. The Canadians suffered over 1000 dead and wounded during their dash toward the German line—only 188 men and five officers of the 10th and 260 men and five officers of the 16th reached the wood and dug in. During the charge the commander of the Camerons company in the 16th Battalion, Captain John Geddes from Winnipeg, was mortally wounded but continued to crawl forward, urging his men on.[5] Those who actually made it to the objective were in no mood to take prisoners, and some Germans who surrendered were shot.

The next day the Canadians were forced to withdraw from their positions, losing more men as they moved back through the open fields. Meanwhile, another costly attack took place further west, as the 1st and 4th battalions advanced on the German lines on Mauser Ridge. The Canadians had no artillery support, and a promised French attack failed to materialize. Once again losses were terrible—about half of those who attacked—but the German plan to push south and cut off and surround the Canadian and British troops in the Salient had to be abandoned.

The headquarters of the Canadian brigades and the British headquarters overseeing the battle were frequently cut off from the chaotic fighting, and commanders often had no clear idea of what was happening. It was left largely to officers and non-commissioned officers at the battalion level to decide how to resist the German advance. Two

Canadian brigadier generals, Arthur Currie and R.E. Turner, were under unbelievable pressure during the battle, and their headquarters were under fire a good deal of the time. Both men, at different points in the fighting, personally went back to British headquarters to try and get reinforcements to shore up their sections of the line, and both were unsuccessful. Like all other officers in their situation, they were learning the rules of this new and terrible form of warfare as they scrambled to block the German advance.

On Saturday, April 24, the Germans mounted another gas attack, this time directed at the Canadian front line. At four in the morning a heavy artillery barrage began and a gas cloud, smaller than that of the first attack, drifted across the section of line held by the 15th and 8th battalions. It was most dense at the junction point between these two units and many of the men there were poisoned and died in the trenches. The Canadians were marginally better prepared than the French had been two days before. The advice had been circulated that if you soaked a piece of cloth with urine and held it in front of your mouth and nose the chlorine would be partly neutralized by the ammonia in the urine. This remedy was suggested by two Canadian Army doctors, Colonel George Nasmith and Captain F.A. Scrimger, and commanders like Colonel Lipsett of the 8th Battalion made sure their men knew what to do.[6]

When descriptions of the gas attacks reached Canada, the Red Cross immediately made patterns available to women all over the country and they began to sew an early type of gas mask for the men. Enough material to make 6000 respirators was sent to the Winnipeg Red Cross, and Mrs. Bond, of the Red Cross executive and an experienced army nurse, and her committee cut out the pieces that were sewed by volunteer groups in Winnipeg and Brandon.[7]

Minnie Campbell received letters from many IODE members offering to help: Mary Graham of Craik, Saskatchewan, wrote to say that she would make some if Campbell sent her a pattern. At about the same time, Alma Cliff of Mortlach, Saskatchewan, wrote to say that the women of her town would do the same. This sort of action, while it may not have produced the best possible gas masks, did a great deal to relieve anxiety and stress among women and gave them a way to have a direct, immediate role in the war.

The Germans had lost the advantage of surprise and their advance was not as easy as it had been on April 22, although they massively outnumbered the British and Canadians, twenty-four battalions to eight. They hoped that this gas attack too would trigger a wholesale retreat and allow them to realize their objective of pushing south to cut off and encircle the Canadians and the two British divisions in the Salient. But the Canadians and British put up a fierce resistance on April 24 and 25, struggling to establish a new line of defence as they were pushed back by the Germans.

The Winnipeg Rifles history of the fighting describes the scene immediately after the gas attack:

> Half the 8th Battalion succumbed to the poisonous fumes. The battalion on the left was obliged to retire and the 8th found itself in danger of being surrounded. But it held on. Asked by headquarters if he wanted to retire Colonel Lipsett answered "The 8th can hold its bit." While supporting battalions were preparing new defenses in the rear, the men of the regiment kept up a withering fire on the enemy, drove off an attack on its front and withstood a fearful enfilade fire from left and right, and this from an enemy force five times its size...Thus began a tradition of never losing a trench to the enemy, a tradition never to be broken throughout the war's duration.[8]

Those men of the 8th who escaped the worst of the gas continued to fight. To their left the 15th was hit hard by the gas and remnants of the 13th Battalion were also still in place along the Poelkappelle Road, where they had been resisting the German pressure since Thursday. These troops held on until 8:30 in the morning when they were ordered to begin pulling back to Gravenstafel Ridge, about a mile behind the original front line. The 8th maintained their positions in the front line until later in the day when they, along with the 5th Battalion on their right, withdrew to the ridge. It was during this phase of the battle that Sergeant Major F.W. Hall of the 8th earned the first Victoria Cross for bravery given to a Winnipeg man. Hall had been carrying a wounded comrade out of no man's land to safety when he was shot.

O.1285

Canadian troops in a trench on the Western Front.

During the afternoon, confusion over orders transmitted from the rear led General Turner to withdraw his troops to a line closer to Ypres. This was a costly mistake—men were killed in large numbers as they drew back into new trenches, which offered little cover. Another Victoria Cross was awarded to Lieutenant Edward Bellew of the 7th Battalion for bravery during this battle. He fired his machine gun at the advancing Germans until he was out of ammunition and then continued to fight with his bayonet until he was captured. He would spend the rest of the war in a prisoner-of-war camp, learning of his medal only in 1919.

St. Julien was lost during the day on April 24 and a counterattack to recapture it was ordered at 6:30 p.m. The attack was delayed until daylight the following day, and once again troops were slaughtered when advancing over open fields with no artillery support. The next day Canadian and British troops were driven back from Gravenstafel Ridge by a massive German attack, and the following day the remains of the Canadian force were relieved and sent back to the reserve trenches.

The men of the Canadian Expeditionary Force had endured a terrible introduction to the war, but had proven their bravery as they frustrated the German goal of eliminating the Salient, capturing Ypres, and advancing to the coast. The Canadian losses were 6036 wounded and killed, one-third of their fighting strength. Only six officers and 231 other ranks of the 1000 Winnipeg Rifles reported for the first parade after the battle, and the 10th and 16th battalions lost a total of 1500 men as casualties.

1' War has struck home "/mourning the dead

Back home, the papers carried news of the battle, but people with relatives or friends in the fighting had to wait several days for news of their loved ones. For Winnipeggers it was not until Sunday evening, April 26, that, in the words of the *Free Press*, "the news of the heavy casualties spread over the city with wonderful rapidity and the Free Press was besieged all evening with telephone calls and with anxious relatives who came direct to the news room in a desire to hear the worst. There were many sleepless ones in Winnipeg last night. The war has struck home." The paper announced that casualty lists would arrive "in the next few days" and promised that families who had lost loved ones would be told before the lists were made public, a promise they were not always able to keep. But even the *Free Press* admitted that its information was limited. The paper asked people who "receive notifications of casualties" to telephone the paper with the information "as soon as possible."

The chaos at the front made it difficult to establish who was wounded, who was dead, and who was missing. In this, as in most of the battles of the Great War, the identification of the dead was made difficult by the fact that bodies were scattered over a wide area, some of it now behind enemy lines, and shelling often mutilated or buried corpses. Lists were printed daily over the next two weeks as official information trickled in, and the *Free Press* noted that some families belatedly receiving bad news had "assumed their boys were safe, not having seen their names in the lists earlier in the week."

In her novel *Aleta Dey*, Winnipeg journalist and suffrage leader Francis Marion Beynon described the emotional turmoil people experienced while they worried about a loved one being killed or wounded. The title character is at work when a telegram arrives: "It was from the military office at Ottawa. Lieutenant McNair had been gassed and wounded. I sat down dumb and stricken." Unsure about her friend's condition, "three days passed in a vain effort to learn further details. I cannot tell what I suffered during those days.... Impotence is the peculiar sting of this particular form of ordeal, combined with uncertainty, which gives the tortured imagination free rein to create its own hell of horror. For three days and nights I traversed the battlefields of France. I found McNair in No-Man's-Land, with an arm blown off and gasping for breath." She continued to imagine all sorts of dreadful things until finally another telegram arrived: "I stood with the ugly yellow thing in my hand, choking, until it suddenly came to me that the certainty that McNair was dead would be easier to bear than the awful anguish of the past three days." The wire was from McNair himself, saying he was in hospital and out of danger. She fainted.[9]

Day after day the papers listed the casualties:

Killed Captain John Geddes, 33 Middlegate, born in Chicago, educated in England, grain trader and most recently manager of the Winnipeg and Suburban Development Company. His wife and two children had gone to her home in Ireland when he left for the war.

Killed, Private Allen Ingalls, 116 Colony Street, nephew of Mrs. J.W. Dafoe, electrician with the Winnipeg Street Railway, twenty-two years old.

Wounded, Lieutenant George Richardson of Kingston, older brother of Winnipeg grain trader James Richardson and a well-known hockey player. He was killed about a year later, in February 1916.

Killed, Sergeant N.J. McKenzie of the 16th Battalion. Twenty-four years old, 127 Kennedy Street, an inspector for the Bank of Montreal,

*a member of the rowing club and a well-known rugby player. His brother
was listed as missing.*

*Suffering from the effects of gas, Private Stanley Foreman, 620
Dudley Avenue, a well-known and popular fireman with the Canadian
Northern Railway. He had played football for many city teams.*

*Wounded, Dr. G.S. Mothersill, the Medical Officer of the 10th
Battalion, a crack shot and a member of the Winnipeg Rowing Club,
thirty-five years old.*

*Wounded, Private Archy Macdonald of the 10th Battalion, an
iron worker in the CPR shops in Winnipeg.*

*Wounded, Gerald and William O'Grady, sons of the former
colonel of the Winnipeg Rifles, who died in November 1914. They were
both lieutenants in the 8th Battalion.*

*Missing, Lieutenant J.K. Bell of the 8th Battalion, 516
Dominion Street, barrister, thirty years old.*

*Missing, Captain George Northwood of the 8th Battalion,
architect, 218 Oxford Street, thirty-seven years old. His wife and three
children are staying in California.*

*Killed, Lieutenant R. Hoskins, 32 McAdam Avenue, a lawyer
called to the Bar in 1912, twenty-eight years old.*

*Killed, Lieutenant G.A. Coldwell, 10th Battalion, son of George
Coldwell, minister in the Roblin government, twenty-two years old, a
"well known and popular young man."*

*Killed, Lieutenant J.E. Reynolds of the 8th Battalion, twenty-
four years old, known to his friends as "Brew," about to be admitted to
the Bar when he joined up. He had played rugby and hockey at St. John's
College.*

*Killed, Captain H.A.C. Wallace, 18 Hill Street, Manager of
Houston, Murray and Simpson Real Estate, thirty-five years old with a
wife and two children.*

*Killed, Lieutenant Struan Robertson, of the Princess Patricias,
twenty-seven years old, stepson of W.H. Gardner of Oldfield, Kirby and
Gardner. His brother Harry was with him when he died. He was "very
popular with all he met and the news of his death came as a sudden
shock."*

Killed, Lieutenant G.F. Andrews, of the 8th Battalion, twenty-two years old, 95 Academy Road. Worked with his father as a real estate agent. His father, mother and sister are living in England.

Wounded, Private Charles Liddle, 288 Smithfield St., a printer, Private Archibald Barber, 186 Smithfield Street, Private Robert Allan, 78 Lusted Avenue, a clerk, Private M. McSloy, 488 Elgin Avenue, Private George McLeod, 138 Walnut Street, Private James Ferrier, Disraeli Street, a Motorman for the Winnipeg Street Railway, all of the 16th Battalion.

Killed, Private Oscar Lebean, a clerk at the Vivian Hotel, Private Edwin Cecil Holloway, Private William Irvin, a clerk in Eaton's Store, Private John Gloag, 864 College Avenue, a teamster, Private John Ballantyne, 379 Graham, a mason, Private Douglas Gordon Wilson, 477 Spence Street, a shipper at Dominion Lumber, all of the 8th Battalion.

In four days of fighting, from April 22 to 25, Winnipeg had lost hundreds of young men and with them untold promise and future potential for the city. And this was just the first major engagement in a war that would last another three and a half years.

Canadians, shocked by the loss of life, began to mourn their dead, gathering together for public services. In Winnipeg on April 29 there was a huge memorial service at Happyland Amusement Park, between Aubrey and Garfield streets, a place with rides and games associated in normal times with innocent fun. Over 4600 troops then stationed in the city attended along with a similar number of civilians. It was a cold day, but people stood in a gigantic hollow square to sing hymns and pray and listened to a sermon by Dr. G.B. Wilson of Augustine Presbyterian Church.

Reverend Wilson touched on most of the themes that Canadian speakers would return to on such occasions throughout the war. He claimed a special sort of virtue for the Canadian troops who fought at Ypres, adding that they "were not filled with the lust of conquest, that they had no chant of hate to sing, that they were not a military but a pastoral and commercial people; that they coveted no people's silver or gold or land; that they detested aggression and loved to walk in the path of peace and stable progress." He talked about the noble sacrifice made by the Canadian troops and called on his listeners to "rejoice that the Canadian citizen soldiery, in such terrible circumstances, showed so glorious a courage and fidelity." In explaining their courage, he pointed to Canada's rugged environment, saying that "the history of Canada had been a history of struggle against adverse natural conditions and perhaps we are now learning that the victories of peace prepared men for every eventuality of war."

The often-repeated theme of sacrifice was the language of a strongly Christian country, and one still greatly influenced by the romanticism of the previous century. Images of Christian knights, dedicated to defending the weak, were common in the propaganda of all the combatants. The dead soldier, held *Pietà*-like in the arms of a female angel, often appeared in magazines and newspapers, and later in stained glass windows and memorial statues. The object of the sacrifice was the preservation of British democracy and the rule of law, contrasted with the kaiser, the militaristic tyrant who wanted to destroy these things. For the men fighting for this cause, no price, not even their lives, was too great to pay.

Some fighting men may have been influenced by these lofty ideas, but their real motivations were often more down-to-earth. Some, like Alec Waugh, were driven by the desire to avenge the deaths of comrades. He wrote to his parents, on hearing that a friend of the family had been killed in France:

> I have just received yours and mother's telling me of Roddy's death. As you say, it brings things very very close to home, and just as long as I can work a machine gun or pull the trigger of a rifle I'll show no mercy to any German. Damn them all. We have a lot to wipe out. Doug is a cripple, Jamie Dawson a prisoner in Turkey, Alex Waugh with a smashed thigh, Fred Richie killed and now Roddie. That's our own little Honor Roll and just as soon as those remaining, Frank Mathers, Jim Butters, Jack Dawson, Mac and myself can get the chance, a few deeply rooted scores will be settled.

A few days after the May 5 service, there was a service at St. Stephen's Presbyterian Church for Captain Geddes and other members of the Camerons who had died at Ypres. Many of the Camerons in Belgium were parishioners of St. Stephen's, so the service had a special meaning to those present as the 79th Cameron Highlanders and the newly formed 43rd Battalion marched to the front pews of the packed church.

On Sunday May 9, 1915, another large public act of remembrance took place with the first Decoration Day parade of the war. Decoration Day was an American holiday established in the 1870s to commemorate the men who died in the Civil War, but for thirty years in Winnipeg Decoration Day had been celebrated on the Sunday closest to the anniversary of the victory over Riel at the Battle of Batoche. Like the American observance, it involved a military parade and the decoration of the graves of the fallen with flowers. The parade always ended at St. John's Cathedral cemetery at the graves of the Winnipeg Rifles members killed at Batoche. After the South African War the focus of the day had shifted and it became a commemoration of all Canadian wars.

The parade had enormous significance in 1915, falling as it did so soon after the fighting at Ypres. There was an outdoor church service at the University of Manitoba grounds on Broadway, led by Canon Murray, Reverend Loucks of All Saints' Church, and Reverend W.B. Heeney of St. Luke's Church. Present were Lieutenant Governor Douglas Cameron, his aide-de-camp, Count de Bury, and Mayor Lachance of St. Boniface. Those attending formed a hollow square with the four sides made up of active service units, veterans, cadets, and bands. They sang "O God Our Help in Ages Past," prayed using parts of the Anglican service, and ended with "God Save the King." Then the whole company marched to St. John's cemetery. On the way they laid a huge wreath at the base of the 90th Regiment memorial column in front of city hall. It bore the message, "In affectionate memory of our boys who have fallen at the front in the great European war, and in sympathy for their relatives."

Captain S.H. Williams of the Strathcona's Horse took part in this parade and remembered it many years later: "It was the first war time Decoration Day and the parade was nearly all khaki. With several battalions all in kahki, the Field Artillery with their guns all horse drawn and with the squadron of the Lord Strathcona's Horse, it was a very colorful parade. We picked our smartest men and best horses for the occasion."[10]

Nurses watch as a wounded soldier arrives at the Queen's Canadian Military Hospital in Shorncliffe, England, c. 1916.

The veterans of 1885, led by Hugh John Macdonald, marched in front of the Lord Strathcona's Horse, and then came more veterans, the lieutenant governor and General Ruttan, the commanding officer of Military District Number 10, in cars. The IODE members filled eleven cars along with patients from the convalescent hospital operated by the order. The 79th Cameron Highlanders cadets and a contingent of Boy Scouts also marched in the parade. At St. John's cemetery they laid wreaths on the graves of 1885.[11]

On the day after the parade, the *Free Press* noted the propaganda value of parades, commenting that the sight of the veterans marching in the street "is calculated to instill a lesson of loyal patriotism and self sacrifice that the school children, the alien within our gates and the citizens generally will not easily forget." Continuing on the symbolism of the parade, the report added that "the presence of the men in khaki will link the past with the stirring things of the present, most vividly in the minds of the spectators."[12] Communities across the country held similar ceremonies and funerals as Canadians, shocked by their first personal experience of the costs of this war, struggled to make sense of the slaughter.

Even in England, the courage of the Canadian troops was being recognized. In London, at St. Paul's Cathedral, a special service was held to recognize the Canadians' bravery at Ypres. The bishop of London said that "the manhood of Canada shone out like pure gold," when they refused to retreat before the German gas and the onslaught that followed. British publications, from *Punch* to the *Times* noted the bravery of the Canadians in slowing down and ultimately stopping the German advance. The reputation of the Canadian soldiers was in no small part the work of Sir Max Aitken, soon to be Lord Beaverbrook. The Canadian millionaire had migrated to London before the war and begun to build his newspaper empire. He was elected to the House of Commons and would be a minister in Lloyd George's Cabinet. By 1915 he had assumed the job of being Canada's "eyewitness" to the war. Among other things, he provided a steady stream of favourable news stories to the press, describing the exploits of the Canadians.

The positive propaganda probably saved the morale of the fledgling Canadian Army from a complete collapse and gave them the strength of purpose to overcome the mauling they had received. The fighting at Ypres was, for those who survived, a short course in war as it was now fought. The officers and men who came out alive would provide the Canadians with a cadre of experienced fighters on which to build what would, by 1918, be one of the best armies on the Western Front. Men like Louis Lipsett and Arthur Currie carefully noted what they had learned and shared their insights with newcomers. Because the Canadians stayed together as a fighting unit, this knowledge and experience was more efficiently passed on to new recruits than was the case in larger conscript armies.

The fighting in April 1915 was in many ways the birthplace of the Canadian Army in World War I. The troops acquired a reputation for tough, stubborn bravery that they kept throughout the war, and the officers who survived would provide the Canadian Corps with many of its best leaders. General Arthur Currie, speaking to the troops in 1918, portrayed the battle as the beginning of the Canadians' war: "Beginning with the immortal stand at the 2nd Battle of Ypres, you befittingly closed, by the capture of Mons, your fighting record in which every battle you fought is a resplendent page of glory."[13]

A sadder result of the second Battle of Ypres, and many more like it, was that many young Canadians were badly wounded, and these men now had to survive and learn to live with injuries that might never completely heal. For some, dealing with the memories of battle would cast a permanent dark shadow over their lives. Many men who survived the war would die relatively young, during the 1920s and 1930s, as a result of both physical and mental disabilities.

Within weeks, the papers began to carry graphic letters written by the survivors of the second Battle of Ypres. Private M.G. Mahood wrote from hospital to his mother and father who lived in Elmwood. He was recovering after having shrapnel removed from his head. He told them how he was wounded and bandaged up by a Red Cross man, only to be buried when another shell exploded near him. When his friends dug him out, his bandage was gone and he was covered with blood from head to toe. "Mother, it was only nerve that was keeping me up," he wrote. He told his parents how he saw a friend killed next to him: "I miss my chum very much. He got killed outright on the 22nd and died never saying a word. Dear mother it is an awful sensation when you see your chum getting killed. You neither care for shot or shell." He described walking back to Ypres through a landscape that was constantly shelled and littered with dead horses and men.

Douglas Waugh, the son of the mayor of Winnipeg, Richard Waugh, was badly injured, along with many other members of the Strathcona's Horse, in the fighting as infantry at Festubert on May 24 a few weeks after the second Battle of Ypres. By August, Waugh was in England, in a military hospital at Fazakerley outside Liverpool.

His younger brother Alec, also in the Strathcona's Horse, was able to get leave to visit. At this time Alec had only recently finished training in Canada and he stopped to see his brother on his way to Shorncliffe Camp, where most Canadian troops were trained before crossing to France. His expenses for travelling to see a badly wounded relative were covered, but he told his father that "we have to thank Mr. Rogers for hustling things in my case." Robert Rogers, minister of the interior and member of Parliament for Winnipeg, was, as a good constituency politician, anxious to help Alec Waugh in any way he could.

This would not be the only time he "hustled" things, for the young Winnipegger Alec's first letters from England that summer describe his brother as being in a "very bad way" with a serious infection in his wounded shoulder. He slowly recovered, and Alec attributed this to one of the nurses, Sister Dando. She was the one, Alec wrote, "to whom he owes his life and I cannot say enough for her self-sacrifice and devotion to duty in this one case. She is an ideal nurse."[14]

The care they received from army nurses often made a deep impression on wounded men. Douglas would eventually marry a Canadian Army nurse. He recovered and returned to Winnipeg, but he was disabled by his wounds and could not return to the fighting. The following year he began working as purchasing agent for the Greater Winnipeg Water District, of which his father was the chairman. For him the war had been mercifully short; his brother would serve for another two years.

The 800 Canadian nurses who served in hospitals in France and England were in some ways better off than their colleagues in other armies. They were all officers, beginning at the rank of lieutenant, and this brought privileges and respect. Nurses served in the forward casualty clearing stations close to the line, in the larger hospitals like the Number 3 Canadian General Hospital at Boulogne on the French coast, and in long-term hospitals in England like the Duchess of Connaught Hospital at Taplow. Regardless of where they were stationed, day after day they would see the horrible results of machine-gun fire and shrapnel.

Clare Gass, a young nurse from Nova Scotia who was stationed in Boulogne, has left us her diary, in which she recorded the shock and pain she felt while treating the steady stream of wounded men. In July 1915, only two months after leaving Montreal, she wrote:

> I shall never forget the sound of the motor ambulances as they bring in the convoys. The continual burr as they pass our tents, as one follows the other from the siding to the highway, some slower than others according to the severity of the wounds of the patients they carry. Sometimes they seem to continue all night long and when I waken with them I cannot go to sleep for hours listening and thinking what it all means and the condition of these

poor lads, tired in body and spirit, sick of the war, sick of France, aching for their homes and dear ones.[15]

Deeply shocked by what she was seeing, she wrote:

> Some of these new patients have such dreadful wounds. One young boy with part of his face shot away and both arms gone and great wounds on both legs. Surely death were merciful.... The men are all so good and patient, and so grateful for even the smallest attention. These are the horrors of war but they are too horrible, can it be God's will or only man's devilishness. It is too awful.... Heads shattered to pieces or limbs hanging by a thread of tendons. Oh why must such things be. All are so brave and yet those who are not badly wounded are so tired of war, at least those who have been long in the trenches—tired in such a hopeless way.[16]

In October 1916, after a year and a half in the service, she recorded the story of a soldier called Edney, a shell-shock case on her ward: "Tonight he told me his story, poor laddie—a gentle sweet faced boy from whom war has claimed its own." In a whisper in the night while others were sleeping he told her of carrying his friend Reg for three miles on his back; they were knocked out by an exploding shell and when he woke his friend was lying beside him, his head severed from his body. The nurse's diary continues, "Then when we both had wept a little over it he became silent again and I gave him a sleeping draught and he had a dreamless sleep til dawn."[17]

Cecily Galt, the daughter of Judge Alexander Galt, was one of many Winnipeg women who served as a nurse during the war. In August 1915, when the *Royal Edward*, a transport ship belonging to the Canadian Northern Railway, was torpedoed in the Aegean Sea, it was thought that Galt was on board. The ship was carrying troops, many of whom were members of the Royal Army Medical Corps. About 1000 people died when it sank. A few days later it was confirmed that Galt and another Winnipeg nurse, Katherine Scoble, had not been aboard. Both women served on a hospital ship anchored in the harbour of Moudros on the Island of Lemnos. The wounded they cared for were brought from the front at Gallipoli, usually in open boats, and conditions were harsh because of the "flies, heat, sand and filth," according

In 1915 parades of troops had become common sights in downtown Winnipeg. This group marches east on Portage Avenue past streetcars led by cyclists.

to letters from the women published in the *Telegram*. They were short of mosquito nets, water, and good food. The hospital cook, a veteran of the Canadian Northern Railway, did his best to provide a diet of boiled eggs, bully beef stew, dry bread, and tea with condensed milk.

Patriotic Week / "nothing but contempt"...

A few of the badly wounded began to return home to Canada after the battles of the spring of 1915. Winnipeg was the first place in Canada to organize a Returned Soldiers' Association for the care of these men. They met for the first time on July 1, 1915. Mayor Richard Waugh was the chair and G.F. Carruthers, W. Cross, and W. Martin were the other executive members. Federal minister Robert Rogers joined them at their first meeting in the rooms of the Army and Navy Veterans' Association and congratulated them on being the first community in the Dominion to start organizing for the returned men. The group told Rogers they had already found jobs for a few of the men coming home from France.

Earlier in the day the mayor and Rogers had taken part in the Dominion Day parade, which in 1915 marked the opening of Winnipeg's National Patriotic Week. Planning for the Patriotic Week had begun in January when the city council had voted not to give its usual grant to the Industrial Exhibition, the annual fair that would have normally started on July 1. The exhibition had lost money in 1913, when it had been reinvented as the Winnipeg Stampede, an event that would later move to Calgary, where it had a wider appeal. There was a loss again in 1914, in spite of record attendance, and the council had had to pay off the exhibition's debts. To the debts was added the projected cost of repairing the exhibition buildings and grandstand, making the continued funding of the fair too expensive for the councillors. The directors of the exhibition agreed to cancel the event for 1915. Soon afterward the Winnipeg Industrial Bureau—a branch of the Board of Trade—proposed a National Patriotic Week instead. The bureau's first step was to set up a large representative committee, the way Winnipeg's middle-class handled every such task. At the first meeting T.R. Deacon expressed doubts that due to the war "the project might not meet with the necessary support." Judge Meyers answered him with an enthusiastic patriotic address, pointing out that such an event might convince more people to enlist and help the Empire win the great battle currently going on, and his remarks "met with the full support and applause of the meeting."[18]

The week began on Dominion Day with a parade so large that it was said by the *Telegram* to have "blazoned forth to all that Winnipeg is nothing if not enthusiastically patriotic, loyal and full of national and imperial fervor." Winnipeg, the Dominion's third largest city, was always anxious to demonstrate that she was as rich, as dynamic, as lively, and now as patriotic, as her older rivals, Montreal and Toronto.

The Eaton's store displayed its patriotic fervour by draping the front of the building with a forty- by sixty-foot Union Jack, carried in the parade by the Loyal Order of the Moose. The *Telegram* had been selling smaller Union Jacks—$1.10 for the flag alone or $1.48 for the flag and a pole that could be attached to one's house—so throughout the city one could find similarly patriotic decorations.

At 1 p.m. the parade started in Market Square and went south on Main Street to Portage Avenue. After the usual circuit around Portage, Sherbrook, and Broadway, it proceeded up Main to Dufferin and then west to the exhibition grounds. The organizers had created a parade that was a celebration of the city's united effort to win the war. It began with the mayor and council members in open cars, followed by the enormous Union Jack, and a float depicting the "Friends of Britain," with people dressed in the costumes of the various Allied nations. Next came an IODE float, with a woman dressed as Britannia, a military band, and a float carrying veterans. The recently formed Winnipeg Women's Rifle Association was in the parade as was a float with a huge model of the new British warship, HMS *Winnipeg*. The Highland Cadets came marching next, followed by an armoured car. A float with CPR machinists and blacksmiths making shells reminded the crowd that Winnipeg had been given a contract to manufacture shell casings in March 1915 and the work was being done in the machine shops of the CPR and Grand Trunk Railway.

The fraternal societies also demonstrated their support for the war—Independent Order of Odd Fellows, the Maccabees, Knights of Pythias, Knights of Columbus, Sons of England, and many others marched. There was a Women's Christian Temperance Union float, a university float, and a Winnipeg School of Art float. An Icelandic history float, a Polish history float, a troupe of Polish athletes marching, together with the local Norwegian men's choir, demonstrated the widespread support for the war effort in the city's immigrant communities.

The industries of Winnipeg, including Crescent Creameries, Gordon Ironsides, and Fares meat packers, and dozens of others, sent decorated floats. There was a T. Eaton float showing Canada and her provinces. Then there were horse-drawn delivery wagons and horses entered in different categories in the horse show, which would form part of the week's events. Five hundred Boy Scouts marched in the parade, and many bands played, including a burlesque house band. Bringing up the rear was Kershaw's steam calliope, a slightly melancholy reminder of happier days at the exhibition.

As the parade entered the exhibition grounds on Dufferin Avenue the marchers were greeted by the cheers of 5000 people who had come to see the grandstand show. The crowd was entertained with demonstrations by the Boy Scouts, St. John Ambulance, and some drill squads, but there were also the usual vaudeville acts to lighten people's spirits.

Patriotic Festival events were distributed around town all through the week, and included a horse show at the amphitheatre on Colony Street and the Dominion Track and Field Championships. There were horse races in front of the grandstand, and on July 3 there was cricket at Assiniboine Park all day, and a water carnival at the Canoe Club. On July 10, the last day of the Patriotic Week, there were final playoffs for many of the events and a car race at the exhibition grounds. The car races were always held on the final day because they ruined the track for horse racing. Whether the events of the week moved anyone to join the army is not known, but the event was a financial success: a final profit of $7134 was donated to the Patriotic Fund, the Red Cross, and the St. John Ambulance Society. It undoubtedly cheered people up after the shocking events of the winter.

Events like the Patriotic Festival would provide only momentary relief, and enthusiasm for the war had begun to flag in Winnipeg by the middle of 1915. The shocking losses of the second Battle of Ypres had a chilling effect. As early as February 1915, the *Telegram* had commented that, unlike those who had volunteered in the first burst of enthusiasm the previous summer, new recruits were fully informed of "the terrible agonies endured by soldiers in the trenches of Flanders." Before censorship—much more comprehensive in Canada than in either Britain or the U.S.—clamped down, letters appeared in the papers from Winnipeg men who had gone to France with the Princess Patricias, with horrific descriptions of trench warfare. But it was the first appearance of lengthy casualty lists in the newspapers after the fighting in April and May, when the Canadians were first in the thick of the fighting, that brought home to Winnipeggers the shocking cost the country would have to pay in order to win this war. By June, fully three-quarters of the original Canadian Expeditionary Force had been either killed or wounded.

Clearly more troops were needed if Canada was to continue to contribute to the war effort. Yet over the two and a half years that passed before the introduction of conscription there was a slow, steady de-

cline in the flow of volunteers. Though many strategies would be tried
to arrest this trend, nothing could restore the enthusiasm of 1914.
The introduction of conscription in 1918 would only partly solve the
problem of declining enlistment, and widespread opposition to the
policy meant that the troops were sent overseas at a much higher cost
in social disruption than expected.

Recruiting took on a grimmer, more aggressive tone in mid-1915
as clergymen talked from their pulpits about joining up and returned
soldiers spoke at rallies. The Methodist *Christian Guardian*, a pacifist
paper before the war, said that every young man must account for
himself "to his Empire and to God why he is not in khaki," which was
now a sacred colour.[19] During the summer of 1915, for the first time,
women in Britain and Canada shamed men in public by putting white
feathers on their lapels if they were not in uniform.[20]

In July 1915 George Foster, at the time acting prime minister, engaged three advertising agencies to undertake a poll of Canadians,
asking them "what is wrong with the recruiting system and how can
we fix it?" Significantly, this survey found that what was holding up
recruitment was "lack of a sufficiently deep realization of Canada's
interest and stake in the war."[21] Many Canadians, both French and
English, were unconvinced that their country should fight. Many
people found it worrisome that fully two-thirds of the men who went
overseas with the First Contingent were not born in Canada but na-
tives of the British Isles.

The survey results illuminated a basic split in Canadian society.
Some viewed Canada as a part of the British Empire and Canada's
role in the war as that of an adjunct to the British Army and the Royal
Navy. In the first few days after the outbreak of war some people, such
as Robert Rogers, a federal Cabinet minister, lamented that the former
Laurier government had failed to institute a naval policy that would
have seen Canada making a major contribution to the Royal Navy.
The other point of view, and one that would develop further during
the war, was that Canada was a separate nation and should decide
whether or not to fight based on whether or not there were compelling national reasons. From Foster's survey, it is clear that quite a few
Canadians did not believe there were any such compelling reasons.[22]

Foster proposed a major advertising campaign to inspire people to enlist, but Sam Hughes, in his quixotic fashion, rejected the idea, saying recruits must decide to go because of an "inspiration from within."[23] Hughes was not above attempting to inspire from without, as long as he was doing the inspiring. The following month he approved the expenditure of $27,000 for war posters, and in January 1915 alone he travelled 7000 miles, making twenty-two recruiting speeches in fifteen days.

A recurring issue in Canada's recruiting campaign was Sam Hughes's insistence on creating new battalions instead of simply raising troops to reinforce existing units, a policy opposed by Canada's few professional staff officers. Major General Gwatkin, the chief of the General Staff, favoured a Canadian Corps capped at 50,000 men, "rather than adding to the number of regiments, batteries and battalions at the front." He argued that this would enable Canada to more easily maintain and reinforce the existing battalions at full strength.

He reminded the minister that the men had to be trained, armed, and equipped, and the units they formed had to be reinforced once there were casualties. He pointed out that, with casualties as heavy as they had been, it took 3000 men to keep a 1000-man unit up to strength at the front for a year.[24] Hughes disagreed, and by 1917 the Canadian Expeditionary Force had over 250 battalions, many created in response to lobbying from local militia regiments like the Cameron Highlanders and Winnipeg Grenadiers.

In September 1915, Sam Hughes announced an innovation: organizations, communities, and individuals could also attempt to establish fighting units. Inspired by the British Army's "pals" units, groups of men from the same ethnic group, club, or with the same opinion on some social issue would form the nucleus of a new battalion.

Hughes implemented this policy in his usual highly personal fashion, sending out telegrams to prominent men in Canadian communities. Many were known to him personally and some at least were Conservative Party friends. This was the case with W.T. Egecombe, a Winnipeg alderman, who announced that he would raise and command a battalion composed entirely of members of the Orange Lodge. His colleague, Alderman Lineham, was the medical officer. This unit would have been welcomed by Sam Hughes, long one of the Orange

Lodge's representatives in the Conservative Party, who saw the members of the lodge as ideal Canadian soldiers.

The headquarters for this new 184th Battalion were in the Olympia Hotel, which had been standing empty since the bankruptcy of its owners. Newspaper ads placed by the battalion featured pictures of the hotel and stated that "Men of the best type are being recruited." The battalion had a businessmen's company and an athlete's company. Readers were given the message that the 184th was "without class distinctions and without appealing exclusively to any one class or social section it is filling up with the best class of men from all walks of life." It is likely that few Roman Catholics signed up.

Lendrum McMeans, a former Conservative member in the provincial legislature soon to be appointed to the Senate, also offered to raise a battalion. In January 1916 he wired Robert Rogers that he was "willing to offer my services in the army and I am willing to raise a Battalion at once and put my money into it."[25] He had lost one son at the second Battle of Ypres and another was at the front. His daughter was an army nurse serving at Shorncliffe Camp in England. W.H. Sharpe, the former Conservative member of Parliament for Lisgar, had received approval to raise a battalion and Colonel A.G. Fonseca had been given permission by Hughes to raise a battalion of Scandinavians in Winnipeg. He was a salesman and the son of William Gomez Fonseca, one of the early businessmen and settlers of Winnipeg.

The strategy, which "proved to be Ottawa's last nationwide strategy to increase volunteers and maintain a system fast reaching its absolute limit," failed to raise large numbers of men.[26] Many of the new battalions did not attract a full complement of men and ended up as reinforcements for other units. When the efforts of Colonel A.G. Fonseca fell short, his 500 recruits were used as reinforcements and he and his officers all took lower ranks in order to be able to go over to France. Fonseca, then a captain, told the *Telegram*, "You can tell the people of Winnipeg that while I am sorry to lose them as friends, I am real glad to be beginning my journey which I hope will end in Berlin."

Not everyone was willing to take a lower rank: "the privates went to the front in composite units in the new divisions or as reinforcements for battalions already there, while the lieutenant colonels, majors and company sergeant majors often piled up in England, complaining to their MP's or to Hughes, drawing their pay, and feeling much too embarrassed to tell the folks at home what had happened to them. The mess, for mess it was, was another of Sam Hughes's many gifts to Canada."[27]

Recruiting rallies began to feature speeches by veterans and the relatives of soldiers in mid 1915. At a meeting on July 21 at the Industrial Bureau auditorium, Colonel James Kirkcaldy spoke about the second Battle of Ypres, where he was wounded fighting as a member of the 8th Battalion. He thundered that "I have nothing but contempt for the man who can go but does not." He said he was sorry for people who had lost sons, but "had you been privileged to see as we saw them, you would have been pleased that their death was glorious. I know no better way to die than to die for your country."[28]

Mayor Waugh spoke next, reminding the crowd that the Magna Carta, the cornerstone of British democracy, was 700 years old and must be defended. He said the kaiser, who threatened their freedoms, was so evil that beside him Nero seemed like an innocent child. He chided the young men in the audience, saying that if they did not go to war he would have to go instead, with his friend Hugh John Macdonald, and they would take the girls with them. Referring to his two sons in the service, one of whom was still recovering in hospital in England, he said, "I know what it means to let a boy go to the front. It was a great sacrifice, but this is a time for great sacrifices." Waugh's words illustrate the grim determination that was setting in as people put winning the war ahead of their own feelings. A few days earlier at a service to remember two men killed at Ypres, Waugh had made the point even more strongly: "I would ten times rather have my son lying dead on the field of battle than have him a coward and turn his back on danger...Those that have sent boys to help fight for the British Empire will always be proud that they helped to keep the old flag flying."

Such statements were not uncommon during public events during the war. In July 1916, for example, Winnipegger William Fisher spoke about losing his two sons to the war: "it is a sad blow. Our home is desolate without them. But we would rather that our boys lay—as they do—in their honored graves among the brave dead in the fields of Flanders than have them walk the streets of Winnipeg with the coward's brand upon their brow."

Judge P.A. Macdonald made a similar comment in a speech in November 1916: "I would prefer to see my son who is now at the front dead rather than showing the white feather in the streets of Winnipeg."

In a private letter to E.L. Drewery, the Winnipeg brewer, written in January 1917, Mrs. Acton Burrows thanked him for his letter of condolence on the death of her son in France. She expressed sentiments similar to those of Waugh and Macdonald: "It is a terrific blow but I well realize that I am only one of many who have been bereaved and that I must be brave.... Much as I shall always miss him I have no regret that he went, entirely of his own free will.... I should, however, have always had regrets had he preferred to stay at home and be a slacker."[29]

Did these statements, that seem so harsh now, mean that these people did not have normal feelings toward their sons? We know that in private Waugh's grief over the death of his son Alex at the end of 1917 was profound and genuine. Placed in the context of the time we can only conclude that these statements demonstrate their determination not to let their sons down by showing weakness and to make sure that Canada was on the winning side in this terrible war. Community leaders like Waugh also knew that they had to be seen to be patriotic. They were not alone in expressing these sentiments and significant criticism of the war's enormous waste of life did not really begin until the later 1920s.

We can get a further sense of the atmosphere in Canada during the war from a speech delivered at the IODE annual meeting in May 1917. The president, Mrs. Gooderham, told delegates they had all suffered and denied themselves and felt fear. But, she asked, had they simply felt these things as an inescapable part of being at war, or "have we been willing to go further than the force of circumstances made it necessary for us to go? Have we felt as never before the oneness of Empire? Have we realized that the individual has a great responsibility to society?" Mrs. Gooderham's questions serve as a sort of definition of patriotism as it was seen by people who were completely focussed upon winning the war. She called for self-denial and absolute dedication to the country and, of course, to the Empire.

Members of Winnipeg's Polish community contributed this float to a parade supporting the war effort in 1915.

Of course, people were not always able to live up to these sorts of almost inhuman standards. In a letter written to Minnie Campbell by a fellow IODE member, Rosalie Creighton, who had lost a son, said, "the sense of loss is so great that one's pride sometimes seems absolutely submerged in grief and pain."

❧

Training

Recruiting by the established militia regiments continued in the summer of 1915. The Winnipeg Grenadiers regiment was busy raising the 78th Overseas Battalion. J.B. Mitchell had gotten an agreement from Sam Hughes that if the Grenadiers "recruited a full battalion of one thousand officers and men, it could go to France as a Grenadiers unit."[30] When he gave his approval, Hughes insisted that the new battalion be commanded by an officer who had seen service in France. Colonel James Kirkcaldy was chosen to take that role. Kirkcaldy had been the tough chief of police in Brandon for many years and had served in the militia before the war. His experience in France placed him in a select category of officer who had actually experienced the realities of the war at the second Battle of Ypres and survived to apply the lessons learned. Many of the senior officers of the Canadian

Corps would share this pedigree. Kirkcaldy led the 78th through 1916 and 1917, ending the war as a much decorated brigadier general.

Kirkcaldy was an aggressive recruiter, visiting workplaces in the city. When he went to the Ashdown Warehouse and addressed a group of the employees, four men joined the army on the spot. He later spoke in other firms, such as the Royal Alexandra Hotel, where seven more men joined up.

The 190th Battalion, raised by the 90th Winnipeg Rifles, began recruiting in February 1916 under Colonel A.W. Morley. Morley, a lawyer in civilian life, had gone overseas in 1914 with the 8th Battalion and, like Kirkcaldy, he had returned to Winnipeg when he was wounded. He announced that he would use new recruiting methods, such as a professionally produced advertising campaign, to attract men. The first advertisement addressed employers, telling them that the battalion had "greater work" for their workers than they could ever offer and asking them to call a meeting and get the men to sign the recruiting "Roll of Honor" printed in the advertisement. Upon request, the battalion would send a car to pick up the men and take them to the battalion headquarters for their medical examination and to sign their attestation papers. Gone were the excited crowds of August 1914, crowding into the regimental offices to join up.

All over the country, during the last half of 1915 and first months of 1916, civilian recruiting organizations sprang up to support the local military authorities. In February 1916 a Winnipeg group, the Citizens' Recruiting League was established with sponsorship from the Board of Trade. The league was governed by a Committee of 100, including representatives from commercial, financial, educational, and labour bodies. They informed the public that "there is an urgent need for a recruiting campaign through the province of Manitoba...the methods that have hitherto been effectual are less than satisfactory...and there is a general desire in the community to help the military." Convener Lendrum McMeans expressed the hard-nosed approach the league would take: "I believe that a man who has not offered his services as yet has some very strong reason for his action. It will be the duty of this recruiting league to find the cause of his refusal and, if possible, remove it." Judge Mathers, who was the vice-president, suggested that the league could get lists of employees working for the larger firms and contact each of the men individually. They organized meetings where officers and returned soldiers could talk to the public, and they arranged for speakers to give short talks in churches and theatres.[31]

The league's most ambitious project was a census of potential recruits. Using the method devised by Lord Derby, Britain's commissioner of recruiting, the men were divided into three categories: bachelors and widowers (ages eighteen to thirty), bachelors and widowers (ages thirty-one to forty-five), and married men or widowers (ages eighteen to forty-five) with children.[32] Next, the city was divided into districts, and on Wednesday, March 8, 1916, soldier canvassers from the 78th, 90th, 101st, and 184th battalions spread out into their assigned areas. Cards were distributed on which the name, residence, business address, age, and nationality of men between eighteen and forty-five were recorded along with the name of the person giving the information. Citizen volunteers picked up and dropped off cards at the league's headquarters in the Curry Building on Portage Avenue.

While it had been anticipated that the census would be completed in a few days, problems soon emerged. In many cases information about single men was refused, and much of the data was supplied by neighbours so that it was of questionable accuracy. Many people told the census takers that the single men in the house had already tried to enlist but were rejected as unfit by the army doctors. The league gave these men a lapel pin so that they would not be bothered on the street, another idea borrowed from the British. The census, imperfect as it was, identified 5094 eligible Winnipeg men who were not in the forces. All these men, except those registered as enemy aliens, were sent circular letters and each of them had personal visits from recruiting officers.

A major impediment to recruiting was that, now with a reviving economy, employers did not want to lose workers. On March 22 the Recruiting League set up a Women's Registration Bureau to gather the names of women willing to take on the jobs of men wanting to go to war. Sixteen women had signed up by the end of the first day. One woman expressed the ambition to be a streetcar conductor and a Russian woman said she would work as a postman. Eva Crane, of Sydney, Manitoba, became the first woman truck driver in Winnipeg. She had family members at the front and she said, "I took this job so that some healthy, physically fit man could go overseas and fight alongside my husband and brothers."

On April 14, 1916, a delegation of volunteer recruiting officials, including Winnipeg's Judge Mathers, met with Prime Minister Borden in Ottawa. They asked the prime minister for a comprehensive national census of men to be followed by universal conscription. Mathers told Borden that volunteerism was inherently unfair because it took the very best men in society rather than spreading the burden equally. He worried that the country was being drained of its "best blood," as, presumably, Anglo-Canadian volunteers were killed in the trenches. Anglo-Canadians had wanted to take the lead in the army and in fighting the war, but by 1916 it was clear they could not win the war alone without sacrificing an entire generation of their children. They began to call for other ethnic groups, previously not really welcome in the fight, to do their bit.

Mathers also argued that the pressure being put on civilians was unfair: "we have under the present system compulsion in its most obnoxious form. It is absurd to speak of enlistment at the present day as voluntary. In the cities of the west the man who is not in uniform is made to feel that he is a sort of social outcast. No man who joins the ranks today does so voluntarily. He does so because he can no longer resist the pressure of public opinion."[33] Of course, Mathers's own recruiting league was not above using this sort of pressure.

Borden listened carefully, but he answered that there was no need to make changes at the moment because enough volunteers were coming forward. Later in the day, Minister of Trade and Commerce Sir George Foster spoke to some of the group and told them it was impossible to consider conscription because of the resistance from Quebec.[34] But conscription was unpopular all across the country. Farmers argued that their sons were needed on the home front to produce food for Britain; labour leaders spoke out against conscription of workers without conscription of wealth; and many Canadians who had immigrated from places such as Russia or the Austro-Hungarian Empire had come, in part at least, to escape the conscription of their children and were against it in their new home. Some, like the Mennonites and Doukhobors, had been promised, as a condition of their coming to Canada, that they would never be conscripted into the army. For others, conscription was a betrayal of the very traditions of British liberty and democracy that Canada was fighting to defend.

For those who did volunteer, the first taste of army life was a period of training at Camp Sewell, 180 kilometres west of Winnipeg. In the spring of 1915 men who had volunteered for the second and third contingents as well as some regular units, including a squadron of the Strathcona's Horse, began to gather there for training. This camp had been the location of summer militia exercises in Military District 10 since 1910. Each summer, including the summer of 1914, militiamen converged on Sewell for two weeks to learn how to drill and shoot and take orders.

By the spring of 1915 the camp had been greatly expanded, with water lines, latrines, and showers, many permanent buildings, and a shooting range that could accommodate 500 riflemen. That year 10,994 men lived under canvas and trained there. In the fall of 1915 the name of the camp was changed to Camp Hughes, and the following summer 27,754 soldiers were stationed there, served by amenities like movie theatres and stores, a swimming pool, and photo studios. In that summer the camp was the second-largest community in the province and on weekends civilians swarmed in to visit. In 1917 and 1918 the sharp decline in the numbers of volunteers meant that the camp was again much smaller.[35]

The battalions in the camp in the summer of 1915 normally did physical training in the morning followed by a run and bayonet drill. There were night patrols with blank ammunition and hours of marching and inspections. Sports were encouraged. Jimmy Robinson, later a sportswriter and hunting guide, had enlisted in the 61st Battalion and was at Camp Sewell that summer. The 61st was called the "Athletic Battalion" because of the large number of well-known sportsmen in the unit. Robinson wrote that he played baseball and hockey with stars of the time like "Bullet" Joe Simpson, Spunk Sparrow, Jocko Anderson, Pork Rommeral, Roddy Smith, the three Morrison boys from Selkirk, Bobby, Crutchy, and Alf, some of whom would go on to play professional hockey in Canada and the United States. A team organized by the 61st and led by Simpson won the Allen Cup in 1916. After the war, during which he was wounded twice, Simpson played for the Edmonton Eskimos and the New York Americans and was on

In 1915 Camp Sewell had been renamed Camp Hughes, in honour of Sir Sam Hughes. These young troops are likely part of a contingent of recruits from universities.

the 1932 Canadian Olympic hockey team that won the gold medal at Lake Placid. But the men not only played sports, as Robinson remembered: "I had never played poker or black-jack before my enlistment, but it didn't take me long to learn. I was a soft touch for the slickers from Winnipeg."[36]

The summer of 1915 began with cold, wet weather, including a snowstorm in May and rain in June. Alec Waugh, while still in training at Camp Sewell, wrote to his mother, "for the love of mike get me a slicker, one of those yellow oilskin ones and send it by parcel post at once. You can get one cheap at Eaton's. In a couple more days I'll be down with pleurisy if the rain keeps up."[37] In another letter, Waugh told his father that he and his fellow troopers were supposed to get up at 5 a.m. and run down a hill to take a cold shower before dressing in the cold and rain. "You bet your life the officers don't even get up to

see if we go. It would kill them."[38] He complained that he had not been paid because "our officers don't give a damn."

Captain Williams of the Strathconas had more positive memories of that summer: "We had a most enjoyable time at Sewell Camp, but of course didn't appreciate it as we should have done. The air was so clean and pure that when you got up in the morning it made you feel glad to be alive. When it rained, as of course it sometimes did, it dried up very quickly as the ground was so sandy."[39] Williams also wrote about pet bear cubs in the camp: "nearly every other unit in Sewell Camp had one... The men had a lot of fun with him. They are very playful." The most famous bear cub of World War I, the regimental mascot of the Fort Garry Horse, never saw Camp Sewell. He was named Winnie and was acquired in the fall of 1914 in northern Ontario by Captain Harry Colborne, during the trip to Valcartier. Probably the only Canadian bear to accompany the first contingent overseas, he soon found himself in London Zoo, where he eventually became the inspiration for A.A. Milne's *Winnie the Pooh*.

Aside from such momentary amusements, the Strathconas and other units would spend the summer of 1915 fighting mock battles. Machine guns were represented by a stick with red cloth tied to the end. When it was waved around it meant it was firing, and umpires would tell recruits if they had been hit. By the following year the experience of the fighting in France and Belgium—and the real threat of the machine gun—would begin to influence training, and an extensive system of trenches was constructed.

The 27th and 43rd battalions had left the city for England in May 1915 without spending time at Camp Sewell. On May 13, the 27th Battalion boarded the CPR train for the first part of their journey. They had officially become the 27th City of Winnipeg Battalion in a ceremony in Market Square where Mayor Waugh handed out special shoulder patches with the city crest. As they marched to the CPR station thousands of people lined Main Street to cheer them. The 43rd and 44th battalions lent their bands for the occasion, and the 28th Battalion formed up at the station to salute their comrades.

Two weeks later, the 43rd Cameron Highlanders Battalion, including forty officers and 998 other ranks, left Winnipeg under the command of Colonel R.M. Thompson. Lance Corporal James Low remembered, "We marched all the way from Minto Street right down to the CPR depot where the freight sheds were. There was so much crowd, excitement and everything that, my God!, you couldn't move." The Reverend Charles Gordon, their chaplain, wrote in his memoirs that the "departure of the Cameron Highlanders brought 50,000 people to line the streets of Winnipeg to watch their swinging kilts and hear the wild, weird shrilling of their pipes, and bid them God speed." A new set of pipes, imported from Glasgow, had been presented to the 43rd earlier in the month by local businessman Alex Macdonald, and the St. Andrew's Society had presented them with a set of band instruments at a "crowded function" at the Industrial Bureau. The battalion was also given several field kitchens paid for with money donated by Winnipeggers.

When the 27th and 43rd battalions reached England, they were billeted at Shorncliffe Camp near Dover. There they found a familiar officer, General Sam Steele, in command of the Second Division of which they formed part. But the old soldier was not destined to lead the division at the front. The British objected to him due to his advanced age—he was seventy-seven at this time—and his lack of battle experience. In reality, he had as much experience as most senior officers in the field at that time, having fought in the South African War as the commander of Lord Strathcona's Horse, but there is no doubt that his advanced age was an impediment. He would have received little support from Sam Hughes, being the sort of hard-drinking professional soldier the minister disliked. In August the question was settled when he was injured in a car accident near Shorncliffe and he was soon after replaced by J.J. Creelman, a militia colonel of artillery. Never to fight in France, the old soldier spent the rest of the war as an inspector general of Canadian troops. By the middle of September 1915 the Second Division of the Canadian Expeditionary Force was complete and ready to cross the channel. On October 1 they went into the trenches near Ypres.

At home in Manitoba on October 18, the 44th Battalion, consisting of thirty-seven officers and 1097 other ranks, most of whom were from Winnipeg, climbed aboard two trains at Camp Sewell. They were bound for England where they would receive further training before being moved to France. There had been a good deal of frustration in the ranks of the 44th because many of the more experienced men had been sent as reinforcements to France before the battalion was fully trained. But the battalion recruiting office had brought the unit back up to strength.

When they reached England the men of the 44th were among the first Canadian units to be stationed at Bramshott, a new training camp that would accommodate Canadian troops in both world wars. The battalion history spoke well of the new camp: "The quarters at Bramshott, though not ideal, are infinitely preferable to the muddy tents of the First division at Salisbury Plain in the winter preceding."[40]

Jimmy Robinson, now serving with the 44th Battalion, remembered that when they arrived at Bramshott they met some of the men they had trained with in Manitoba: "There was a large hospital...which received thousands of wounded soldiers sent back from the battle front in France...To see many of our former comrades legless, armless, blind and otherwise maimed gave us our first realization of the horrors of war. Also to hear their accounts of hand-to-hand fighting and myriad gruesome incidents in the trenches, served to prime us for the trial by fire that was soon to be our common lot."[41]

Around this time, Alec Waugh would leave his brother in Liverpool to join the Strathconas in the much larger Shorncliffe Camp near Bramshott. He was one of a group of Strathconas attached to the Fort Garry Horse and the callow twenty-year-old was not happy about it. He did not take well to being given orders by officers of what he called a "sixth rate militia outfit." He criticized the Fort Garry commander Lieutenant Colonel Patterson, "who showed what an errant coward he was when he visited the firing line a short while ago."

As a result of a disagreement with a Fort Garry officer, and, in all probability, because of his general attitude, Alec was demoted from sergeant to private. He sulked that the rank "will be permanent because I'll never take another stripe in this outfit as long as I am connected with it." A few days later he complained to his father that "we feel like a bunch of convicts or prisoners and the Fort Garry officers encourage the delusion. We have no horses and are general fatigue men for a militia outfit that isn't fit to keep our boots clean."

Alec's life took a positive turn when General Sam Steele, the former commander of the Lord Strathcona's Horse, came on a tour of inspection. Steele moved the Strathconas into a squadron "separate from all the militia outfits here, an immense advantage to us." He wrote that Steele was a "real soldier" and that "his face has more character in it than any other I have ever seen," and Alec enjoyed the dressing down Steele gave Colonel Patterson for saluting with his riding crop. Steele was not every Canadian officer's cup of tea, but he was popular with the rank-and-file soldiers.

The strength of this animosity may seem a little surprising in that Alec, like most Canadian soldiers, had only been in the service a short time, but he had quickly developed the loyalty to his own regiment that was the mark of a soldier. As a Strathcona, he already thought of himself as a permanent force soldier, a different breed from the militiamen. He wrote to his father that "quite naturally the permanent forces hate the militia like poison and the hatred is finely developed between ourselves and the Fort Garrys."

Another young Canadian, Clifford Wells, was experiencing many of the same feelings as Alec Waugh as he became integrated into the Canadian Army. He was a native of Montreal assigned to the 8th Battalion Winnipeg Rifles. Wells quickly came to feel a part of the 8th, proudly explaining in letters to his parents that they had received their nickname, Little Black Devils, from a Métis fighter at Batoche. He recounted the unit's exploits in the spring of 1915 at Ypres: "they made a wonderful stand with the Germans all around them."[42] He said he was glad to be going to France with the 8th because their officers were kind and considerate to newcomers, while many veterans of the Princess Patricia's Light Infantry, to which he was previously attached, were rather "snobbish."[43]

Like most young soldiers, Alec Waugh developed a special bond with his regimental comrades. He wrote to his father, "Yesterday night we sang songs, wrote letters and finally wound up around the big open fire. Occasionally our thoughts will all turn together across the seas. We compare experiences.... It is on these occasions that we bring out the now well worn pictures of the best little mother in the world...or pictures of our sweethearts, if we have one. It is this mutual trust and interest in each other that makes me so loyal to my squadron and we stick to each other as no other unit in camp does."

Alec settled into the routine that, for a private, consisted of hard work. He was not paid for some time because of a bureaucratic mix-up and wrote to his parents that some money and a food parcel would be appreciated, since they were not given a lot to eat. He had a fatigue in the kitchen of the officer's mess, which meant that he got a decent meal, but only, he complained, after being interrogated by the chief cook, who was a former bar tender from the Queen's Hotel in Winnipeg.

He wrote to his father in mid October that he was taking a musketry course with the Lee-Enfield rifle, which, he said, was "splendidly sited and much superior to the Ross." He expressed the view of many Canadian soldiers that the Ross was a substandard weapon. With the Lee-Enfield, he wrote, "there is no danger of the bolt jamming under rapid fire, the danger of this in action being illustrated by Doug, who told me of men hammering open the Ross bolt with their entrenching

The Women's Volunteer Reserve organized by Dr. Ellen Douglass.

tool, to cover a German advance. Supplying men with faulty arms such as this is, I believe, nothing short of deliberate murder."

He was proud of his good health and eager to prove to his father that he was now a man like his older brother. He wrote, "When Doug left for France he weighed one hundred and seventy pounds, my present weight. This is all bone and muscle in my case and I am quite confident that I can stand the same cruel strain on my constitution that Douglas did...My arms, with work and exercise, are as firm as rock and I'll bet that my forearm is as big as yours. Ten and a quarter inches around it. When I had my last medical examination the doctor said I was in absolutely perfect health, in fact he expressed surprise that all our men were so perfectly constituted. I told him that we made real men in Canada, even out of some very poor material."[44] Untested in battle, he tried to be confident about his fighting abilities: "I guess we have inherited some good scrapping blood we two, particularly of what the Strathcona casualties tell me of Doug."

Still, he wrote often about going home: "Perhaps Doug and I will make it together, but this would be really almost too much to expect of providence.... Say Dad, if I hadn't been in the game, I wouldn't have ever wanted to live in Winnipeg. My one ambition now is to finish up with some German helmets, about a hundred notches in by gun and a brass band to go home with." With the touch of melodrama that often marked his writing, Alec told his father that "some day I shall see you and mother, with Doug, safe at home...broken and crippled perhaps, but happy in knowing that we've fought for our home, our mothers, sisters and sweethearts, and the world is right again."

For Alec, as with many Canadian soldiers, close exposure did not necessarily strengthen his love of the mother country. Although he liked the English countryside, the towns and cities did not compare favourably with home for Alec. The cities, he wrote, were a "succession of dirty, narrow streets" and middle-class houses were all alike, "with trim well kept hedges and tidy back yards but I cannot possibly see how genius can flourish in these rows of red brick villas.... I want a street where one is able to breathe, and where a wagon does not need to occupy the walk while another passes."

In the fall of 1915, in a letter to his father, Alec gave an amusing description of the ministrations of an English barber, which may indicate a more general impatience with the ways of the mother country:

> After a wait of anywhere from forty minutes to an hour you climb into a chair, just an ordinary chair, with a slide in the back topped with a cushion of plush in which is concealed a piece of cord wood. The plush is invariably red on the ends, but in the center the nap is worn away and greasy with brilliantine and hair oil, not to mention the accumulations from necks of the great unwashed of ten generations.... After serving a few customers and prognosticating all meteorological conditions at length, the gentleman who is to operate on you appears, bearing a huge earthen pot and a sloppy looking brush. He carefully spreads a half inch of soap on your face, rubs it into your nose and ears, being very careful to wipe your mouth with a large and capable hand, ending in a finger of unusual proportions, reminding one of a helping of ham and sausages. This operation is gone through several times. Finally after you feel that after all time is money, and that in a few minutes your neck will be permanently fixed in an uncomfortable position, a razor is brought to bear on your face. At the imminent risk of cutting your throat it is brought down the sides of your face, rubbed over your chin and with a few "finishin" swipes at your neck, is removed. The hay is mown presumably. A

sponge is next brought to play and dexterously inserted into your
ears, slopped around your face while you wonder why barbers
wear huge Masonic watch fobs and invariably have the remains
of several meals spread down the fronts of their "weskits." The
talcum is done up in bricks and applied to the face with the same
rotary motion used in holystoning a barrack room.

The new Winnipeg Battalions in England and France at the end
of 1915 waited for their chance to prove themselves. In France
the 27th City of Winnipeg Battalion was in rest billets at Locre.
Constance Nanton and her committee members had been busy packing Christmas parcels for the men: "Over 2000 parcels arrived from
the 27th's Women Auxiliary Guild. Not one man went without a gift
of comforts that holiday. Concerts and sports were the order of the
day, culminating with turkey with all the trimmings served by the
Battalion's officers."[45]

Officers serving their men was a traditional Christmas departure
from the usual hierarchy of the army. Although everyone suffered
hardship in the trenches, the situation of officers was better than that
of the men. Officers did, however, have a fairly short life expectancy in
the trenches where their uniforms made them prime targets for snipers.

Promotion from the ranks was relatively common in World War I,
because of the terrible casualties, and promotion brought with it a
change in a man's life. In June 1915 Alec Waugh had been promoted,
while still at Camp Sewell, from private to sergeant in the Lord
Strathcona's Horse, as we have seen, a rank he later lost. He proudly
explained to his father that "the appointment as sergeant carries with
it a great many privileges, the main one being that of dining in the
sergeant's mess, wihich is a heaven of epicurean delight compared
with the usual run of grub-eaters who answer the cook house call and
consume their meals from their knees on the ground."

Toward the end of 1915 he was promoted to the rank of lieutenant. This advancement came partly through the political influence
of Robert Rogers, federal minister of public works and member of
Parliament for Winnipeg. Rogers was able to arrange Alec's promotion as a favour to the Waughs, who, although they were Liberals, were
still prominent Winnipeggers and Rogers's constituents. In a letter to

Alec, he wrote, "I was very glad indeed to receive your letter of the 11th of December and to know that you are getting along so well. I may say that General Carson sent me a very flattering report of your conduct and work, which is very much appreciated and he was very pleased indeed to take advantage of the opportunity to give you a well deserved and well earned promotion."[46] J.W. Carson had been Sam Hughes's personal representative in England since 1914, managing the Byzantine political side of army affairs.

Although Waugh did not try, as some did, to use his relationship with Rogers to avoid fighting, being promoted to lieutenant brought many benefits: he would have more money, better food, and a batman to keep everything "up to scratch." He and another officer shared a large room in the Shorncliffe camp. He also received a fifty-one pound allowance for a London-made uniform, but life in trenches required more practical clothing like woolen socks, waterproof coats, and good gloves. Months after Alec's death, his father received a bill from a London tailor for a trench coat he had ordered.

In his classic Canadian novel of the First World War, *Why Stay We Here?*, George Godwin describes how his main character, Stephen Craig, got a commission, although he had been turned down as unfit to serve by the army doctors. Disheartened and worried because he had brought his wife and children to England to live while he was in the army, Stephen had lunch with his brother Ricky, who was a captain in the British Army. His brother advised Stephen,

> "You want a commission? Right, I'll explain how you can get it. You've got to go straight to the Minister. Old Sammy is at the Savoy surrounded by chocolate majors. Never mind them. Shove in.... And now the important part. You must bear in mind that old Sam is only a man under his Piccadilly chest. And quite a good old scout too.... Now what you've to do is to appeal to him for a commission. 'Your well-known good heart, sir, has brought me here. Everybody told me I should get a square deal from you.... I want a commission in the C.E.F.'"[47]

In the novel, Craig, like many men in real life, got his commission as a lieutenant, with its comparatively good salary and better allowance for his wife and children.

Clifford Wells was also promoted from the ranks around this time and wrote to his parents about similar improvements in his living conditions. In Wells's case, his new servant was a former florist from Winnipeg who was unable to fight in the trenches because of wounds he received at Festubert. Wells had been promised a commission when he joined up as a student at McGill and he had often expressed his impatience to his parents that the promise was not kept. On one occasion he asked his father, a prominent Methodist minister, to "pull whatever strings" he could.

In November 1915 the future premier of Ontario, Leslie Frost, wrote to his brother about the same subject. He had been recommended for a staff officer position. He told his brother that "now this looks pretty good with what pull I can exert and if Dad will use his best diplomacy, I'm out to get a good job."[48]

Men who had been in the fighting since the beginning of the war did not like the role politics played in Sam Hughes's army. In his letters, Princess Patricias Major Agar Adamson expressed disgust to his wife about the officers who received their commissions through politics. In January 1916 he wrote that "Men every day in this and other Regiments are receiving telegrams from Sam Hughes through Carson to return at once and get their commission. Most of them have only been out a few months and good Sergeants and men who would make excellent officers are not considered."[49]

Clifford Wells, although he wanted his father to use his influence on his behalf, also recorded the negative perception of politically connected officers among their comrades. In June 1916 he wrote, "There is...at present a lieutenant who came to England as a civilian and through friendship with General _____ secured a commission...he knows absolutely nothing about soldiering, most of the officers will barely speak to him."[50]

Winnipeg Women in England

Many Winnipeg women crossed to England to live out the war closer to their relatives fighting in Belgium and France and to support the war effort. The wife of Grain Exchange secretary C.N. Bell, who had two sons in the Army Medical Corps, spent a large part of the war in England. Lieutenant Governor Cameron and his wife moved to England after the end of his appointment to be closer to their sons who were in the service.

Likewise, Margaret Tupper, Charles Tupper's wife, lived in England while he was serving with the Camerons in France in 1916. He was a Winnipeg lawyer and the grandson of Sir Charles Tupper, a long-time Conservative Cabinet minister and, briefly, prime minister. He was wounded and she wrote that she had been trying to get him transferred to a hospital in England. In a letter to her husband she reveals that there were limits to what one could accomplish by asking Sam Hughes for favours. She had called on Major General G.C. Jones, head of the Canadian Medical Corps, and other officials, and in a letter to her husband she agreed with him that she might only "mess things up if I pursued my efforts beyond General Jones—namely to our old friend Sam, who has arrived in London. You are not in a Canadian hospital, so Sam might be only officious as he usually is. If General Jones can't manage to get you over I don't know who could...I understand it is very difficult to get through the red tape of English Hospitals by our usual 'colonial methods.'"[51] By colonial methods she meant the use of political influence through their friendship with Sam Hughes.

Journalist Mollie Glenn published several stories in the *Telegram* about the Canadian troops in England. On January 1, 1916, she spotlighted Lenore McMeans of Winnipeg, who was working in the Field Comforts Commission headquarters at Shorncliffe. This organization was responsible for receiving and sorting gifts sent from a 1000 women's organizations spread across 872 Canadian towns and villages and then forwarding them on to the troops in France. Glenn reported that the staff barely had time to eat during the busy Christmas season. The work of supplying field comforts like cigarettes, wool socks, books, razors, and a wide range of other items was extremely important for the morale of men who spent their days either in the horror of the trenches or in often uncomfortable billets during their time out of the line. The commission was the smaller of two such agencies, the other one being the Canadian War Contingent Association, in which women also played a large role.

Glenn wrote about Winnipeg women among the volunteers in hospitals in the area of the Shorncliffe camp. She reported that they spent time each day "sitting at the bedsides of our wounded boys, talking to them of home and the future and leaving in their wake heaps of good things to eat, plenty of cigarettes and the most cherished of all gifts, papers from home." Every day Mrs. G.W. Andrews of Winnipeg went to see wounded men of the 90th Winnipeg Rifles Battalion and Mrs. F.E. Mackie, wife of Colonel Mackie of the Lord Strathcona's Horse, and Mrs. Murray Ross, wife of Captain Ross, visited hospitals in the Folkstone area. Mrs. Hugh Walkem visited patients from the 43rd Highlanders, and Miss Florence Steele, General Steele's daughter, who had completed St. John Ambulance training, was soon going to leave for Malta or Egypt to work in hospitals there. In the meantime she worked in the Bevan Hospital in Folkstone.

Mollie Glenn described the Canadian women in London who operated the Maple Leaf Club, originally established by Montrealer Lady Drummond. For two shillings and six pence a Canadian soldier on leave could get a clean bed and pyjamas and a good breakfast at the Maple Leaf Club. During the war, 881,450 visitors used the club's facilities, the women volunteers served 767,781 meals, and made up 443,539 beds for the men. There was a smoking room and a recreation room, and two blocks away there was an annex in a former private home that offered all the same services. The matron of this annex was Mrs. A.C. Shaw, the widow of a Canadian officer killed in action. Mrs. Graham Watson of Winnipeg went to the club each day to clean the rooms. Glenn added that the Canadian women were "working and working hard; and are looking on life from an entirely different viewpoint since they have taken up their new tasks." One of the women said, "here again is an example of the executive ability of women whose lives have fallen in pleasant places and who had never an opportunity to demonstrate their power owing to the fact that she was not obliged to earn her living."

Not everyone was able to find volunteer work. In January 1916 Minnie Campbell received a letter from Mary Benning, a Canadian woman in London. She was living there with her daughter, and her son was in the field ambulance corps near Ypres. Her daughter, wrote Benning, wanted to move into London so that there would be more chances for her to do useful volunteer work, but there are "more helpers than work to be done," leaving her with little to do.

Toward the end of the war the close to 50,000 Canadian women living in England were seen as a problem, both because of the food shortages suffered by the British public and because of the fear that when the war ended they would take places on ships that could be used to repatriate the troops. For these reasons the government would eventually ban almost all women from travelling to England.[52]

City Politics in 1915

In Winnipeg, the unemployment problem persisted in the spring of 1915. There were still 12,000 jobless men in the city, 5000 of them non-residents. Many of these were eastern Europeans who were considered enemy aliens, ineligible for military service.[53]

In response, the city embarked on what Mayor Waugh called "possibly the largest municipal work in Canada"—spending $2 million to link Shoal Lake with the city with the new aqueduct and another $1 million on a number of smaller improvements. "All things considered," said Waugh, "we will take care of the unemployment situation as well as can possibly be expected."[54]

By the end of April the city had 1000 men working at the old Agricultural College site in Tuxedo, planting vegetable gardens. These men got tickets they could exchange for meals and a voucher for a bed, which the city redeemed when a landlord turned it in. The city would also be paying men to break rock in the City Works yard on Ross Avenue in Elmwood. Married men were welcome to work for wages. The hope was held out that the railroads would be employing 4500 men after May 1.

Waugh hosted a conference of twelve western Canadian mayors on May 21 to discuss the unemployment problem. He encouraged the provincial governments to send representatives as well, as Saskatchewan had already done. The delegates presented a memorial to the federal

government recommending that land grants should be made available
to unemployed men, that public works and highway construction be
used to provide employment, and that foreign trade be expanded.[55]
They also recommended establishing labour exchanges and restrictions on immigration. Later, Waugh was instrumental in planning a
similar conference in Ottawa to discuss unemployment with the federal politicians.

In spite of these measures, men who were classified as enemy aliens
continued to find it difficult to get work. A large group of these men
had left Winnipeg to march to the American border at Emerson on
Friday, May 14. The *War Measures Act* made it illegal for men from
enemy countries to leave Canada, and on Monday 182 men, all that
was left of the group that left Winnipeg, were stopped at Emerson
and sent to Brandon where they were interned in the city arena, one
of the federal government's internment camps.

The great need created by the war resulted in the increasing intervention of governments at all levels into the business of helping the
poor and needy, something that, up to now, had been taken care of
by the churches and voluntary groups of middle-class people. At the
same time professional social workers and nurses began to take over
the day-to-day work of these organizations.[56]

Early in 1915 the Patriotic Fund requested that the city council
take the $5000 it had been giving the fund every month and instead
use $3000 of it to do sewer work and to give the private Associated
Charities $2000 for relief payments. The secretary of the Associated
Charities, J.H.T. Falk, asked the city to go further by taking more of
the responsibility for soldiers' families and by paying off his organization's deficit. Falk, like many others across Canada, was finding that
charitable donations alone were not enough to support relief programs.
Too many chose not to donate, said Falk: "There are people in the city
of considerable affluence who will not voluntarily subscribe to such a
cause as this and whose only contribution to charity consists of what
is indirectly...drawn from them...Those callous citizens who recognize
no duty towards their less fortunate fellow men, together with non
resident tax payers should be quietly forced to do their share."

About the same time, Augustus Nanton, chair of the Manitoba
Patriotic Fund, was also speaking to Manitoba municipal leaders

The formidable and capable Minnie Campbell organized the Winnipeg branch of the IODE.

about the need to add tax funds to the money being raised by voluntary donations. In Winnipeg the city responded by taking a larger role in managing relief and in October 1915 offices were being prepared at the city hall for a new civic commission that would replace the Associated Charities and the relief program of the Patriotic Fund.

The economic slump of 1914 created by the outbreak of war was slowly transformed in 1915 and 1916 into a boom as the business of supplying the Canadian, British, and other Allied armies began to pro-

duce large profits. Western businessmen were anxious to share in this
business, and Winnipeg organizations mounted a campaign, beginning
as early as October 1914, when the Winnipeg Board of Trade passed
a resolution demanding that supplies for western units be purchased
in western Canada. The Patriotic Fund executive passed a similar
resolution, wanting to create jobs for people who would otherwise
be dependent upon the fund and other charities to survive. Troops
training in the city were also seen as a source of income and jobs for
Winnipeg. In March 1915 the Industrial Bureau began lobbying for
troops to be trained in western Canada. Since Camp Sewell was "considered the best in Canada for field work" and since "Western Canada
has contributed largely in men and money," the organization argued
that training troops in the west would stimulate further recruitment.[57]
These appeals were successful and Winnipeg benefitted, especially in
the winter when large numbers of men were billeted in the city.

In the first months of war contracts for supplies and equipment
were often awarded as patronage with political input from Minister
Sam Hughes and the officials he appointed to manage the process. In
the spring of 1915 the inevitable scandals began to emerge, and in
April Prime Minister Borden announced that war purchasing would
now be managed by a commission composed of the "best businessmen
in Canada" who would award contracts strictly on the basis of tenders
and lowest bids. Many applauded this change, including the *Canadian
Finance* newspaper, which opined that "the ancient order of political
patronage in Canada is un-British and that 'practical politicians' like
Bob Rogers and Frank Oliver, who have steered the Conservative and
Liberal Party machines should not have a hand in public business."[58]

In spite of the condemnation of Robert Rogers, minister of the interior, and Winnipeg's representative in the Cabinet, it was to him that
the Board of Trade appealed when they wanted the War Purchasing
Commission to include a western member. Soon after, the membership of the commission was announced and it included Winnipeg
wholesale grocery merchant George Galt, along with chairman A.E.
Kemp, a Toronto millionaire and Conservative member of Parliament,
and H. LaPorte, a former mayor of Montreal.

The Board of Trade continued to be dissatisfied with the amount of
war material produced and purchased in Winnipeg. By August, the

board had conferred with Galt and the War Purchasing Commission, the Shells Committee, the CPR, and the Department of Militia in an attempt to secure a change. They were ultimately unsuccessful, partly because military supplies were distributed from the supply depot in Ottawa, meaning that western suppliers were forced to offer uncompetitive bids, which included the price of shipping to Ottawa. As a result, Winnipeg was unable to secure a share in the manufacturing boom resulting from the war that was proportional to its size and potential.

Between a quarter and a third of all the shells fired by British and Dominion artillery on the Western Front were manufactured in Canada. Fortunes were made by Canadian businessmen involved in making shells, and many new jobs were created for men and women, but the factories were almost all located in eastern Canada, close to the ports from which the material was shipped. Sam Hughes had created the Canadian munitions industry in the same hurried way in which he raised the First Division. With a hand-written memo of September 7, 1914, he established the Canadian Shell Committee. The membership included military officials and some of the managers and owners of Canada's small iron and steel industry. The chair was Colonel Alex Bertram, owner of a steel works in Dundas, Ontario, a militia officer, successful businessman, and a friend of Hughes—exactly the sort of person Sam Hughes preferred to work with as he rushed around creating his army and all its supporting institutions.

One of Bertram's functions was to meet with people who aimed to get some of the munitions business for their companies or communities. Of course, in Sam Hughes's world, this was how government contracts were awarded: handed out by a trusted political operative to ensure everyone got their share and friends of the party got the largest share. Bertram talked with many petitioners every day. Even former prime minister Wilfrid Laurier visited him in his office to support the case of one of his constituents. Winnipeg delegations also visited him and were successful in getting a contract for shell production.

The Shell Committee operated from the fall of 1914 until the following autumn. The committee was a Canadian organization whose responsibilities, authority, and lines of reporting were not clearly defined—not unusual with Hughes's creations. The members appear to have been honest men who worked long hours to lay down the foundations of a new Canadian munitions industry. But not all of Hughes's political cronies were honest, and one of them was caught making excessive commissions on deals he negotiated. Hughes survived this scandal but it weakened the position of the Shell Committee. When the shortage of artillery ammunition became a much larger scandal in Britain in 1915, the result was Lloyd George being appointed British minister of munitions. One of his initiatives was to replace the Canadian Shell Committee with the Imperial Munitions Board, controlled from London but chaired by Canadian businessman Sir Joseph Flavelle, one of the talented individuals Borden recruited in his effort to replace patronage with rational business methods.

The Imperial Munitions Board operated on a much larger scale and by the end of the war had built many new factories in Toronto and Montreal and supplied the artillery with close to 44 million high-explosive and shrapnel shells of various sizes. Canada's steel mills tripled steel production capacity from 800,000 to 2.5 million tons per month. The board's factories made shells, explosives, brass shell cases, and fuses. The fuses, the most intricate and complex part of the shell, were produced by skilled women workers. The marshalling of Canadian plants and workers to produce munitions was one of the great success stories of the war. The board also built aircraft and ships for the war effort.

Winnipeg participated in the production of munitions beginning in 1915, when Mayor Thomas Deacon secured an order from the Shell Committee for 1.5 million high-explosive shells to be manufactured in the city's machine shops. This contract employed 500 men for a year with a payroll of $1 million.[59] In February, Deacon established a western shell committee with representatives from Vulcan Iron Works, Dominion Bridge, and the Grand Trunk Pacific, Canadian Northern, and the Canadian Pacific railroads, all of whose shops and staff would be involved in the contract. The shells were made here and shipped empty to eastern Canada or Britain, where the explosives were added. By August 75,000 shells had been produced in Winnipeg and by the fall 100,000 shells a month were being shipped from the various western plants, with Winnipeg producing the largest share.

When the Imperial Munitions Board took over, production was concentrated at the Transcona Shell Company, formed in 1915. The company produced 18-pounder shells in the former coach painting shop
of the Grand Trunk Pacific shops in Transcona. This factory achieved
the largest daily output of these shells—3672 on a single day—and had
the largest total production of any facility in Canada—476,566. Brass
shell casings were also made in Winnipeg, beginning in 1915.

Some other Winnipeg firms did benefit from war contracts, but
not to the same extent as eastern communities. The most important
categories in which Winnipeg participated were uniforms, tents and
canvas supplies, medical supplies, and leather goods, including har-
nesses, all items that could be shipped cheaply to the eastern ports. At
the end of January 1915, John Hadden's factory at 261 Fort Street
received an order for 6000 tunics and 6000 pairs of pants—the first
war contract won by a Winnipeg firm. Hadden said it would allow
him to employ about 100 out-of-work tailors. Tailors in the city also
enjoyed a small increase in trade because of the demand for officers'
uniforms. As in the British Army, Canadian officers received an allowance for uniforms and equipment and were expected to have their
own uniforms made for them. Burns and Co. Military Tailors advertised that they would make an officer's tunic for twenty-three to thirty
dollars, breeches for from ten to thirteen dollars, and trousers for from
nine dollars to $11.50.

But even in the area of clothing manufacture Winnipeg was far behind Montreal and Toronto, with their large, long-established factories
and extensive labour force. In 1917 alone Toronto factories received
orders for uniforms amounting to $3.1 million and Montreal had con-
tracts for $4.8 million, while Winnipeg produced only $311,000 worth
of military clothing.[60]

During the first three years of the war, the Winnipeg share of the
total Canadian government expenditures under the *War Appropriation
Act* were 0.9, 0.8, and 0.3 percent, respectively. In 1916–17, by com-
parison, Toronto and Montreal plants received 8 and 12 percent of the
money expended by the government.

On May 11, 1915, at the annual meeting of the Board of Trade,
Winnipeg's business leaders attempted to find some hopeful signs in
the generally gloomy business situation. Railroad construction, once

a major employer, was slowing down. The CPR was planning to build twenty-six miles of new line in Manitoba, the Canadian Northern planned to finish the last part of its transcontinental line, and the Grand Trunk Pacific had completed its main line. The Hudson Bay Railway was still under construction, and workers had laid 130 miles of track from June to October 1914, pushing the end of steel 220 miles beyond The Pas. The railroad planned to go to within forty miles of Fort Nelson or York Factory on the shores of Hudson Bay in 1915. The project did provide jobs, but working conditions on the Hudson Bay line were so terrible that many men died.

In Winnipeg building permits for only $1.8 million worth of construction had been issued, compared to ten times that amount in 1912. The city's construction projects for the year were for less than $1 million compared to the $5 to $7 million that had been the norm before the war. A few large projects continued—the completion of the Minto and McGregor armouries, the Provencher Bridge, additions to the Royal Alexandra Hotel and CPR office building on Higgins Avenue, and the Shoal Lake aqueduct.[61] But the days of massive infrastructure spending in the west were over.

The Greater Winnipeg Water District aqueduct was one of the few large projects that continued to provide employment throughout the war. Construction had begun in 1914, after some years of planning. The aqueduct would bring fresh water from Shoal Lake to Winnipeg, solving, at long last, the city's serious water problems. Winnipeg's water came from artesian wells and was high in minerals so that people had to use water softeners and collect rainwater for household and industrial uses. The aqueduct, like the City Hydro dam, was an example of the great public works programs that the young and ambitious city undertook in its first half century. The hard-nosed businessmen who dominated civic life were not averse to public utilities, especially if the government was providing infrastructure that would make their businesses more stable and profitable.

By the end of 1914, $1.7 million had been spent on the aqueduct, and during 1915 a rail line connecting Winnipeg and Shoal Lake was completed. As well as supporting the construction project, the line opened the heavily wooded country to settlement and logging and made money transporting logs and freight. In January 1916 work on the aqueduct itself ceased after cracks appeared in the concrete pipe. It had been built more cheaply than the original plans stipulated and was not properly reinforced to prevent cracking when the ground settled and heaved in the cold. City council set up an inquiry with a complete reconsideration of the plans.

Some aldermen were upset that the original plans, which called for reinforcement if building on clay or muskeg, had been changed. Some blamed Mayor Richard Waugh, who was accused in the *Winnipeg Telegram* of knowing about the problems ten days before the news was made public and doing nothing. In February 1916 Waugh wrote a letter to the *Telegram* asking for an apology and denying he knew about the problem earlier. He called for an investigation, and the paper apologized.

An inquiry commission, which included General Ruttan, Winnipeg's long-time city engineer, recommended returning to the original plan. Work continued, and on March 20, 1919, when the water was turned on in Winnipeg, the city finally had "an ample supply of soft water for all uses." Still in use, the aqueduct is ninety-six miles long and drops a total of 300 feet from the source at Shoal Lake to the City of Winnipeg. The total cost of the line was $36,000,000, paid for with bond issues and taxes.[62]

In the summer of 1915 there was hopeful news about western agriculture. Because sources of wheat in Russia and western Europe were cut off by the war, prices were rising. Canadian farmers brought 25 percent more land under cultivation than in the previous year, and the weather cooperated to produce a record western Canadian crop of 393 million bushels of generally good quality. This was the greatest crop ever harvested to that time and surpassed the previous record by 70 percent. By August 1, Winnipeg wholesalers, anticipating demand from farmers, were making large shipments to country stores across the west.[63]

An additional boost to the farm economy was provided by increased sales of draught and riding horses to the Canadian, British, and French armies. The surge in farm income led to renewed optimism in Winnipeg and all over the west. Land values rose, and 229,419 Americans crossed the border to take up Canadian farms between 1915 and 1918.

Manitoba Bridge and Iron Works was one of the Winnipeg firms that participated in the first shell contract awarded to Winnipeg in 1915.

In August 1915, however, the huge crop presented western farmers with a serious problem—they did not have enough men to help with the harvest. The hot weather had ripened the grain prematurely and men were urgently needed to help bring in the crop. Harvesters from the east were not expected in as great numbers as in previous years because of the war. Men wanting to work on the harvest were asked to go to the Immigration Building beside the CPR station or to the Industrial Bureau. The entire staff of the Department of Agriculture were sent to the bureau to assign work to the men, and by August 11, 4300 men had been dispatched. W.F. Hepburn was hired by the department to recruit harvesters. One of the places he went in search of men was Camp Sewell, and soldiers training at the camp were given leave to go work on the harvest. Military authorities grumbled that this severely hampered their training, and, in fact, some soldiers did not even return to the camp after the harvest.

Jithney's + the Winnipeg Electric Railway

Despite the war, life continued on in Winnipeg. Like the reality of an early harvest that required labourers, Winnipeg was still adapting to its stunning growth of the last decade, and the growing pains could be seen in issues like public transportation. Friction between the city and the privately owned Winnipeg Electric Railway Company came to a head during the years from 1915 to 1918, when the company found itself facing a major crisis.

The Winnipeg Electric Railway was, in 1914, one of the most successful enterprises in Winnipeg, paying its shareholders dividends of close to $1.1 million and closing the year with a surplus of $994,000. Nearly 60 million tickets were sold to Winnipeggers, triple the number for 1904. Owned by Sir William McKenzie of the Canadian Northern Railway, the Winnipeg Electric Railway and its associated companies also had Winnipeg directors like the banker Augustus Nanton, McKenzie's business associate Hugh Sutherland, and hardware wholesaler F. Morton Morse.

Horse-drawn streetcars had first appeared on Winnipeg streets in 1882, and in 1891 Winnipeg became one of the first municipalities in North America to have electric streetcars. The original company was owned by Toronto businessman A.W. Austin. McKenzie and his partners, tough veterans of the bare-knuckle world of railroad contracting, began moving into the streetcar business in Toronto and Winnipeg and won the right to operate a competing line in 1892. By 1894 Austin admitted defeat and sold out to his rival. McKenzie entered on a period of growth and consolidation, acquiring several other companies— the Suburban Rapid Transit Company and the Winnipeg, Selkirk and Lake Winnipeg Railway—after which he had a monopoly of streetcar service to Winnipeg, St. Boniface, and the surrounding country.

In the years before the war Winnipeg was a typical "streetcar city," and the extension of the street railway lines was automatic under an agreement with the city once enough people lived along both sides of a street. Subdivision lots were advertised as being near the car line and thus just "minutes from City Hall." By 1914 the company provided the sole method of transport for most Winnipeggers, constructed its own wood-frame streetcars in its Fort Rouge car barns and employed a large and relatively well-paid workforce. Ensconced in their quarters in the magnificent Street Railway Chambers building at the corner of Albert and Notre Dame, company directors could be excused for feeling pleased with the success of their business.

Since the acquisition of the Manitoba Electric and Gas Light Company in 1904, the Winnipeg Electric Railway had also enjoyed a monopoly on the supply of gas for cooking and lighting in the city. This domestic gas was produced in two coal gasification plants, one by the Assiniboine River at the end of Ruby Street and the other on the banks of the Red River near Victoria Park.

In one important sector of its business—the supply of electric power to homes and businesses—the company did have a competitor: the Light and Power Department of the City of Winnipeg. In 1912 the city's new hydroelectric dam at Pointe du Bois had begun delivering electricity to Winnipeg homes and businesses. The Winnipeg Electric Railway, which had completed its hydro dam at Pinawa in 1906, had been charging seven and a half cents per kilowatt hour for electricity. The city light and power rate was set at three and a half cents, and the company was forced to match the lower rates. Suddenly, electric power, which had been something of a luxury, was within reach for most families, and many people began wiring their homes and buying electrical appliances to replace the gas stoves and lamps they had been using. In its 1918 annual report, the Board of Trade estimated that the new rates had saved Winnipeggers $3 million in the years since 1912. The city advertised itself as an ideal place to locate manufacturing businesses because of its cheap electricity.

The city derived some income from the Winnipeg Electric Railway under a contract that gave the city 5 percent of gross earnings and an annual licence fee of twenty dollars per streetcar—an arrangement that produced $122,000 in income for the city in 1914 alone. But the relationship between the company and the city was not a happy one. There were disagreements over a range of issues, and lawsuits were a common way of resolving differences.

Added to the larger issues were a myriad of day-to-day complaints of the sort that every public transit utility always receives—crowded cars at rush hour, long waits in cold weather, and the suspicion that drivers shut off the heat to the passenger areas of the cars in cold weather so their own areas would be warmer. All these matters made their way to the city council meetings with the expectation that the aldermen would solve them. As streetcar riders themselves, they often joined in with complaints of their own. Since nearly everyone took the streetcar to work and to recreational activities on their days off, grousing about the service was one of the things that bound Winnipeggers together. Sir William McKenzie was seen by many to be a high-handed eastern capitalist who did not care about the problems of lowly streetcar passengers.[64]

Even the simple matter of changing routes could lead to a major confrontation. After making a number of route changes in 1914 the Winnipeg Electric Railway and city council were deluged with letters of complaint. Council placed the problem before the public utilities commissioner, Judge Robson, who gathered evidence at a public hearing and issued his own route changes in the form of an order. The company did not like the judge's changes but was obliged to implement them. For several years the company registered its dissatisfaction by printing the statement "According to order number 170 of the Manitoba Public Utilities Commission" on its schedules.[65]

Then, on February 2, 1915, the *Telegram* carried a story on its front page about a new phenomenon—the jitney—which had recently begun appearing on the streets of American cities and was now starting to operate in Winnipeg. A jitney, explained the paper "from a circus term meaning a 5 cent show, is nothing more nor less than an auto operated by a private owner and carrying passengers for a 5 cent fare in active competition with the street railway."

Jitneys were very popular with Winnipeggers from the first day they began operating. The newspaper described them as the next stage in the natural evolution of urban transportation, "just as the mule car superseded the stage coach and the trolley superseded the cable car. Evidently now the motor industry has reached such perfection that we are on the eve of another big development in the transportation industry and the motor car will supersede and take the place of our trolley system."

The capital-intensive street railways, cumbersome and slow to respond to criticism, were often not popular institutions; the jitneys on the other hand offered a maneuverable and much more responsive form of transport for commuters. Personal cars were not yet within reach of most people and riders loved the novelty of a car ride home.

Several conditions encouraged the jitney explosion in late 1914 and early 1915. Henry Ford's strategy of selling his little cars at lower and lower prices was making them affordable for a vast new market. The majority of jitneys were Model T Fords, which could be purchased new for about $850. By 1914 dealers were beginning to have second-hand models of more expensive cars available for purchase.

In cities all over Canada and the U.S., including Winnipeg, men out of work because of the economic downturn got a jitney licence and took to the streets. In Winnipeg at least some of the operators were Ukrainian, Polish, or Jewish people who seized this opportunity to have their own business in a city where it was difficult for them to establish one. Some women also took the opportunity to create a job for themselves. On February 15, the *Telegram* carried a photo of Mrs. Leonard Sintzel, the first female jitney driver in the city. Taxi companies, which had only recently made the transition from horses to motor cars, also jumped in because they saw jitneys as an opportunity to expand their business.

The jitneys earned their owners a living, although a 1915 economic analysis of the jitney business—one of many at the time—predicted their demise because drivers would never earn enough to pay off loans, account for depreciation, keep up with repairs, and give themselves a decent wage. Some economic studies predicted that once the economy recovered jitney operators would go back to solid factory jobs that paid a good wage.[66] These sorts of predictions were music to the ears of the street railway companies, who often commissioned the studies and quoted them in their advertising.

In Winnipeg the cost of a jitney licence was twenty dollars, and there were soon many jitneys on the street, including several belonging to A.M. McLeod of the Exchange Taxi Company. McLeod ordered a fourteen-passenger bus built on a Packard chassis from the Lawrie Wagon Company factory at Portage Avenue and Wall Street. By March 1915 the bus was running all day on a regular schedule from the Maryland Bridge down to Portage and Main and back starting at 8 a.m.

McLeod took the lead in forming a Jitney Association in Winnipeg, which, like associations in other cities, offered services to the drivers and represented them in dealings with the city government. At the founding meeting of the association the operators discussed such things as whether the Street Railway was making plans to block their progress and whether, when the warm weather came, there would be many more jitneys on the street. A local representative of the Ford Motor Company spoke, telling the assembled jitney owners that he was with them all the way. The association developed a "Safety First" policy that required members to pass a test and become licensed as chauffeurs and carry a standardized red and white sign in their window indicating that they would abide by the safety rules.

Many people, including Mayor Waugh, were now taking jitneys to work, and Waugh declared himself to be enthusiastic about the new innovation. The *Telegram* reported that "the City Controllers and other council members look to these vehicles to solve, once and for all time, the problems that have necessitated unending anxiety and thought for years" as the city dealt with the streetcar company. But Wilford Phillips, the general manager of the Winnipeg Electric Railway, was soon complaining that jitneys "work the centre of the City to death without going out far into the suburbs the same as the cars of the street railway are obliged to do."

The Street Railway estimated in spring 1915 that it was losing $500 a day because of the jitneys. Over the next three years the company's losses reached $1 million, resulting in operating deficits and the collapse of its share price. City council, however, was not inclined to sympathize with the complaints about "unfair competition." Phillips soon proposed a reduced streetcar schedule to match the reduction in the number of passengers being carried. He also requested that the city take over snow clearing on the street railway lines in all areas outside the central city—work the company claimed it could no longer afford to keep up. After a heated debate, city council agreed. Things were to get much worse for the company before the jitney challenge was finally dealt with in 1918.

Provincial Politics / The Fall of Rodmond Roblin

The most significant events of the Manitoba government's legislative session that opened on February 9, 1915, did not take place in the legislature, but in the meetings of the Public Accounts Committee. In all legislatures in post-confederation Canada, such committees were often the scene of dramatic attempts by opposition parties to root out government mismanagement and corruption.[67] During the month of March 1915, the Liberal members of the committee, led by E.B. Hudson, had asked for plans and documents concerning all the government's public works projects. The Liberals were especially interested in some very expensive changes that had been made to the plans for the massive new legislature, changes that seemed to stand out as the best point of attack.

The Conservative chair of the committee, A.B. Taylor, kept the discussions narrowly focussed, and on March 30 the Conservative majority moved approval of a committee report that concluded "any changes in plans and method of constructing these buildings were absolutely required." Hudson moved a lengthy amendment, charging that the contracts had been violated and the province had been defrauded of close to $800,000 by Thomas Kelly, the contractor. One of his examples was $25,000 worth of concrete that had allegedly been paid for but never delivered.

Hudson's amendment stated that the committee had not been able to do its job because certain key witnesses and many documents had not been produced, and he ended by asking for a Royal Commission to inquire into the matter. In the House, the debate on this amendment dragged on through the evening of March 31 and into the morning of April 1. At 1:30 a.m. members went home to bed. It was assumed that Premier Roblin would use his majority to defeat the amendment the next day and then ask the lieutenant governor to prorogue the legislature, effectively ending the business of the session and the ability of the Liberals to attack his government until the next session in a year's time.

Events took an unexpected direction, however, when, the following morning, Roblin went to see Lieutenant Governor Douglas Cameron, a Liberal who had been appointed by Wilfrid Laurier. While their conversation was not recorded, we know that Cameron made proroguing the legislature contingent upon Roblin's requesting a Royal Commission. Cameron may have threatened to dismiss him as premier and to ask Norris to form a government.

Whether or not Cameron overstepped his authority is certainly de-
batable. There is no doubt that he was disturbed by what he had been
reading of the Public Accounts Committee sessions. He later wrote
that he had suspected "something might be wrong in connection with
the contract for the Capitol Building," since the previous September,
when Minister of Public Works Dr. Montague first announced that
the project was hugely over budget.

Cameron had taken some steps that were certainly controversial
before meeting Roblin. For example, on the evening of March 31
he had met with Opposition Leader Tobias Norris, who went to
Government House with a petition signed by twenty-two Liberal
members of the legislative assembly. The petition was essentially the
Liberal amendment to the Public Accounts Committee report with its
request for a Royal Commission. For the lieutenant governor to meet
privately with the leader of the Opposition was unusual and some
said it was improper.

Because he said he no longer had confidence in Roblin's government, including Attorney General James Howden, Cameron took the
unusual step of consulting with Chief Justice Howell on the legali-
ties of the situation before meeting with Roblin. What the judge, who
was also a Liberal appointee, may have told him was that a central
principle of the parliamentary system is that the governor general
and lieutenant governors must act "in accordance with the advice
of his ministers who must always have the support of the House of
Commons."[68] Roblin, with his majority, could claim to have the confidence of the legislature. It was, however, also possible that if the
representative of the Crown disagreed with the government on some
vital question he could either "recede from his own position or accept
the great responsibility of dismissing them."[69]

If the government was to be dismissed there had to be an alternative government available and willing to take responsibility. Chief
Justice Howell may have quoted the words of Alpheus Todd, the great
Canadian nineteenth-century authority on parliamentary government
who wrote that the lieutenant governor must not interfere in the affairs
of the elected government except in certain specific circumstances.
One of these is when he is being asked to sanction "any ministerial act
or proceeding which infringes upon an existing law."[70] Bourinot, an-

other important Canadian authority, wrote that, unlike the sovereign, the Crown's representative cannot be "freed of responsibility for his acts or be allowed to excuse a violation of the law on the plea of having followed the counsels of evil advisors."

Cameron may, therefore, have concluded that it was his responsibility, as the, in Todd's words, "especial guardian of the law," to use his power when he believed that the government had acted illegally. Todd states that the governor is entitled to stipulate "whatever conditions he may deem essential for the promotion of the public interests before he proceeds to exercise the power of dissolution."[71] And so, Cameron may have felt justified, when asked by Roblin to prorogue the legislature, in refusing unless there was a proper inquiry into the contracts for the construction of the new legislative building.

As a result, on the afternoon of April 1, Premier Roblin stood in the legislature to announce that a Royal Commission, chaired by Chief Justice Mathers, would be set up. It was to be the last time he spoke in the chamber where he had spent over twenty years as a member.

Testimony before another Royal Commission held at the time revealed details of the resignation of the premier. Toronto lawyer F.H. Phippen, acting for the Conservatives, proposed to E.B. Hudson that the premier, who felt that the charges made by Hudson were "at least substantially correct" saw that he must resign or be dismissed. Phippen said Roblin would resign if the Royal Commission were dismissed and the Liberals instead pursued a civil action against Kelly to recover any overpayments. Hudson agreed, but with the conditions that Roblin had to state in his resignation letter that the charges of corruption were correct.

The agreement fell apart because Roblin's letter did not contain the promised admission, although he did say he felt there had been irregularities and that he had lost the confidence of the public. He invited T.C. Norris to his house and told him that he would resign on May 12. It was noted at the time that "Sir Rodmond and Norris, although strong political opponents, were warm personal friends."[72] On May 12 the lieutenant governor called upon Norris to form a government that would serve until the provincial election on August 6.

By July, transcripts of the Royal Commission hearings were being published every day in the newspapers, and at the end of the

In 1915 the Winnipeg Street Railway's long dominance of Winnipeg streets was
about to be challenged by the jitney.

month the text of the final report was printed. Mathers concluded
that an election fund was created for the Conservatives by overpay-
ing Kelly a total of $822,963, an amount that he donated back to Dr.
Simpson, an official of the Conservative Party; that Kelly was shown
the estimate of competitor Thomas Lyall, so that he could underbid
his rival; that Roblin was the person who showed Kelly the bid; that
the Conservative ministers W.H. Montague, James Howden, and
George Coldwell did not know about these practices at first but became parties to them later; and that Dr. Simpson would dictate the
dollar amount or the percentage to be added to a contract for the election fund and that amount would be added by Victor Horwood, the
provincial architect. It was concluded that George Coldwell and later
Dr. Montague would instruct Horwood to do this and that Roblin
signed inflated contracts for some of the work in the building. Some
time between October 18, 1914, and January 1, 1915, Roblin and Dr.
Montague destroyed an order in council and all the paperwork on

one of the contracts with Kelly. The damning report destroyed the reputations of Roblin and his ministers.

On September 1, Roblin, Montague, Howden, and Coldwell were brought into court before Hugh John Macdonald, charged with defrauding the people of Manitoba. On September 16 the preliminary hearing of the case of the former ministers got under way, but their trial did not begin until the summer of 1916. It ended in December of that year with a hung jury. Another year passed before the charges against the former premier and his ministers were finally dropped because Roblin was declared to be extremely ill and in danger of suffering a heart attack if he had to go through the stresses of another trial. Dr. Montague had died from a stroke in November of 1915.

On Wednesday, July 14, 1915, the beleaguered Conservative Party held a convention in Winnipeg in preparation for the provincial election to take place on August 6. About 1000 delegates met to elect a new leader and agree on a platform. They chose Sir James Aikins, a leading Winnipeg lawyer who had been the Conservative member of Parliament for Brandon since 1911. Aikins was a prominent temperance advocate and untouched by any of the scandals that were filling the daily papers.

The convention busied itself with abandoning many of Rodmond Roblin's policies: they voted to resurrect the Macdonald prohibition law of 1900 and to support women's suffrage; they abandoned the Coldwell amendments and resolved to work for clean government and an end to corruption in public life; they stated their support for publicly owned abattoirs and for cooperatives. They even changed their name, calling themselves the Independent Liberal Conservative Party.

On August 4 Aikins spoke to a large audience assembled in the Walker Theatre. He emphasized the difference between the party of Roblin and the new Conservative Party. He told the audience that the platform was developed by the delegates to the convention, before he was elected as leader—it was a true "people's platform" and not the product of backroom deals. He contrasted Conservative promises with those of the Liberals: his party promised to enact the 1901 prohibition law of then Conservative Premier Hugh John Macdonald while the Liberals were promising only to hold a referendum. He said his party would "enforce the law" in dealing with the wrongdoers in the legislative building affair. He specifically mentioned Victor Horwood, the provincial architect, whose testimony had been so damning for the Conservative ministers, and who, Aikins said, had been accused of perjury. This comment was greeted with cheers from the crowd.

But none of these changes helped convince Manitobans to vote Conservative. When the election was held on August 6, only five Tories were re-elected in a province where they had formed majority governments for the previous fifteen years. With one exception, all the Conservatives members were from predominantly French ridings, probably because of Roblin's support for bilingual schools.

The Liberals swept into office with an unprecedented thirty-nine seats. But the popular vote suggested that their victory was not due to any great increase in support for their party. The Liberals' 64,363 votes represented only a small gain of 1565 on their 1914 tally of 62,798 votes. The Conservative vote on the other hand fell precipitously from 68,352 in 1914 to only 38,623 in 1915, a loss of 29,739 votes. The Liberals, then, appear to have won because large numbers of people who had previously voted for Premier Roblin simply stayed home rather than cast their ballots for Aikins and his reinvented party. The Conservative *Telegram* reported that Aikins was a gentleman about the defeat, which the paper said was no surprise. The Conservative Party would not form another government until the 1950s.

The contrast between the revelations of political chicanery at home and the heroic sacrifices being made by Canadian troops at the front sickened many Winnipeggers. S.R. Tarr, editor of the Winnipeg paper *Canadian Finance*, wrote that he hoped Norris would administer the province in a businesslike way and abandon partisanship. He condemned his counterparts at the *Free Press*, *Telegram*, and *Tribune* for slinging endless insults at each other. He said that "the public is sick of that."[73]

But the partisanship did continue as the Liberals pursued their enemies and made the usual political appointments at the beginning of their term in office. At the federal level real change was coming though, and at the end of 1917 the Conservatives and part of the Liberal Party would form a coalition government focussed on winning the war. In Manitoba, the early 1920s would see the election of a Progressive government that ushered in a thirty-year period during which traditional party conflicts were largely absent. It was as though, for a time at least, Canadians had grown tired of political feuding so characteristic of the early years of the war.

1916

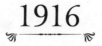

At 4 a.m. on November 21, 1915, a troop train pulled into the CPR station loaded with men who had been wounded in the bloody battles of the past year. As the train, which was hours late, entered the eastern side of the city the men crowded to the windows and said, "there she goes," "Good old Peg," "Thank God we're home again." In spite of the hour, Mayor Waugh, his wife Harriet, and hundreds of others were at the station to greet the returnees. Some were taken home by the Returned Soldiers Association, and men from out of town were put up in hotels until they could continue their journey.[1]

Harriet Waugh met the train with a small group of volunteers from the Returned Soldiers Association. She would meet many trains carrying returning soldiers during the rest of the war, ready to offer them tea and something to eat and help with finding a place to stay if they needed it. She made sure the returning soldiers were welcomed properly. Later, she would be working in the station on the day she learned that her own son, Alec, was dead, but would keep on pouring tea and answering questions until all the troops were taken care of.

Edward Drewery wrote to Waugh when he finished his term as mayor at the end of 1916, saying: "The kindly interest shown at all hours and upon all occasions by yourself and Mrs. Waugh in our returning soldiers will always stand out as one of the many splendid activities of your term. It was felt that the welcome home to our wounded boys could not be in better hands."[2]

Troops marching in Winnipeg, c. 1916.

Many of these men came home haunted by their experiences at the front. A Private Cary told the *Telegram* that a series of pictures was always in front of him: "I see a big fat fellow aiming. I get him and he jumps like a big jack rabbit performing in a pantomime. I laugh as I see him come down on his shoulder with his heels sticking up and wiggling funnily. But nevertheless I fire again and the wiggling stops." Cary also told of how his friend was shot through the head right next to him.

Stories like these brought the painful realities of war home to Winnipeggers, and in turn the numbers of volunteers were declining. Nevertheless, Winnipeg was crowded with new recruits in the winter of 1915–16 as men were brought into the city from Camp Hughes. The *Telegram* carried pictures of the 90th Battalion's uncomfortable accommodations in the drafty, thirty-year-old drill hall at the Fort Osborne Barracks. Bunks had been erected on the floor of the main arena. In one corner there was a canteen and an area with mess tables where the men ate. Also pictured was "Fatty" Brown, the "star cook" of the outfit. The 100th Battalion, the only soldiers in the city sleeping on spring beds rather than bunks or cots, was billeted in the Johns Mansville Company warehouse at 92 Arthur Street. The buildings of the old Agricultural College in Tuxedo and the display buildings at the exhibition grounds were once again pressed into service.

A great many social events with a military flavour were arranged over the winter months to keep the new recruits occupied and get them out of their uncomfortable barracks. The Horse Show Amphitheatre on Colony Street was the scene of the Grand Military Carnival sponsored by the Ladies' Auxiliary of the 61st Battalion. There was skating, waltzing to the Battalion Band, and prizes for the best men's and women's costumes. On February 8, at the Royal Alexandra Hotel, a banquet was hosted by Colonel Kirkcaldy and the officers of the 78th Battalion. Following dinner, guests enjoyed a dance in the ballroom with music by the band of the 100th Grenadiers. Early in March a vaudeville show was staged at the Walker Theatre to raise money for the 184th Battalion. Dinner parties were arranged for before each show, which included a performance by women from the battalion auxiliary. A one-act play called "For France" was on the bill. Also around this time, the 179th Camerons were having dances every two weeks at the Minto Armoury. Meanwhile, Colonel Kirkcaldy's speeches at recruiting meetings had made him something of a celebrity and he became a popular lecturer on the war, addressing groups such as the Lady's Aid at Grace Methodist Church.

Entertainments such as these for the most part benefitted the officers and non-commissioned officers, who also had their own messes as places for socializing. Most common soldiers sought their entertainment in the beer parlors and pool halls in the centre of the city. Along Main Street between William and the CPR station and hotel at Higgins Avenue there were many small hotels with beer parlors catering to the soldiers. There were at least ten such hotels within a five-block radius of the police station at Rupert and Martha.

It is not likely that the soldiers had much time or even opportunity to meet young women of Winnipeg who were their own age. Some of the soldiers undoubtedly frequented the brothels in Point Douglas. More respectable young women who were in the city working at wartime jobs may not have had much opportunity to fraternize. Dr. Ellen Douglass, speaking at a Council of Women meeting on February 12, 1916, where the morals of the city's young women were being criticized, suggested it was not young men that they had to fear:

> We've talked too long and too much about girls and girls' behavior.
> It is about time we looked after the men. I do not wish to insinuate
> that the majority or even a large percentage of the businessmen of
> this city are anything but the most desirable of citizens, but I have
> discovered in the practice of my profession that some offices are
> not fit for girls to be working in, especially girls away from home
> and out for themselves for the first time. These human sharks of
> men to whom I have reference are not the young men of our city.
> They are older men and in many instances are married. If we had
> some central information bureau to which girls would apply to
> discover what offices to avoid and what homes many tragedies
> might be avoided. And also with such authentic information, we
> could boycott the men involved.[3]

The majority of young troops quartered in the city had little to do
in their off hours but visit the hotels and drink, a situation that at times
resulted in major outbreaks of violence. The Main Street hotel bars had
given Winnipeg a bad name ever since the 1870s and, although they
had recently been cleaned up and brought under stricter control with
tougher licensing regulations, they were still rowdy places where men
often drank themselves into a stupor. The liquor license commissioner
had received complaints about at least one of these establishments,
the Selkirk Hotel. Soldiers were getting drunk there and then passing
out in the snow and freezing. One man lost both hands to frostbite.
Women complained of being accosted by drunks in the street.

There was a strong and widespread feeling that soldiers should
not be drinking at all. In October 1915, the captain in charge of a
company of 500 soldiers out on a route march phoned E.L. Drewery
at his Redwood Brewery to ask if "that offer" was still good. Drewery
asked him "what offer?" and the captain replied, "Why, to give my
men a drink." Drewery agreed and treated all 500 men to a cold
beer. The uproar over this simple incident was immense. Temperance
campaigners complained to General Ruttan, commanding officer of
the military district. The Reverend W.J. Hindley lamented that boys
from "good Christian homes" were being corrupted with beer. Ruttan
answered that the men had broken no rule of discipline but allowed
that the captain had probably been unwise.

But the days of the Main Street bars were numbered, and the temperance movement would soon achieve its longed-for goal. On March 13 Manitobans registered their approval, with a 23,000-vote majority, of the new Liberal government's prohibition legislation. The new Act, which would, among other things, close down all bars, was to become law on June 1, 1916.

For those who saw the war as a sort of crusade of good against evil, banishing liquor from the lives of Canadian troops was a great victory. At the front most soldiers saw the rum ration as an essential part of their day, and even that great temperance man Charles Gordon acknowledged its value once he had served as a front-line chaplain. Prohibition was just one area where the rather pious social reformers showed their naïveté about the brutal realities of the war in Europe and the disruption it was causing at home.

"Lost their heads entirely"...

That spring, the restlessness after a long winter was resulting in violent incidents among the troops. On March 22, there had been a brawl at 49 Austin Street, a boarding house belonging to a Mr. Chorney and located just south of the CPR station on Higgins. This house had a restaurant on the main floor where working men could come for their meals and rooms for rent upstairs. A group of men from the 144th Battalion, led by Sergeant Walker, entered the house searching for a Private Kortan, who had been absent without leave for about a week and was reported to be staying in the house.

Walker and his men were interrupted in their search by military police from the provost marshal's office, located a short distance away in the Immigration Hall on Higgins Avenue. When it was established that the search had not been officially ordered, Walker was arrested and one of his men was struck in the head with a nightstick by a military policeman. City police constables were also present because they had been alerted by phone of the disturbance, but they did not intervene except to tell a crowd of soldiers gathered in the street to leave.

Later the same evening a larger group of soldiers came to the boarding house and stormed in. Witnesses said that they had marched down

Main Street four abreast. These men appear to have been looking for someone who had had a fight with a soldier at the nearby Maple Leaf Hotel. There were estimated to be 300 to 400 men in and around the boarding house. Some threw bottles and ice chunks that broke the windows on the main floor. Mr. Chorney, an Austrian national and a registered enemy alien, claimed that the soldiers stole his cash box with twenty-seven dollars. He claimed not to know why they had been there. As a "foreigner" his boarding house was no doubt considered to be fair game by many of the soldiers.

These events suggest that many of the troops in the city were not really under the control of military discipline. New recruits, often led by inexperienced officers, were quick to take the law into their own hands. The city police, and no doubt many Winnipeggers, must have been anxious about their ability to control these thousands of young men. They were used to policing a city that still had some of the flavour of a frontier community where men outnumbered women and there were always plenty of young unattached males crowding into the beer parlors on payday. But the troops greatly increased the numbers who might potentially get into fights and cause a disturbance.

On Saturday, April 1, conditions were ripe for trouble. The bars were still open and doing roaring business selling drinks to soldiers who had just received their pay. There were men from all the battalions in Winnipeg along with about 500 more from the 108th Battalion stationed in Selkirk. They came into town on the electric railway, the bars in Selkirk being closed that day. When constables John McBeth, Leonard Morrison, and James McSkimming of the city police came down Main Street around 6:30 p.m., they saw a crowd of soldiers and civilians in front of the Imperial Hotel on the northeast corner of Main and Alexander. When they went to investigate they found a man lying down in the hotel doorway, very drunk. They "caught hold" of him, intending to take him to the police station a block away on Rupert Avenue.

The crowd objected, and one man in particular was quite agitated, shouting, "Let go, you cock-sucking bastards" and "come on boys, we won't let these cock-sucking bastards take him." He is also reported to have said that the police had beaten up one soldier the day before and they would not beat up this one. Constable Morrison later tes-

tified, "we tried to arrest this man making the disturbance but the
crowd forced us so much that we could not arrest him at all—they took
him away."

Two military policemen, privates Letewin and Steadman of the
144th Battalion, were also outside the Imperial Hotel and tried to take
control of the prisoners, shouting to the city police that they would
take care of the matter. But the crowd was too dense and they too
were pushed aside.

McBeth struggled to a nearby police call box and phoned for a patrol wagon. The wagon came quickly but had trouble pulling up to the
curb because of the crowd. It finally was able to pick up the drunken
soldier and take him back to the police station. Constable McBeth
said that by the time he came out of the station after delivering his
prisoner, Rupert Avenue was full of soldiers and civilians, packed in
a crowd that extended back across Main Street. At its largest, the
crowd was estimated to number close to 3000 and completely blocked
Main Street so that only the streetcars were making their way through.

Captain Goddard, the assistant provost marshal for the Winnipeg
Garrison, arrived on the scene about 7:30 p.m. from his headquarters
in the Immigration Hall by the CPR station. But, as Sergeant James
Lucas of the 78th Battalion, an experienced military policeman and
ten-year veteran of the London Metropolitan Police, testified, "we
could not handle the crowd, we did not have sufficient men." General
Ruttan, the officer commanding the 10th Military District, arrived
but could not make himself heard. Later in the evening a company of
men from the 144th Battalion arrived, and Lucas said "that is when
we got them in shape." The crowd, then, was in control of the street
for several hours.

One of the conclusions of the resulting inquiry was that the riot was
the result of confusion in the minds of most soldiers over the jurisdiction of the military as opposed to the city police. Many seemed to
think that city constables had no jurisdiction over the troops at all.
Lucas called this "the old grievance," but in fact the military police
worked with the city police and often turned prisoners over to them
to be kept in the cells on the second floor of the police station.

On the night of the riot, however, there was little evidence of cooperation between the two forces. When two military policemen tried

to arrest a soldier knocked down by a city policeman in front of the McLaren Hotel, the city constable shouted, "I want this man, keep away.... Keep your hands off him or I will hit you too."

At about 7:30 in the evening the police charged into the crowd in front of the station and used their batons to drive the crowd back toward Main Street. At least one military policeman was arrested, and another testified that "they [city police] used their batons pretty freely—I got hit wearing the badge (the military police armband), the badge was no good at all." Sergeant Mills of the 144th said that "[city police] apparently lost their heads entirely; I was dodging batons for about 3 minutes myself." The veteran Sergeant Lucas described the police knocking people down indiscriminately, including a man with one leg who may have been a returned solder. Private Letewin said that when the disabled man was struck, "the people saw it and were raving."

Some time later—different times were given by different witnesses— the police charged the crowd again. Many of the soldiers were now armed with bricks and chunks of ice and wood they had picked up by the livery stables and in the empty lots that surrounded the police station. This charge was much more violent because the crowd was angry and "wanted to put it over on the police."

Finally, late in the evening, companies of infantry and the Lord Strathcona's Horse were able to gain control of the streets. A company of the 90th Battalion stood in front of city hall and another from the 144th stood in front of the police station. Many of the rioters fell in when ordered to by their officers and marched back to their barracks. Troops patrolled the streets to make sure there was no more trouble. There is no evidence that the troops were ordered to use force, in contrast to other times when they were called out, during the streetcar strike of 1906 and the General Strike in 1919. Clearly it would have been disastrous for morale if the recruits, who had volunteered of their own free will to serve, were manhandled by their comrades.

A number of soldiers had been arrested and those whose units had no cells of their own were put into the cells in the police station. The rest were taken back to their quarters around the city. There were several men from the 108th Battalion from Selkirk, as well as those from Winnipeg units, in the police cells on Rupert. Some of these men

Richard Waugh was mayor of Winnipeg in 1915 and 1916. He and his wife Harriet participated in various volunteer organizations, his sons all served in the forces, and his daughter was an army nurse. He is pictured here with members of St. Johns Ambulance.

testified that they were beaten by the police. Private John Hill said that "a policeman nearly choked me going up in the elevator and he hit me with his baton after he got me into the cell." Clifford Reynolds was badly beaten, and one of his officers, Major Willets, said that Reynolds was covered with blood when he arrived back at the barracks.

On Sunday morning a crowd of soldiers and civilians again gathered on Rupert in front of the police station and began shouting for the release of the men in the cells. The crowd began throwing pieces of ice, bricks, and rocks, and soon every window in the station was broken. The city later presented a bill for a little over $600 for the broken glass, but the Department of Militia and Defence declined to pay.

A company of the 90th Battalion arrived, marching with fixed bayonets, to remove the soldiers being held in the cells. When the men came out of the station the crowd broke through the line of troops and began pulling them away. By the time the soldiers gained control of the situation many of the prisoners had disappeared into the crowd. Some of these men later testified that they did not understand what was happening when they were "rescued."

W.A. Campbell was called as a witness because he had been outside the police station on Sunday morning. A real estate broker with an office in the Nanton Building, he was at the Carlton Club, of which he was a member, when word came that there was another disturbance at the station. He and a friend drove to the scene, taking a roundabout route to avoid the crowds. They stopped at the corner of Louise and Rupert, and, like a lot of other people, stood looking at the broken windows. Soldiers and civilians, men, women, and children milled around to see the sights. Suddenly, said Campbell, the garage door, which opened onto Rupert, was raised and a squad of police charged out.

Campbell said "they began hitting right and left...they struck one soldier who went down on his hands and knees and one of the policemen got his baton up and struck him again." His companion tried to stop the beating, but Campbell felt they were in danger and shouted, "we better get out of this or we won't be worth five cents." As they were getting back into the car they saw a soldier opening a clasp knife. Campbell saved the man from real trouble by calling to him: "I said 'Come over here, I want to talk to you.' He answered 'I can stand some things, but I can't stand to see a woman knocked about.' I said 'come up town,'" and the man rode as far as Portage Avenue on Campbell's running board. Campbell described the police as being in a "brainstorm of hysteria." Other witnesses to the riot, including two men who operated businesses on Main Street, were critical of the police and their response to the riot. Finally the military convinced the police to withdraw from the street, and they began patrolling with infantry and cavalry pickets. Troops would remain in the streets for several days.

All the troops in the city were confined to barracks and leaves were cancelled. Bars were off limits for some time after the riot. Four soldiers, one with a fractured skull, and one civilian were taken to

the General Hospital for treatment. Over the next two weeks rioters, civilian and military, were brought before Magistrate Hugh John
Macdonald in the Police Court located in the Rupert Avenue Station.
Macdonald told men claiming to have been beaten that they could
make a formal complaint to the Police Commission. He gave most of
the men five- and ten-dollar fines for creating a disturbance—not a
trivial amount for privates earning very little. Macdonald declined to
hear the cases of men already tried by the military.

The officers of the Military Court of Enquiry were Colonel A.L.
Bonnycastle, in civilian life a police magistrate, Major D.A. Ross, a
Winnipeg engineer, and Captain G.S. Thornton. These conservative
gentlemen, at least two of them members of the Winnipeg establishment, tended to downplay the riot. Their findings were that there was
no real conflict between the military and civil police; that the civilians
at the scene, "curious or otherwise," added to the "difficulties of the
situation"; that a few police were "over zealous" in their efforts; and
that the army furnished pickets when asked and "materially assisted
in restoring order." The stories of police violence, the length of time
it took the military to restore order, the fact that hundreds of troops
had been rampaging in the streets while their officers seemed pow-
erless to stop them, was not commented upon in the findings of the
court. The Winnipeg establishment, represented by the men in charge
of the inquiry, was certainly not interested in having this scandalous
incident talked about across the country, and especially in cities like
Toronto and Montreal, still seen as Winnipeg's rivals. The presence of
so many troops in the city made matters more volatile than in normal
times. Large numbers of young men with little to do but drink created
perfect conditions for a riot.

There can be little doubt that the experience of seeing the centre of
the city in the hands of an unruly mob had a profound effect on the
Winnipeg middle class. The riot of 1916 probably helped shape their
responses to later disturbances like the 1918 strikes and the General
Strike of 1919. On these occasions, citizen groups led by organizations
like the Board of Trade would take an active part in trying to control
the city. In 1919 volunteer police—the city police were on strike—and
the Royal Northwest Mounted Police used force and even fired their
weapons, killing one man, to clear the streets of demonstrators.

News of the April riot was censored until mid-week and the story was not given much prominence in the Canadian press outside Winnipeg. It was picked up by the Associated Press and stories ran in many papers in the U.S. Most of these followed the Associated Press story, which stated that a "war whoop" from an Indian soldier trying to prevent the arrest of a comrade started the trouble. There is no mention of an Aboriginal soldier in any of the Canadian sources.

Things quickly returned to normal in the city, at least on the surface. Various attempts were made to reassure the local population that the soldiers in their midst were just normal, spirited boys. The 203rd Battalion put on a concert at the King's Theatre in St. James; 78th Battalion paraded downtown and it was announced that their band would give a concert on the following Sunday at the Pantages Theatre. By the end of the week the *Free Press* reported that all seemed quiet in the city. Companies of troops continued to patrol the streets and to stand guard at the police station.

"It was simply Hell"...

The effects of the riot were as nothing compared with the devastating results of facing the Germans in battle. Winnipeg men, like all the others serving in the Canadian Expeditionary Force, experienced danger, horror, boredom, the loss of friends, and incredible emotional and physical stress during the time from April 1915 until November 1918. The fighting and day-to-day life in the trenches took their toll in dead and wounded. The men were tested in impossibly difficult situations. If we are to understand the true effect of the war on the city and the people who greeted these men when they returned home, we must look at some of the experiences they went through.

The first action in which the 27th City of Winnipeg Battalion fought, at about the same time as the riot in Winnipeg, was the Battle of the St. Eloi Craters. St. Eloi is a small village south of Ypres. It was here that the British exploded six mines under the German front line on March 27, 1916. The explosions were enormous and remnants of the huge craters, which changed the landscape radically, survive today. British troops moved forward and over the course of the next week, captured some but not all of the cratered area. Then, on April 4, the exhausted British were replaced by the men of the Second Canadian Division.

The 27th Battalion took over a section of the line between the Germans and the craters. It was the first time the battalion had been on the front line. In the first few hours, the trenches the 27th Battalion occupied were leveled and the battalion lost 230 men in the German bombardment. Poor communication between the forward line and headquarters, and overcast weather, which prevented air reconnaissance, combined to hamper the Canadian efforts. The craters completely changed the landscape, making the existing maps useless and leading to costly mistakes about the actual location of the troops. After two brutal weeks the Germans were successful in gaining possession of the craters.

The fiasco led General Alderson, the British commander-in-chief of the Canadian Corps, to criticize General Turner, in command of the division, and General Ketchen, in command of the 6th Brigade, whose battalions, including the 27th, had been mired in the fighting. Alderson and some others argued that the two Canadian generals should be removed from their commands, but both men were politically connected: Ketchen would be elected as a Conservative MLA in South Winnipeg after the war, and Turner, who won a Victoria Cross in South Africa, was one of Sam Hughes's ideal militia colonels—the sort of successful businessman who Hughes believed would transfer his business talents to the battlefield. Others realized that firing them might lead to a deepening of the rift between the Canadians and British. And so, in the end, it was Alderson who was moved from his post. He went to England to be inspector general of Canadian troops, and General Julian Byng took command of the Canadians.

Colonel Snider of the 27th Battalion also lost his command and was given a training post in England. A sympathetic modern historian has said of Snider's performance: He was relieved of his post "because of 'nervous exhaustion.' Snider's medical file noted that he had 'no sleep for 6 days and nights and naturally felt the loss of his men personally. On retiring to billets felt naturally depressed and fatigued, but it was only when he saw his bed that he went all to pieces and broke down and cried.' There is genuine poignancy in that medical case history, and Snider is owed our understanding. He continued to serve

Winnipeg police officers such as these men used their billy clubs to clear the streets during the spring 1916 riot.

in Britain, passing on the lessons he had learned to reinforcements."[4] Snider was a victim of the chaos of the fighting on the Western Front, where even an experienced officer's skills could turn out to be irrelevant. Everyone was trying to learn the rules of this new kind of fighting as quickly as possible and each battle was studied for lessons it could teach. Louis Lipsett, who had been stationed in Winnipeg with the Strathcona's Horse at the war's outbreak, kept a notebook in which he recorded his experiences and what changes he would make as a result of them. Notes like his were used to train officers and develop new tactics.

That said, a comment about learning from mistakes written by Colonel Dubuc, the commander of the 22nd Battalion during the Battle of the Somme, reminds us of the reality of the trenches: "It is no easy matter to express opinions as to the lessons to be derived from the above operations, as the great majority of the actors were either killed or wounded. Only four of the original eleven officers remained with the unit. The difficulties of communications were also highlighted: 'Once the attack is launched the Battalion Commander is practically impotent ... the trouble seems to be that casualties amongst officers are usually so large proportionately that nobody is left to send this information."[5]

In June the Germans detonated a mine under part of the Canadian trenches near Mount Sorrel, a short distance from St. Eloi. The Princess Patricias lost an entire company when the mine went up. Dick Richardson, a recent graduate of the Manitoba Agricultural College, was one of the few survivors. Recovering later in hospital in Leicester, he wrote to a former classmate in Canada:

> Perhaps you have heard something about the time we have been having. I hope I never have to go through it again. It was simply hell!... Our regiment was almost obliterated. About 40 of us came back out of the two companies that held the front line. Number 1 Company on our right were all either killed or taken prisoner, not a single man came back. Number 2, which is the company I was in, were able to hold them off all day and all night until their artillery leveled all our trenches and left us with only 40 men, many of them wounded. They got through the trenches on our right and got behind us opening up machine guns from both sides so that we were forced to retire on our left over 400 yards of broken country, the whole of it a mass of flame from bursting shells and swept by machine guns. I had to crawl most of the way as a piece of shrapnel early in the day had put me out of commission opening up my right side to the depth of my ribs and about 5 inches long

> and two inches wide.... it is such a relief to get away from bursting
> shells that even as helpless as I am this is like heaven.

Richardson described how a friend he calls Steve helped bandage him up. They found a fellow student from Manitoba Agricultural College, so badly wounded that they did not recognize him at first. They bandaged his wounds and moved him to as comfortable a position as possible. They had to leave him, and Richardson concluded he must have died. He had to walk almost all the three miles back to Ypres. He lost track of his friend Steve, who was shot through both arms. In his other letters Dick Richardson seems a decent, optimistic, and intelligent young man, a new graduate who in normal times would have just been starting out on his life. The profound effect of the nightmarish scenes he describes can only be guessed at. If he had lived—he was killed at Vimy Ridge—there can be no doubt that he would have been haunted by memories of his lost friends.

The 43rd Battalion, Cameron Highlanders, experienced their first fighting at Mount Sorrel. They had finally embarked for France in February, ending a period during which the 43rd had been used as reinforcements. Now they would fight as a battalion in France and "the desire of all Camerons was at last accomplished."[6] From then until armistice the 16th Battalion with its Camerons company and the 43rd would serve in France, and a total of 3891 men would be sent by the Camerons organization at home as replacements to fight with these units.

The Camerons were anxious to prove themselves. One night Colonel Griesbach of the 49th Battalion met a group of Camerons led by a sergeant who wanted to know "Where the hell is the fechtin line": "With difficulty he persuaded these Highlanders, who wanted the enemy to know the Camerons of Winnipeg were coming, that there was no fechtin to be done at the moment."[7]

At Mount Sorrel the 43rd played a role in retaking captured ground known as Maple Copse. A description survives of a meeting between the 43rd commander, Colonel R.M. Thomson, and General A.C. Macdonnell before this action. The two men had known each other in Winnipeg, when Macdonnell was commanding the Lord Strathcona's Horse. He was now in command of the Third Division.

He later recalled the following scene: "Lieutenant Colonel Thomson came into my cubicle in the ramparts and reported. I said, 'You thoroughly understand your orders.' He replied 'Yes General.' 'Well,' I answered, 'Old friend, you'll just go in and clear Maple Copse completely with the bayonet to the old highland cry, "We'll hae nane but Hielan Bonnets here," and keep bearing to your left until you join hands with the 42nd Highlanders, and when you do make sure of the touch.' He grasped my hand and left in high spirits, repeating the slogan as he went."[8] They attacked at midnight and by dawn they were in control of the copse.

This scene illustrates not only Macdonnell's skill as a commanding officer and warmth as a friend but also the power of Scots ethnicity to motivate fighting men. Both men were Canadian born but when it came to facing difficult fighting they drew on their Scots heritage for courage.

Thomson was probably one of the oldest colonels in the Canadian Corps. He was born in Ontario and was involved in militia work all his life in Winnipeg. He fought in the Riel Rebellion in Saskatchewan and was one of the founders of the 79th Cameron Highlanders and its first colonel. He had even paid for a company of Camerons to go to London for George V's coronation. A bachelor most of his life, he had married Charles Gordon's widowed sister-in-law in 1913. In May 1916 Thomson offered his large house in the Winnipeg neighbourhood of Wildwood Park for use as a convalescent home for soldiers. It would later become St. John's Ravenscourt School.

The 27th was also engaged in this battle and supported the First Division as it assaulted and retook Mount Sorrel on June 13 and 14. General Julian Byng brought his particular style of leadership to the fighting at Mount Sorrel, and under his leadership the Canadian attack was carefully planned, with the staff, the artillery, and the infantry all working together as an integrated force. A heavy barrage preceded the advance of the troops early on June 13. Thick smoke was spread and the Canadians followed the barrage closely, catching the Germans still in their dugouts.

The next day the inevitable German counterattack was expected and planned for, and the Canadian artillery broke up two German advances. In many ways their success at Mount Sorrel indicated that the Canadian Corps' costly learning phase was now over. Under Byng's and then Sir Arthur Currie's leadership they were putting into practice the lessons they had learned in the bloody fighting of 1915 and the first months of 1916.

Byng tried to control political meddling. When a new divisional commander was needed to replace General Mercer, killed at Mount Sorrel, Sam Hughes wanted his son, General Garnet Hughes, to be appointed. Byng instead gave the job to General Louis Lipsett, a proven officer. Privately he said that the Canadian Corps was "too good to be led by politicians and dollar magnates."[9]

Of course, in many of the chaotic battles of the war, no amount of planning could bring order out of the chaos. The Battle of the Somme, a diversion intended to take pressure off the French Army at Verdun, raged for close to six months and cost more Canadian lives than any other engagement of the war as thousands died in often futile attempts to capture a small piece of muddy ground.

On July 1, 1916, the first day of the Battle of the Somme, Sir Douglas Haig's army went over the top. On that day, 20,000 British soldiers died and 40,000 were wounded, the heaviest losses in the history of the British Army. The Newfoundland Regiment, which had already suffered through months on the Gallipoli front, lost 600 men on July 1 and their objective was not taken. It was said that not one home in Newfoundland was left untouched by the slaughter.

Winnipeg battalions like the 8th, the 16th, the 44th, and the 27th were not engaged at the beginning of the battle, but went into action in September. The Allies pushed slowly eastward, paying a terrible price for each yard of ground. Some of the worst fighting for the Canadians took place before a section of the German line nicknamed Regina Trench.

From September 21 to October 21, 441 Winnipeg men were killed at the Somme. The Camerons had the heaviest losses, seventy-two men including their colonel. By November, when the Regina Trench was finally captured by Canadian troops, Canada had suffered 25,000 casualties in the battle of the Somme, 16,000 of them trying to take the Regina Trench. The description of the feelings of the men of the 44th Battalion was likely typical of the entire Canadian Army: as Ed

Russenholt writes, "Lloyd George pictured the Somme as the 'mouth of hell'—and for the 44th this has been true."[10]

In the novel *Why Stay We Here?* one of George Godwin's characters, a survivor of the Somme, suffers from an obsession with the battle: "And now he talked about the Somme. His mind always came back to that battle. He talked about the war impersonally; but about the Somme he spoke in a proprietorial way. There was even affection in his voice. The battle, in memory, had become dear to him. He went over, again and again, every phase of it as he had lived and suffered it. It was the morbid affection of the leper for his sores, of the bereaved for the afflicting sorrow.... He was dyed in the battle. Its living memory coloured his thoughts by day, his dreams by night."[11]

All the Winnipeg units were eventually involved in fighting at the Somme. On October 8, the 16th and 43rd Battalions were both involved in another unsuccessful attempt to take the Regina Trench. Charles Gordon, the 43rd Battalion chaplain, had wanted to go up to the front line with the men, at least one-third of whom were members of his church, St. Stephen's, in Winnipeg. Lieutenant Colonel Thomson, commander of the 43rd and one of Gordon's elders in St. Stephen's, prevented his going, and he was assigned to the battalion's dressing station instead.

The Camerons attacked but found that the German wire, reported broken, was actually intact. Caught in the wire they suffered 500 casualties, including their colonel. Thompson was killed when, being transported back to a dressing station to have a wound looked at, his ambulance was struck by a shell and he was killed.

The next day Gordon conducted a burial service for the colonel in the presence of the remnant of the battalion. He described the scene in his memoirs: "the 43rd officers stood round the open grave in silence for a few moments. Then each dropped a sprig of evergreen onto the coffin and turned away.... the little company formed up, the big drum struck a startlingly heavy beat, the pipes shrilled into the silent air the regimental march 'Pibroch o' Doniul Dubh' and with heads up, chests out and kilts swaying that gallant remnant swung away ... to meet whatever it was their duty to meet and do whatever it was their duty to do."[12] Pounded by a seemingly endless number of cruel blows, men stopped feeling and relied on their sense of duty to keep them going.

A little over two weeks later, on October 25, the 44th Battalion also attacked the Regina Trench at 7:00 a.m. There was no covering barrage because the runners sent back to order it were both killed. Advancing on German troops that had not been shelled, the 44th were shot to pieces, losing 200 dead and wounded. Jimmy Robinson remembered that "we had not advanced more than fifty yards when machine guns began sweeping our lines. The bullets whistled through the air and our men were mowed down like wheat before a binder. One bullet crashed through my steel helmet an inch above my head; two hit my water bottle and one glanced off my rifle. Only a miracle left me unscathed."[13] Pinned down all day, some crawled back to their starting line and they managed to repulse a counterattack by the Germans. Robinson lay all day in a shell hole and after dark he and his companion Axel Green, before the war a clerk with the Empire Elevator Company, crawled back to their front line trench which was "full of dead and wounded. Misery, death and agony mingled in a turmoil that even in hell I am sure one could find no equal.... Dozens of our men died in that trench. We first moved those we thought had a chance to live and whose wounds were located so that carrying them out would not prove fatal." He went out and rescued Lieutenant Brown, who had lain all day in no man's land with a smashed ankle. They carried him a mile and a half in ten hours through mud up to their waists.

After the fighting, Jimmy Robinson was overcome with a "sense of loneliness and desolation" as he realized that many of his close friends were dead and "I would never see them again." He continued, "Later when I left the trenches on the way to Albert, accompanied by Tommy Gordon, both of us gave vent to our trials and tribulations in no uncertain words. Tommy remarked that he had 'a bellyful of this damned war' and did not care if he lived or died. I backed him up and added a few consoling outbursts of my own. We were both ready to go West and felt the good Lord would have performed a noble deed if we had been left in the Valley of Death with our comrades."

The horror of the Somme had a similar effect upon many of the men who survived and some did "go west" or desert. Two British soldiers who left the front and tried to escape on a Swedish ship were arrested and executed for desertion. At their court martial, Albert Ingham and Alfred Longshaw both said things very similar to Jimmy Robinson

Canadian troops during the Battle of the Somme, 1916. People at home seldom grasped the true horror of conditions on the Western Front.

and his chum. They gave as their reason for deserting that "practically all my comrades were gone" and "I was worrying at the time about the loss of my chums."[14] Private Longshaw also said, "my service on the Somme had reacted on my state of mind, which had become morbid and irrational."

At least two men from Winnipeg were executed for desertion. Stephen McDermott Fowles enlisted in February 1916 in the 107th Battalion. From his attestation papers we might conclude that the nineteen-year-old was a little unsure about things. He first said that he was married, but that was crossed out and he said he was not. He first said he had no occupation and then wrote in "farmer." Fowles went to England in the fall of 1916 with the 107th, but he was soon sent to France with reinforcements for the 44th Battalion. Arriving in France in the fall of 1916, he would have been with the 44th during the battle of the Somme. He was charged with desertion and on February

12, 1917, he was tried in front of a field general court martial and sentenced to death. This sentence could be overturned higher up the command structure and, as often happened, his punishment was commuted to ten years penal servitude. This sentence was then suspended and he was sent back to the 44th, by now in the lines before Vimy Ridge, preparing for the battle soon to be fought there.

Later in the year he deserted again, while the battalion was fighting at Passchendaele. He was once more sentenced to death, on December 29, 1917, and once again his sentence was changed to ten years penal servitude, and then to two years in prison. But the army needed men to face the massive German offensives of the spring of 1918, and Fowles was taken back once more to the 44th Battalion at the end of April 1918. Ordered to go and pick up a gas mask before moving up into the trenches, Fowles deserted a third time, only to turn himself in a few days later. He was tried again, and this time he was shot, on June 19. His superiors would, by this time, have seen little alternative to going through with the execution. As Desmond Morton writes, military law sought to maintain discipline more than "to do absolute justice to the individual."[15] Men were, therefore, often executed in order to serve as examples to their comrades.

This seems to have been the case with Dimitro Sinizski, who was executed for cowardice in 1917, the only man sentenced to death and executed in General Louis Lipsett's 3rd Division. Born in Kiev in 1895, he immigrated to Canada and settled in Winnipeg. In December 1915 he enlisted in the 144th Battalion. In September 1916 his unit left for England where it was broken up and sent to France to reinforce other battalions. Sinizki fought at Vimy Ridge and then in the nearby Avignon area. He was moving up with his comrades to raid the German trenches: "On the night of 24/25 August, 1917, he fell out and refused to continue. When ordered to proceed up the line he again refused, saying he would rather be shot. He refused to put on his equipment. Sinizki did the same thing the next night, and had to be marched up to the line under escort. On the way up, he sat down and refused to move, again saying that he would rather be shot than go back to the trenches. He was finally arrested and charged with: 'When on active service—misbehaving before the enemy in such a manner as to show cowardice.'"[16]

Sinizki had never been in trouble before and had no previous charges. He seems to have been a good soldier, but, contrary to usual practice, his sentence was not commuted. He was condemned to death at his court martial and shot soon after. It has been suggested that he was shot to provide an example to other "Russians" in the Canadian Army because the unsettled situation in Russia had led Russian troops in the French Army to mutiny. The Canadians had transferred Russian-born troops out of the front line areas for fear they would do the same. Lipsett may have decided that he needed to make an example of Sinizki to prevent more trouble among the Russian troops.[17]

In all, twenty-five Canadians died in front of firing squads during the war, twenty-three for desertion, two for murder, and one for cowardice. They were tried and sentenced under the *Army Act*, the British law governing all British and Empire forces. Because of a famous case during the South African War, the Australians refused to allow their troops to be sentenced to death in this manner and executions could only be carried out if approved by the Australian Cabinet. The Canadian government had no such hesitation.

~~Deserters~~ The Norris Government

In Manitoba, the political war over the legislative building scandal continued to unfold. After the election of the Liberal government in August 1915 and the release of the Mathers Royal Commission report, the Norris administration set out to extradite Thomas Kelly from the United States and recoup some of the money fraudulently paid to the contractor. In early September, the search for evidence began when police officers, accompanied by government lawyers R.W. Craig, J.B. Coyne, and H.J. Symington, raided Thomas Kelly's office and his house on the corner of Assiniboine Avenue and Carlton Street. Only Kelly's daughter and his Chinese cook were at home and they were made to sit on chairs in the kitchen and not move during the search. Kelly's office in the Lindsay Building was also searched. The police and lawyers brought along an expert who opened the safe in the office with the help of a drill and a sledgehammer. They also searched the home of R.L. Worthington, Kelly's manager and estimator. In all, they carried off several hundred pounds of papers and documents from the three locations. A few days later J.B. Coyne and some police officers arrived at the offices of Kelly's lawyer Edward Anderson but they were "sent packing." Attorney General Hudson stated that he would let the matter drop.

A.J. Andrews, a Conservative and one of the lawyers for the former ministers, successfully applied to Magistrate Macdonald for access to the papers and books seized by the prosecution from Kelly's house and office. It is an indication of the high level of tension surrounding the case that R.A. Bonnar, one of the lawyers representing the government, was so angry at this decision that he told Andrews he would "slap his face and break every bone in his body." The political backgrounds of the lawyers involved made these raids seem like an extension of the bitter partisan politics of the past. J.B. Coyne and H.J. Symington were both Liberals and R.W. Craig would later be a minister in Bracken's Progressive Party administration.

After many delays the suit against Thomas Kelly went ahead and he was sentenced to two and a half years in Stony Mountain Penitentiary. The amount of money to be repaid was fixed by adjudicators at $1,207,351 with interest of $181,000. In the end, only about $30,000 of this money was ever recovered from Kelly, who moved to the United States after his release from prison in August 1917.

On January 6, 1916, the first session of the fifteenth legislature began with the new government's first throne speech with details of legislation in all the key policy areas in the party's platform. In what was probably one of the most extensive and ambitious agendas in Manitoba history, the government proposed legislation on prohibition, votes for women, and sweeping changes to the education system.

In August 1915, Premier Norris had asked the Social Service Council to draft a new act that "would encompass the total prohibition of the manufacture and sale of intoxicating liquors."[18] The council struck a committee, which soon decided to recommend that the government simply reintroduce the 1900 *Prohibition Act* passed by the Macdonald Conservative government. When the session began in January Norris introduced the Bill that banned the sale of liquor except by druggists and then only with a doctor's prescription. Liquor would also be legal for religious and scientific purposes. People could have alcohol in their homes as long as they purchased it outside the province and had it shipped in. Wholesale liquor stores and breweries were free to continue to operate as long as they shipped to customers outside the province. The law was passed by the legislature, pending the results of a referendum to be held on March 13.

Premier Norris also moved quickly to amend the *Schools Act* and institute the changes the Liberals had long been asking for. The controversy over this issue reveals a great deal about the general atmosphere in Manitoba at the time. The Throne Speech did not clearly describe the extent of the changes the government wanted, only mentioning the removal of the Coldwell Amendments and the introduction of a compulsory attendance law. Interestingly, the much more important change that the government was about to implement—the elimination of Section 258 of the Act and the end of the bilingual school system—was described in the single line, "Other legislation to increase the standard and efficiency of the public schools of the Province and the administration thereof will be laid before you."

It may be that there was some disagreement about the extent of the changes within the Liberal Cabinet. There had been clear promises made to French parents, for example, that the French bilingual schools would be spared. One scholar has concluded that the sweeping changes were the work of a more radical minority in the Liberal caucus, supported by J.W. Dafoe's *Free Press* and other English newspapers.[19]

The day after the Throne Speech was delivered, the Winnipeg *Tribune* encouraged the government to go ahead with the abolition of the Laurier-Greenway Compromise, with an appeal to English Canadian nationalism: "Now is the time to put the British Canadian stamp on Manitoba. Hybridism had its day under Roblinism: it was another name for division and dishonor." For the *Tribune* it was clear that no concessions should be made to non-English Manitobans but that everyone should be molded by the school system into loyal English Canadians. There can be no doubt that the heat of this statement was in part due to the war and desire to safeguard the British system that Canadians were dying for at the front.

On February 4 the *Tribune* commented that "our soldiers are fighting for British ideals. Are our legislators less patriotic that they should shrink from promoting British Canadian ideals by establishing

English schools in every section of this British Canadian province." J.W. Dafoe called Ukrainians who protested against the changes "monuments to the old regime," meaning the Roblin government. He wrote that "We can say with perfect propriety to the Ruthenian and the Pole that if he is dissatisfied with our educational laws he can pack his trunk and go back to his happy home in war torn Europe."[20] A few days later Dafoe expressed the view that support for bilingual schools was being financed by "European powers." In another issue he stated that there was no room in Canada for any nationalism but Canadian nationalism. He said that, "if necessary, blood will flow" to prevent the ascendancy of the sort of ethnic nationalism that had caused the war in Europe.

During the course of the school debate many Manitobans echoed Dafoe's sentiments. Colonel C.W. Rowley, an official of the Bank of Commerce and commander of the 100th Winnipeg Grenadiers, said grimly, "If we do not face it today, our children will have to face it tomorrow, and it may lead to bloodshed."[21] In February, D.A. Ross, a long-time Winnipeg politician, lost his temper at a meeting with a group of his Ukrainian constituents. He reminded them that there was a war on and that they were Austrians, "and if you don't stop this agitation I'll run you all to Brandon,"[22] referring to the internment camp for enemy aliens. Even the unfortunate Bishop Budka, the Ukrainian Catholic leader, came in for another drubbing; Ross accused Budka of "sowing seeds of sedition and disloyalty" and expressed the view that the churchman should be deported.

On January 11, Premier Norris explained the proposed changes to the *Schools Act* in more detail. He said his government intended to remove Section 258—the section containing the Laurier-Greenway Compromise—from the Act. This would extinguish the right of people with mother tongues other than English to have their children educated in those languages and English "on the bi-lingual system." From now on, Norris said, English would be the only language used in Manitoba's schools. The change, along with the removal of the Coldwell Amendments, would ensure that "the national school system shall remain inviolate and unimpaired."[23]

The premier was an experienced politician and knew well what a storm of controversy the changes would stir up. He promised that in

the month before their introduction "representatives of all the nation-
alities would be invited to state their views to the house so that the
best possible compromise could be reached. There would have to be
compromise."[24]

The next day, Minister of Education J.S. Thornton spoke on the
topic to a full house and gallery and he showed little desire to compromise. He was clearly determined to eliminate the bilingual system. He
began by setting out all the problems with the school system he had
inherited from the Roblin Tories. Some English children, he said, had
had their school changed to a bilingual school and now had to learn in
English and another language foreign to them. He said that 42 percent
of Manitobans had a mother tongue other than English, and in districts
with mixed populations it was impossible to satisfy competing groups.
In some cases what had been French-English bilingual schools had
become Ukrainian-English schools because of slight shifts in population. Sometimes there were struggles for control of the local school
boards between competing language groups. He told the legislature
that not all the teachers arrived in the classroom with adequate skills
to do their jobs. Because the province had different normal schools
for teachers—English, French, German, Ukrainian or Ruthenian,[25] and
Polish—it was difficult to ensure standardized training.

Thornton finished his speech with a clear statement of his party's
views: "There should be one common school teaching the things which
are common to all, and leaving to individual effort those matters which
are of private concern." He said there should be one type of training
for teachers and inspectors who were able to inspect all schools and
hold them all to a common standard. He said abolition of the existing school system was "in our own interests" and the interests of the
"strangers within our gates" whose first necessity is to learn the language of the country. He said Manitoba was putting these people and
their children "under a continuous handicap" by not ensuring they
had "a satisfactory education in English."

He continued: "We wish to give them the same consideration as is
accorded to our own children to fit them to earn their way through
life, and to take places as citizens in our Canadian Nationality. This
question must be dealt with looking forward not backward. Each
generation must take its responsibility and act in the spirit of its own

Demonstration trenches at Main and Water in downtown Winnipeg, built as part of a war bond campaign in 1916.

times, yet ever watchful of the result to succeeding generations. We are building today for the Canada of tomorrow, and our common school is one of the most important factors in the work." Thornton's arguments make clear the political underpinning of the changes—the children of the minority language groups were to become like English Canadians and the schools were the place they would be transformed.

In the Winnipeg *Free Press* the following day, an account of the speech was printed next to J.W. Dafoe's editorial column, which supported Thornton's arguments. Dafoe made special mention of "the provision that makes it possible to disrupt an English school and drive out the English teacher by device of colonizing the necessary number of 10 non-English children is an intolerable offence to the English speaking people of this Province: it must go."[26] These sorts of arguments, appealing to the insecurity of English Manitobans who feared losing control of the province to "foreigners," were unwise and unjust but quite effective in stiffening the resolve of the Liberal government.

Toward the end of January, C.K. Newcombe, the provincial superintendent of education, reported on a survey of bilingual schools that he and his staff had just completed. On the central question of how much English the students were learning, Newcombe essentially agreed with the 1913 *Free Press* study: the two French schools in Winnipeg were doing a good job but the same could not be said of all the rural French schools. The Polish and Ruthenian schools had students who were not fluent in English. English-language skills depended upon the teacher's knowledge, the number of English-speaking students who were attending and the proximity of English-speaking communities. In the German schools, all in Mennonite districts, English was the language of instruction and German was used extensively only with beginners and for about one hour a day with the older children.

There were eighty-five districts with only English schools, but even in these districts there were 110 schools that had enough foreign-language speakers to potentially claim bilingual education. "The administrative difficulties arising out of this situation are obvious," Newcombe wrote. While his report touched on all the problems of the bilingual system, it did not go so far as actually recommending abolition, listing instead a number of reforms designed to make the system work more smoothly. This apparent disagreement between the minister and one of his senior advisors is a further indication of less than complete agreement within the government.

The people who wanted to preserve the existing system did what they could to oppose the government. On January 31, 1916, there was a large meeting of Ukrainians in the Grand Theatre at which a resolution was passed against the abolition of bilingual schools. The preamble to the resolution indignantly charged that, "Whereas certain parts of the misinformed press tries to cause discord between citizens of British and non-British descent" and "Whereas this chauvinistic press by baseless and wicked insinuations ... under pressure from fanatical and reactionary elements ... entertains a step calculated to deprive Ukrainian Canadians in Manitoba of their natural rights bestowed on every community through divine and human justice and intends to abolish laws permitting the use of our language in public schools." The attendees at the meeting also condemned "the behaviour of the press as treacherous and non-patriotic and non-christian like terrorism" and appealed to the government to join in stamping out the "undesirable propaganda of rascal firebrands."

A delegation of 150 Ukrainian community leaders went to the legislature the next day to meet with Premier Norris. They had invited seventeen members of the legislative assembly to attend, but only six came. Another group met with Norris on February 3 and presented him with 125 petitions containing over 6000 signatures. Taras Ferley, the independent Liberal from Gimli, introduced the speakers at this meeting. J.W. Arsenych, a young lawyer who would soon be a partner of A.A. Heaps, told Norris that the changes would drive Ukrainian children into parochial schools operated by the clergy, something he personally did not see as progress. He affirmed that Ukrainians wanted their children to learn English but in an atmosphere that was not hostile to their own language and culture. Instead of the government amendments, he suggested changes that were often asked for by the Ukrainian community: more trained teachers who could teach in Ukrainian and English, more school organizers to help set up schools in the rural areas, and a professor of Ukrainian studies at the University of Manitoba.

Soon after this the Ukrainian community invited fifteen Liberals, two Conservatives, and two independents to a special meeting at the Stella Avenue parochial school. Only two of the Liberals showed up but all the other invitees came. The Conservatives and Fred Dixon, one of the independents, told the meeting they favoured continuation of the bilingual school system. The other independent, Richard Rigg, said that while he did not support continuation, he was in favour of using the schools after hours for language education. The Liberals refused to comment on the issue. At the meeting J.W. Arsenych delivered a strong address in favour of retaining the current system. C. Yakimischak, a third-year arts student, spoke in favour of the system as well. A meeting of 500 Polish people in the Queen's Theatre on Selkirk supported similar resolutions. Another Polish meeting passed ·a motion stating that "to have our children given primary education in their mother tongue is absolutely indispensable to their general welfare."[27]

The non-English press opposed the changes. The Polish language *Gazeta Katolicka* claimed that fanatics were behind the determination of the government to "take away the privilege of teaching our language in schools supported by our own money." Some Ukrainian speakers claimed that they had come to Canada with the understanding that they would have the right to teach their language "and we will not allow ourselves to be deprived" of that right.[28]

The French community had representation in the legislature among the French members of the Conservative opposition. Their leader, Albert Prefontaine, regretted that the Liberals had decided to "create dissension in time of war" by opening the old religious and language issues that had torn the province apart in the 1890s. He said that R.S. Thornton was treating the promises made to the Mennonite settlers who came to Manitoba in 1873 like a "scrap of paper," a reference to the German chancellor's words describing the treaty guaranteeing Belgian neutrality in August 1914. Another French member, the Liberal P.A. Talbot, agreed with Prefontaine, stating that the education amendments were "criminal treatment of a minority," and added defiantly that "the French are a distinctive race and they will not be assimilated whether you like it or not."[29]

Another Conservative, Aime Benard, told the house that he was a loyal British subject and no French Canadian *nationaliste,* but "in 30 out of 47 constituencies, voters of other than the English tongue had been deceived into voting for the government upon the pledge that their schools would not be interfered with."[30] Benard was referring to pledges made during the 1915 election campaign by Tobias Norris that French Manitobans would be exempted from any amendment to abolish bilingual schools.

Thornton answered, rather weakly, that the Liberals had decided on the breadth of the legislation only in October, four months after the election campaign. By then they had realized that the situation in the province's schools was "almost out of hand" and virtually impossible to administer. He said that his hopes of "fixing" the system by improving the teaching of English had to be abandoned.

In St. Boniface on February 25, shortly before the vote on second reading of the bill, a meeting of 1500 people from the city and French parishes in rural Manitoba established a committee to oppose the changes. A new paper, *La Libre Parole*, appeared in St. Boniface under the editorship of historian and journalist A.H. de Tremaudan. He traced French rights in British North America back to the Treaty of Paris in 1783, and Archbishop Béliveau of St. Boniface issued a pastoral letter stating, "There can be no peace where there is no justice," and vowing never to cease working for the rights of Franco-Manitobans. About the same time, the Winnipeg Irish Association, whose members understood the importance of preserving one's language, met and passed a resolution in support of "those people who are presently fighting for their native language and for their rights."[31]

The reaction to the proposed changes in the Mennonite areas of the province was also negative, although there were differences of opinion within that community. The proposed changes to the *Schools Act* were seen as a betrayal of the guarantees under which the Mennonites had originally come to Canada: one of the reasons that they had left Russia was an 1870 decree obliging them to teach in Russian in their schools.

Mennonite delegations, headed by the Reverend H.H. Ewert, from 1891 to 1903 the school inspector of the German-language schools, met with the premier and Cabinet in February. It was argued that the Mennonite public schools were not really bilingual but "dual-language" because students were taught in English for most of the day. German-language and religious instruction took place after 3:30 p.m. The Mennonite students had perfectly adequate English-language skills, said the delegates, and their schools should therefore be exempted from the changes. A petition presented to Norris stated, in part: "Give us some further time and we will demonstrate to the country that our schools equal and, maybe, excel all other schools in the Province, and this notwithstanding the fact, nay because of the fact, that our children also learn a second language."[32]

When Norris responded that there would be no exemptions, many of the more conservative Mennonite groups withdrew their children from the public schools and placed them in private, German-language religious schools. Eleven such schools had already been established in response to the Roblin government's directive, in 1907, that all public schools must fly the Union Jack or lose their grants. Now more private schools were established. The appointment of a public trustee, J.F. Greenway, the son of the former Liberal premier, with a mandate to impose English-only schools, was met with passive resistance. In Alt Bergthal, for example, during the 1916–1917 school year the public school teacher spent a lonely winter: "When I hoisted the flag on the first of September there wasn't a child in the school. The old people got together, fixed up a log cabin and hired a private teacher for the 45 children in the district. They paid him the same salary I was getting—$80.00 a month. But I stuck to it and hoisted the flag every one of the 202 days, but I did not have one pupil."[33]

Schools were established by Greenway in districts where the local tax-payers had not asked for them. Land sometimes had to be expropriated for the school because the local farmers would not sell and lumber for the schools had to be shipped from Winnipeg. The government used fines to enforce school attendance, and at one point six Mennonite preachers were in jail because of the boycott.

In 1919, a Mennonite parent, John Hildebrand, was fined with other parents in the Houston School District for not sending his children to the public school. The fines were appealed but the Manitoba Court of Appeal ruled against Mennonite parents and stated the province had the exclusive right to make laws governing schools. Another important finding of the court was that the Mennonites had not actually received any written guarantees about education at the time they came to Canada in 1873, although they had always assumed this to be the case.

The conflict resulted in the emigration, by 1925, of at least 6500 Mennonites to Mexico and Paraguay from Manitoba. They received guarantees from the governments of their new homes that they could control their own schools. Some villages were left virtually empty and, while new immigration from Russia brought Mennonite families to replace those who had left, the province lost many experienced and productive farmers.

None of the protests diminished the determination of the Norris government to abandon bilingual schools. Instead they inspired increasingly vehement counterattacks. Premier Norris told a Ukrainian delegation that they were being selfish in expecting special privileges. A.B. Hudson, the Liberal attorney general, asserted that the French minority in Manitoba in fact had no special constitutional rights. He said he was not impressed when they invoked the Laurier-Greenway compromise because Archbishop Langevin had never supported it in the past, demanding instead that the province return to the old pre-1889 dual school board model. Of the compromise, Hudson said, "it was sacred to us but not to you."

The final vote on the Bill took place on March 8. It passed with limited opposition, from the four French Conservatives and their lone English colleague, F.Y. Newton of Roblin, along with two Liberals, P.A. Talbot and T.D. Ferley. A number of changes followed immediately. The Ruthenian Teachers' College in Brandon was amalgamated with the English normal school there and the Mennonite normal school in Morden was joined with its English counterpart in Manitou. The French teacher-training facility in Winnipeg was now to be staffed by English teachers from the main normal school. While student teachers had previously been allowed to study French history, literature, and composition to prepare for their high-school exams, they would now be required to study English subjects. All teachers would be expected to "know something of the contributions to the world of the great English writers and statesmen."[34] All teachers would now be expected to achieve the same general educational level. The Ukrainian students in Brandon would be supported so that they could pass the grade ten exams and then receive teacher training. The closure of the Ruthenian Teachers' College and the Polish institution were great losses for the two communities. Their students often went on to become community leaders and the students at the Polish college had been seen as good examples to other young Poles, inspiring them to pursue an education.

Troops mass behind city hall as part of a 1916 Decoration Day parade.

School organizers in Ukrainian districts were fired, thirty-five school boards were suspended and their affairs taken over by a provincial administrator, Ira Stratton, a defeated Liberal candidate, postmaster, and long-time school board member in Stonewall. His mandate was to instill patriotism in the students. There were many who felt he was too high-handed in his methods, firing Ukrainian teachers and replacing them with English teachers who were, in some cases, not trained teachers at all. He removed portraits of Shevchenko from some of the schools and generally ensured that the new Act was enforced.

At the same time that the Liberal government repealed Section 258, it introduced the *School Attendance Act*. It stipulated that every child between seven and fourteen was expected to attend school on all the days that the local school was open. Parents were assured that children attending private schools would not be expected to go to the public state schools, provided the private school was offering them an education equivalent to the public school. School attendance officers would be appointed by school boards to ensure that children were in school. Truancy officers who had performed this function during the Roblin period under the provisions of the *Children's Act* were let go.

While immigrant communities in Manitoba were finding it more difficult to express their cultures, the rights of women were expanding. At the end of January the legislature passed an amendment to the *Elections Act* that gave Manitoba women the vote, making the province the first in the Dominion to do so. On February 1, the Political Equality League held a celebratory banquet in the Royal Alexandra Hotel. There were many smiling faces in the room and the mood was buoyant. Dr. Mary Crawford, the chief medical inspector of Winnipeg schools and president of the league, read from a sheaf of congratulatory telegrams and then toasted the premier with a complimentary speech. He replied that his government was simply keeping faith with the people. He too read some telegrams, one from a suffrage group in Chicago. He told a story about a recent trip he had made to Chicago and a conversation he had with a man who did not know he was the premier of Manitoba. The "yankee" said, "Well what sort man must you have at the head of the government. He must be a henpecked husband anyway."[35] The story was greeted with laughter and applause.

Toasts were proposed by the women at the head table. Journalist Lillian Thomas said she had always heard, "You can trust Norris, he's a man of his word." Replying to a toast to the Labor Party by Mrs. A.W. Puttee, R.A. Rigg said that he was confident that women would purify the political life of the province. Mrs. James Munro toasted the Opposition, humorously saying that the Liberals had brought women "to where they could get a glimpse of the promised land, where milk and honey, and nothing stronger, flow." Conservative member of the legislative assembly Joseph Hamelin of Ste. Rose replied, also tongue in cheek, that he wondered "who will mind the baby" now that women are going out to political meetings. He said he was not very good at minding babies. He said that he hoped that now they had the vote women would vote for the Conservative Party. The crowd enjoyed his comments and laughed at his jokes.

Replying to a toast to "Our Friends," meaning the Single Tax League, the Direct Legislation League, and the Royal Templars of Temperance, S.J. Farmer said that the enfranchisement of women was a "genuine, fundamental democratic reform."

The Norris ~~Government~~

Progressive as much of the Liberal program was, the Norris government continued in its efforts to expose the wrongdoing of their old antagonists, perpetuating the old partisanship for which they had criticized Roblin. The inquiry into the legislative building scandal was followed by several more Royal Commissions. In fall 1915 the construction of the power house and the new court house at Broadway and Kennedy were investigated to discover whether or not overpayments were made on the contracts for those projects. Similar investigations of the Manitoba Agricultural College construction and of provincial road construction contracts would follow in 1916 and 1917.

On September 1, 1916, the investigation of the construction of the Manitoba Agricultural College buildings began. The *Telegram* claimed that Finance Minister Edward Brown was not in favour of spending more taxpayers' money on another commission. The paper commented that he was no doubt concerned about how he would explain why so much tax money has gone to lawyers and expert witnesses and "fat fees and easy pickings for party friends." A month later the *Telegram* printed a list of the costs of running the various Royal Commissions, estimating that nearly half a million dollars had been spent up to that time. The *Telegram* may have been exaggerating Brown's concern, but there can be no doubt that the commencement of another commission close to a year and a half after Roblin's resignation must have seemed, to many Manitobans, like a vendetta against the previous government. The target in this investigation was Robert Rogers, who had been minister of public works when the college-building project began, and he was suspected of having profited from real estate transactions that took place before the location of the college was publicly announced.

As the inquiry proceeded, under Justice A.C. Galt, it established, not surprisingly, that Kelly had received overpayments similar to those on the other large construction projects and that he had donated the some of this money to the Conservatives. On September 22, the final day of the inquiry, Robert Rogers was questioned for a full day about the project. At the end of the day he displayed the partisan techniques that had made him such an important tactician for the Conservatives for almost twenty years. As part of his statement, he said that judges should not accept fees for working on a Royal Commission. Galt, who had been receiving $100 a day for his work, on top of his salary, was accused of graft by Rogers, who quoted the law to him. Galt, who was famously short tempered, shouted that Rogers was "involved," meaning he was guilty of wrongdoing. Since he said this before the commission had gathered all the evidence, his statement put the impartiality of the inquiry in question. Rogers smiled, said "thank you," and left the room.

The next day commission lawyer Hugh Phillips called Galt's attention to a story in the *Telegram* that quoted what Rogers had said to him and what he had replied. Galt called Mr. Beck, the editor of the *Telegram*, to appear before him. Beck refused to be sworn or to answer questions, saying that the commission was not legitimate. In fact, he said, it was "illegal, unlawful and without jurisdiction." Galt said he was in contempt, fined him $500, and sentenced him to a month in jail. The news editor of the paper was also fined $100 and sentenced to two weeks, and the reporter who wrote the story was sentenced to one month. Knox McGee, the editor of the *Saturday Post*, which also carried the story, was fined $500 and sent to jail for one month. Judge Galt said, "It is time to let the people understand that the arm of justice is not going to be interfered with either by newspapers or individuals in this province." McGee, a crusading editor who was often involved in controversy, showed no fear, and in the next issue of his paper he called Judge Galt's actions "not only monstrous and archaic but anti-British" and accused the judge of acting as "plaintiff, prosecutor, judge and jury."

The newspapermen were all released on bail after lawyers R.A.C. Manning and F.M. Burbidge appeared before Judge Alex Haggart. Haggart, a former Conservative politician, heard the arguments of the lawyers on October 5 and a few days later gave his decision, quashing the charges against the men and saying that Galt, as a Royal Commissioner, had no more power than an ordinary citizen to punish anyone for contempt. He said that Galt had not acted properly and that people could not be summarily arrested and dragged from the courtroom.

Galt had threatened to arrest Rogers for contempt as well, because of comments the minister had made about regretting having recommended Galt for a judgeship. Rogers, now back in Ottawa, said Galt could go ahead and arrest him, and Galt read out this remark at the commission hearing, adding, "it is idle to deal with questions of contempt if the parties sent down for contempt are immediately released."

Invited to send a lawyer to represent him before the commission, Rogers replied that "the facts have been given clearly and fully by me ... I have no interest whatever in what the Commission may choose to find," since the commission had "already, and before the evidence was heard, announced the verdict." Sending counsel would "only add to the farce."

This type of partisan squabbling was becoming less acceptable to the public who were making huge sacrifices to win the war and were tired of political rivalries. The fact that the Liberals seemed to be just as partisan as Roblin's Tories, although less corrupt, was undoubtedly one of the reasons for their losing support in Manitoba. On the central issue of the legislative building they themselves appeared to act in a partisan manner, awarding a $2.5 million contract loan to finish the building in March 1917 to James McDairmid. This was condemned as political favouritism by the Conservative *Telegram* because McDairmid was a Liberal supporter and had already been doing some work on the building with a small crew of men.

Premier Norris said many times during his tenure that his government had abolished the spoils system and refused to appoint people on the basis of their politics, losing in the process "a few old party friends." But there is no doubt that many Liberals were appointed to government jobs. In September of 1915 the *Telegram*, which had been keeping careful track, charged that the Liberal government had already made 400 changes in the civil service. In the twenty-six weeks they had been in power they had fired 430 officials and hired 741. This represented an increase of 311 people on the payroll. Many of the changes involved the removal of minor officials such as commissioners of oaths, game wardens, and provincial police constables who had been appointed by the Roblin government. They had been replaced with people in favour with the Liberal Party. The deputy minister of agriculture and commissioner of immigration, the Conservative Justin

Golden, was fired and replaced. Roger Marion, for fourteen years the registrar of vital statistics and a Conservative MPP for five years, was fired with six months pay and no pension. A.L. Bonnycastle, the provincial police magistrate and a former Conservative members of the legislate assembly, was replaced by Judge P.A. Macdonald, a Liberal.

As 1916 drew to a close the city was much less united than it had been two years earlier. Revelations about political corruption during the Roblin years coupled with the partisanship of the Liberals produced a low level of support for the old political parties that would lead to the Union Government of 1917. The non-Anglo-Canadian sections of the population, battered by the schools controversy, were much less interested in fighting for Canada at the very time when they were most needed in the fight.

1917

The third full year of the war, 1917 was a time of testing for the combatants, and for those at home. The Canadian Corps would, during 1917, be forged into one of the best fighting units on the Western Front and in battles like Vimy Ridge in the spring and Passchendaele in the fall the Canadians would distinguish themselves with their skill and bravery. But exhaustion and depression set in among the men who had been at the front through the fighting in 1916 and who saw no hope of anything different in the months ahead. In Winnipeg, people were also worn down by the long war, and during 1917 the imposition of conscription would bring frayed nerves to the breaking point. Amidst the growing dissent and despair, most would nevertheless keep their faith in the war effort, raising money, declaring their loyalty and doing what they could to ensure that victory would come.

Civilians had a better idea now of what the soldiers were enduring. On the first day of the Somme fighting a film of the troops going over the top had been made for the War Office. It would be shown all over the Empire, and for millions it was the first moving picture they had ever seen of actual fighting. In November 1916, Richard Waugh wrote to his son Alec that the movie was showing in Winnipeg. Alec responded that they saw the film in his unit, only a few miles from where it was photographed. "You can imagine how interested we were when every corner was familiar to us," he wrote. But he made clear that the novelty was clouded by the reality it displayed, and his words reveal

The Manitoba Agricultural College was turned into the Tuxedo Military Hospital to accommodate the need for recuperation and vocational training space for returning soldiers.

the attitudes front-line soldiers took in order to survive: "while there is always a certain amount of regard shown to the dead, it is best not to philosophize on the subject. If I conjured up all the tears that the battlefields cause, I should be a raving lunatic by now." Clifford Wells made a similar observation, writing to his brother about having seen an accident in the street: "It must have been quite a shock to you when your streetcar killed the auto driver. It would have been to me a year ago, but now bloody death is a familiar sight. I am a different man to the one who enlisted in Montreal fourteen months ago. No one can go through a day's work out here and remain unchanged."[1]

By 1917 Alec had been transformed from a callow youth into a seasoned front-line officer commanding a machine gun squadron made up of troops from the Lord Strathcona's Horse, and he seems to have been well liked by his men. He was attentive to their needs, renting them a piano at Christmas time and asking his father to make sure all twenty-six of them received Christmas parcels from Canada. His almost daily letters to his parents reveal someone who is no longer an immature teenager but a young man who has learned to accept the hardships of the front and is more focussed on his men than himself.

When writing to his mother during 1917, however, Alec shows a growing weariness with the war. He confides in her that he sometimes saw her face: "It is you who walks with me in the Valley of the Shadow, and I grow fearless with some of your spirit." As Alec fought and saw the death and carnage around him, he thought more and more about his mother. He was very critical of his "selfish and thoughtless" English cousins who in spite of their public school manners gave no money to help support their mother. As the fall of 1917 wore on he seemed to grow more despondent and wrote often about death. In November he composed a sentimental poem, "Mother Mine," which was published in the Winnipeg papers:

> Across the threshold of the night it comes, a memory,
> The little loves of baby days, the loves of yet to be,
> Personified in saintly grace, with haloed love divine
> She stops to kiss me ere I sleep
> This little mother mine.
> Throughout the graying dawns and dusks,
> A thousand shadowed fears
> Are stilled by the steadfast mother love
> A burden of the years is lifted
> From a longing heart and with thy hand in mine
> There is no fear, the light has come
> With you sweet mother mine.
> Should Britain ask for all I have, that will I gladly give
> My hopes, ambitions, yes my life that Britain still may live
> And when life's length is fading fast
> And first bright star shells shine
> I'll tell this story o'er again
> I love you mother mine.

On a trip to London, Alec Waugh met an English actress, one of Sir Herbert Tree's repertory company at His Majesty's Theatre in the West End. He describes getting her to sing sentimental songs to him—"Annie Laurie," "Mother Machree," "Loch Lomond," were the songs he was most fond of and which brought him "near tears." Like many young soldiers he had little chance to develop relationships with women. In the fall of 1917 he spent time with another young Englishwoman with whom he had been corresponding. Women often volunteered to write letters to men in the trenches. He wrote to his parents about going out with her to shows and dances: "I think that was the one thing that made the leave a success, someone to go places with and look after, a thing which you will agree, I've had little chance to do for a long long time."

In the middle of November 1917 his squadron was moving into position to take part in the fighting around Cambrai. Alec wrote a heartbreaking letter to his father. He did not expect to survive the coming battle: "If I should die remember that I gave gladly all I had to keep a smile on your lips and sorrow from your hearts. I am only one of the millions who are to know the bitterness, the aching heart, and when the finish comes, the longing for some last kiss or the touch of a hand and a voice to say 'well done my son.'"

Two weeks later, as he was visiting the machine gun emplacements held by his men south west of Cambrai, he was shot through the stomach by a sniper. He said, "I am done for," and told his men not to gather around him or they too would be hit. He said he wanted only to be left alone and not trouble anyone. He died thirty minutes later.

winning at any cost / Hospitals

In Winnipeg, the IODE quietly supported women who had lost loved ones. In 1916 one of them described this in the following way: "scurrying across the prairie on a bitterly cold day in response to an SOS call from a sister in distress...visiting the mother or wife, heartsick with anxiety for some dear one in the thick of the battle, and comforting them in the first dark hours when the dreaded news comes—all such work is being constantly carried on by members...and by such in truth are the bonds of Empire knit tightly together."[2] We might add to this the bonds of human kindness and mutual support developed over the years by women in what was still in many ways an interdependent pioneer culture.

A few months later, Rosalie Creighton wrote to thank Minnie Campbell for sending her condolences over the death of Creighton's husband at the front. "The sense of personal loss is so great that one's pride sometimes seems absolutely submerged in grief and pain," she wrote.

By 1917 there was hospital accommodation in Canada for the men returning wounded from the war. The Manitoba chapter of the IODE had been operating a convalescent hospital since early 1915. It was the first in Canada, located in a former private hospital in a house at the corner of Broadway and Donald. The patients at this time were men in training who had become ill or been injured. The hospital cared for 1462 men in the first year of operation, and in June it moved from Broadway to 71 Smith Street. There the hospital served returned men as the casualties from the second Battle of Ypres started to come home. In January 1916 the hospital moved again, this time to the third floor of the Immigration Building next to the CPR station.

Nationally, the Military Hospitals Commission under Senator Lougheed was established in mid-1915. It was responsible for caring for and training disabled men to, where possible, return to the work-force and earn a living. The commission secretary, E.H. Scammell, considered the hospitals set up in private homes, like the IODE hospital in Winnipeg, inadequate because of lack of trained staff and the short-comings of the buildings. In Winnipeg, the IODE reported in 1916 that all the returned men in their care were to be moved to the Deer Lodge Hospital opened by the Military Hospitals Commission in June of that year. There was some doubt about whether their hospital would continue. They were expecting to lose their space in the Immigration Hall and, the report added, "We shall shortly have to cast about for new quarters in which to carry on our good work, if our Order de-sires to continue it."[3]

But the commission was not able to provide accommodation for all the men who were beginning to flood back into the country, and so the IODE hospital continued to operate. In April 1917 the Manitoba chapter reported that 3545 returned men had been cared for in their hospital in the previous twelve months and at the end of the war they still had 240 patients, eighteen of whom later died in the influenza epidemic.[4]

The Deer Lodge Hospital was opened in June 1916 by the Duchess of Connaught. It was housed in the former Deer Lodge Hotel, which had been loaned to the Military Hospitals Commission by Roderick McKenzie, son of the builder of the Canadian Northern Railway. The IODE paid for furnishing a ward with twenty-nine beds. The new hospital was under the management of Marcella Richardson, an experienced Canadian Army nurse. The main ballroom of the hotel was turned into a classroom where the men could learn useful office skills like typing and receive instruction in apiculture, horticulture, and poultry farming. Teaching the men skills like these was considered by the commission to be the best way to prepare them for their reintroduction into society. A Disablement Fund had been established, with a $100,000 donation from grain dealer James Carruthers of Montreal, and the commission promised that any man returned from the war whether wounded or not would be given vocational retraining. This training would be handled by a committee in each province.

In December 1916 the commission asked that Winnipeg provide accommodation for 1000 wounded soldiers. It had been decided that Canadian long-term patients were now to be brought home from England rather than recuperating in British hospitals. In January 1917 Sir James Lougheed visited Winnipeg and explained the commission's plans: the city would be a distribution centre where bed cases would rest and grow stronger, where long-term convalescents would stay, and where wounded men would receive training. Late in the month plans were announced to build a 600-bed military hospital in Alexander Square near the General Hospital at a cost of $1 million. The square was leased to the Military Hospitals Commission for one dollar by the city council.

But by April 1917 the plans were changed and the commission decided to locate the hospital at the former Agricultural College in Tuxedo. The first building to be occupied was the former dairy building, which had room for 125 men. On the main floor was an office and waiting room, a dormitory for seventeen beds with a large locker beside each one, a bathroom with showers and tubs, another dormitory with fourteen beds and more baths, a recreation room with a billiard table donated by A.M. Nanton, bookshelves, a piano, and a Victrola. On the second floor was more dormitory space and baths meant for the so-called Class 3 men—those who were no longer patients but were receiving vocational training. Men in training who had a home in the city would stay at home. The nurses were also housed on the second floor. Nurse Richardson was the matron of all the convalescent hospitals in the city and was living at Deer Lodge until quarters for her were completed at Tuxedo.

The second floor of the new hospital also had rooms for changing dressings and a storeroom for medicines. On the third floor were two more dormitories. The dormitories in the building were more relaxed than those in a normal hospital because the men were able to have their own possessions around them and there was a lack of rules and regulations. In the basement were the dining room and kitchens and a massage room, and plans called for a medical service department with X-ray room and laboratory. To the west of the building, construction of two new dormitories and a kitchen building was almost complete. The dormitories were long, narrow, two-story buildings, and each floor had a ward for eighty-two beds open to a sunroom overlooking the river and Assiniboine Park to the west.

In addition, an old machinery building was slated to become a centre for vocational training. At the time, training was being offered at different city locations, including the two technical high schools, St. John's and Kelvin. All the land between the college and the CNR tracks to the south would be planted with fruits and vegetables for use in the kitchens and for sale. The farm buildings to the south of the hospital were to be stocked with cattle, sheep, pigs, and poultry. Roblin Hall, the college dormitory, would house another 270 men. The former administration building had an auditorium for 300 and the rest of the building was to be used for training.

By August 1917 it was proudly announced that forty men had been retrained at the Tuxedo hospital and had secured work. At the end of September 1917 there was a field day at the hospital and about 3000 visitors watched a soccer game between the "crutchies," men with crutches, and the "leadswingers," a team made up of men on milk diets. The crutchies won four to one. The nurses and masseuses participated in foot races. At the beginning of October, Lieutenant Governor Aikins officially opened the two new dormitories and the service building with kitchen and dining hall.

But all was not well at the hospital. Fred W. Law, the secretary of the Great War Veterans' Association, had charged that friction

Far from the battlefields, the staff and patients at the Tuxedo Military Hospital were sometimes able to be more light-hearted. Here they are participating in a sports day.

among the staff had led to the resignation of Marcella Richardson and Sergeant Major Angus, who was in charge of training. Law said that the problems stemmed from too great an influence in the administration by civilians. For example, he reported, doctors had to get permission from civilians before ordering supplies. On October 8 Sir James Lougheed sent a telegram to Law promising to investigate the complaints.

Despite the criticisms, the resulting report was quite positive. It explained how vocational training was organized and that only 10 percent of soldiers were so disabled that they could not go back to their former occupations. For the majority, vocational training was designed simply to get their muscles working and teach them some useful skills rather than to prepare them to do a specific job. The report conceded that more had to be done to make agreements with potential employers to provide on-the-job training.

Law condemned the report as "all whitewash," and he promised the veterans that he would not let the issue rest at that. One of their main complaints focussed on W.J. Warters, the civilian hired to work as head of vocational training. In November several hundred of "the boys" at the Tuxedo hospital signed a petition asking that Sergeant Major Angus be reinstated. They claimed that Warters, who taught for the Winnipeg School Board, was better suited to teaching children. Sergeant Major Angus had done a good job and got many men positions in commercial firms in the city.

The dissatisfaction continued, and in November 1917, 250 soldiers in the Tuxedo hospital went on strike demanding that Warters be dismissed. Lieutenant Timmins, the principal of the school, called the men together and asked them what the trouble was. He promised to pass their views on to Ottawa. But, within a week, the strike ended when the men were told that they would lose a day's pay for every day on strike. At the end of January 1918, however, Fred Law was once again complaining, in a speech to the Winnipeg Ministerial Association, that the men were not being taught enough to get a job. Warters did make some positive changes as a result of the strike. He told a Canadian Manufacturers Association meeting that he wanted to place men in local firms as apprentices. The hospital would continue to pay them while they were apprenticing. During 1918 the men began learning marketable skills like auto mechanics, telegraphy, furniture making, and photography.

As the wounded continued to return to Winnipeg, more space was needed. On February 6, 1918, it was announced that two new wings with 300 new beds and a recreation hall would be added to the Tuxedo hospital. For a time there were discussions about moving the hospital rather than expanding further, and in September 1918 Valentine Winkler, the Manitoba minister of agriculture, was in Ottawa to discuss a Dominion proposal that the Agricultural College be moved from the new campus just completed in Fort Garry—the present site of the University of Manitoba—to the Tuxedo site so that the hospital could be housed in Fort Garry. Winkler was in favour, as long as the Dominion paid the real value of the Fort Garry buildings—$4 million. He felt that the Tuxedo site would suffice for the Agricultural College and that some of the teaching could be done by extension if the buildings were not big enough. But on October 26 General Mewburn, minister of defence, said that the Dominion government would not go higher than $3,500,000, to be paid in Victory Bonds. The Manitoba government refused to sell, and the Dominion government prepared instead to put up $2 million in new buildings at the Tuxedo hospital.

In 1918 the Red Cross turned its attention to supporting local hospitals like those at Deer Lodge and Tuxedo. During the summer of
1918 a new Red Cross pavilion was built at the Tuxedo Convalescent
Hospital and funds were provided for supplies, cigarettes, games, and
other "comforts" for the men. The Red Cross also provided the hospital with an ambulance and a car for patient transportation.

The next year the hospital began to share the site with the Fort
Osborne Barracks, which moved from Broadway in 1919. The num-
ber of patients began to decline and long-term care cases were ac-
commodated at Deer Lodge Hospital across the river. The hospital at
Fort Osborne Barracks was reduced in importance until the Second
World War again created the need for military hospital space.

Conscription

During winter of 1916–17, as battles like the Somme and Vimy
Ridge took the lives of thousands of Canadian soldiers, the number
of recruits from all parts of the country consistently fell about 5000
short of the number of replacements needed. February 1917 was
particularly bad—the numbers were 15,000 short. Robert Borden's
government began to prepare the ground for conscription. The first
step was a campaign to register every man from eighteen to sixty-five
and get his particulars on a card. Cards were sent out by the National
Service Board, under R.B. Bennett, and they listed twenty-four questions about the man's health, dependents, and special skills. Eighty
percent of Canadian men registered in this voluntary census, and
based on the returns it was estimated that, nation-wide, there were
still 250,000 able-bodied men who were not in the service.

There was strong support for registration in Winnipeg, but a
determined minority opposed registration and the conscription it
foreshadowed. At its January 8 meeting, Winnipeg city council voted
on a motion approving the National Service Initiative and recommending "the favorable cooperation of the citizens of Winnipeg in the
National Registration Scheme." The position of many labour leaders,
in Winnipeg and across the country, was that men should not be conscripted unless wealth was also conscripted. Pro-labour aldermen W.

Simpson and N. Wiginton moved an amendment to "request the government to nationalize the railways, mills, factories, mines and natural resources for national service." The labour amendment was lost and the main motion passed, but it was a sign that with the increased activity in favour of conscription, opposition would also increase.

At Grace Methodist Church, a meeting of clergy expressed their support for registration. Once again support was not unanimous. William Ivens of McDougall Methodist Church said that "I am a pacifist and I am opposed to war and war moves of any kind." He worried that the church might lose the support of labour if they supported conscription. But there was a range of attitudes toward the question among labour leaders. At an anti-registration rally at the Labor Temple in January 1917, R.A. Rigg, MLA for North Winnipeg, was criticized for supporting registration. Rigg countered that many eastern labour groups were in favour of registration but were saying no to conscription until wealth was conscripted.

On this point the ultra-patriotic IODE and the opponents of conscription were in agreement. At their summer 1917 annual meeting the IODE passed a resolution supporting conscription. The resolution called not only for the conscription of men but also of money, labour, and service, including the service of women, "that all may equally do their duty to their King, country and empire."[5]

F.J. Dixon, who was to be the most effective and courageous of those who openly opposed conscription in Winnipeg, declared that he completely denied the government's right to ask him to register. The local socialist and social democratic parties encouraged working people to refuse to fill out the cards.[6] Dixon, speaking during the Throne Speech debate in 1917, attacked the basic war aims of the government, saying that "the war did not involve the principles of freedom and liberty to the extent some people believed and bore all the earmarks of a struggle for power and possible setting up of a Russian militarism." Dixon's fellow MLA, R.A. Rigg, agreed with him, claiming that Britain did not really enter the war to save Belgium but to gain economic advantage over Germany. He argued that British navalism was just as important as a cause of the war as German militarism and that the basic reason Canadians were fighting was economic antagonism between Germany and Britain.[7] Fellow provincial politicians accused the two men of, like Judas of old, "betraying their countrymen and assisting the Germans."[8]

On January 12, 1917, Dixon spoke to a Grain Growers meeting in Brandon. Local returned soldiers had tried unsuccessfully to convince the Grain Growers to cancel the speech, and on the day of the event a group of returned soldiers came to the hall to protest. Dixon spoke to an attentive audience of 1400, avoiding any mention of conscription and registration. At the end of his speech a returned man shouted, "make him sing God Save the King." "God Save the People," responded Dixon.

Dixon became a sort of lightening rod for the animosity the majority of Winnipeggers felt toward those who opposed conscription. A week after his Brandon speech, the Winnipeg Board of Trade passed the following resolution: "In view of the urgent necessity on the part of all the people of Canada to carry out the country's war undertakings with the utmost vigor and efficiency, the Winnipeg Board of Trade resents the treasonable utterances of F.J. Dixon and R.A. Rigg, members of the Manitoba Legislature, and urges the Attorney General to take proper action under the circumstances." The Board of Trade set up a committee to draft a letter to Dixon, protesting his attitude toward national registration. They suggested that his opposition was not reflective of the views of his constituents in Winnipeg Centre. They sent similar letters to R.A. Rigg of North Winnipeg and to Controller A.W. Puttee and aldermen W.B. Simpson and John Queen, all of whom had been critical of registration. On January 19 both the Great War Veterans and the Army and Navy Veterans organizations petitioned the government to have Rigg and Dixon resign their seats in the legislature. They also condemned Puttee and the three pro-labour aldermen. Rigg was not actually against registration and volunteered to serve in the army a year later.

At the end of January 1917, the veterans groups and some citizens circulated a petition in the Winnipeg Centre riding supporting F.J. Dixon's recall. They also asked Premier Norris and Prime Minister Borden for an Order-in-Council removing him from the legislature. Dixon fought back, saying that recall was not the law in Manitoba and he would only abide by the notion of recall if everyone in the legislature was subject to it. He said that if 25 percent of his constituents signed the petition he would resign and run again. Only fifty people signed the petititon, indicating that his opposition to registration and conscription was quietly shared by many of his constituents in central Winnipeg.

In this same month W.H. Hoop, head of the local postal workers union, was suspended from his job because he counselled union members not to fill out their registration cards. Meanwhile, people officially classified as "conscientious objectors" in the *Militia Act* were concerned that registration would threaten their non-combatant status. Mennonite bishops from Manitoba went to Ottawa to meet with Robert Rogers and R.B. Bennett. They wanted reassurance that if their people filled out registration cards they would not be forced into the army against their religious beliefs. Rogers promised them that the agreement of 1873 under which they settled in Manitoba would be honoured. Their contribution to the war, he said, would be to grow more grain.

The conflict of opinion over the issue continued to be intense in Winnipeg. In May 1917, Board of Trade President Crossin told his members that, in view of the agitation against conscription, it was important for them to express their support and so they passed a resolution that it should be instituted "at the earliest possible moment."

Borden's views on conscription had solidified during a trip to France. His visits with the commanders of the Canadian Corps and with the men who were doing the fighting and paying the price of victory convinced him that conscription was necessary. He was particularly moved by conversations he had with wounded men in the military hospitals. On May 18 he introduced the issue in the House in spite of warnings from his Quebec caucus, Secretary of State E.-L. Patenaude, and Postmaster General P.E. Blondin that it would ruin the Conservative Party in Quebec for thirty years, a prediction that would be out by only a decade: "for Borden, his mind made up that only conscription could maintain the Canadian Expeditionary Force and allow Canada to do its part towards winning the war, political considerations seemed irrelevant."[9]

The situation was grim. In the first half of 1917 there had been about 29,000 casualties. In March there were 125,465 Canadian troops in France and 125,278 in England,40,000 of whom were unfit for service because of wounds. General Gwatkin, Canada's chief staff officer, argued that there were not enough men in England to provide the 20,000 to 30,000 replacements that would be needed in the second half of 1917 and recruiting was producing only 4000 volunteers a month.[10]

On August 29 Parliament passed the new *Military Service Act* that established conscription across Canada. There was strong opposition in Quebec and among the labour leadership and farmers. During summer the debate had divided the country, and the Liberal Party was torn apart as a significant number of newspaper editors and party members turned against Wilfrid Laurier, who continued to oppose conscription. These Liberals would join with Robert Borden's Conservatives to campaign for a Union Government in the months leading up to the federal election in December. Support was very strong in Winnipeg for the Union Government idea: both the Liberal *Free Press* and the Conservative *Telegram* favoured a government of the two parties, led by Robert Borden. J.W. Dafoe and most of the Manitoba Liberal Government supported the Union idea.

The Act passed in the House of Commons by a vote of 119 to 55. Most of the Francophone members of Parliament voted against it, while only five supported the Act—two ministers, one from Saskatchewan, one from New Brunswick, and the deputy speaker. There was a huge riot in Quebec City the night the Act passed and many Francophone Canadians felt disillusioned and betrayed.

The new Act referred back to Canada's *Militia Act*, which provided that if not enough volunteers were coming forward in wartime men could be drafted for military service using a ballot—that is by drawing names at random, as was done in the U.S. This method was seen as unworkable in Canada, because of the large numbers of men needed to work in agriculture and industry, so Canada chose to use a "selective draft." This meant that everyone in a class defined by age and family status would be called up and then would have an opportunity to apply for exemption. Anyone who did not report for duty when called up could be sentenced to up to five years hard labour. The different classes of men set up by the Act were unmarried; widowed and childless men between twenty and thirty-four; men between twenty and thirty-four who were married or widowers with one or more children; and men in the same two categories aged thirty-five to forty-one and

Augustus Nanton, one of Winnipeg's leading businessmen, provided his summer home at Lake of the Woods for convalescing returned soldiers.

forty-two to forty-five. Those eligible for exemption were men whose absence would produce significant hardship for their families or their business, who were ill or infirm, or who belonged to the Mennonite, Doukhobor, or Quaker religions.

The Act provided for a federal military service council and a registrar in each province to administer the Act. Boards of selection were put in place, and there were 1253 exemption tribunals across the country, generally staffed by middle-class businessmen and professionals. The Winnipeg group included the wealthy grocery wholesaler John Galt, grain dealer W.R. Bawlf, confectioner W.J. Boyd, and Great West Saddlery owner W.H. Hutchinson. The decisions of the tribunals could be appealed to the local appeal courts and then to Supreme Court Justice Lyman Duff in Ottawa. Anyone wishing to claim an exemption could pick up a form from the post office and have his employer, business partner, relative, or dependent fill it out.

At the end of September 5 medical boards began examining men in Winnipeg, the first step in the recruiting process. About this time, an official of the Department of Justice told the *Telegram* that a proclamation calling up the first class would be issued soon and all the men in "'Class A' (bachelors between 20 and 34) and passed by the medical officers and have not asked for exemption as well as those whose exemption claims have been disallowed, will become soldiers in 45 days."

The proclamation was issued on October 9, and the exemption tribunals were given a deadline of December 10 to complete all their hearings. No one would actually be expected to serve until after the election in December tested public support for conscription. Among the first round of conscripts, support did not appear to be strong: the numbers of men applying for exemptions were high all across the country—in Montreal only 6.5 percent of men called up came in to join the army. In St. John, New Brunswick, 98 percent of Class A men wanted an exemption, as did 96 percent in Kingston, 90 percent in Toronto, 70 percent in Vancouver, and 86 percent in Calgary.

In Winnipeg the numbers of men applying for exemptions was just as high, at 94 percent. By November 10, only 3050 Manitoba men had reported for duty and there were 19,000 claims for exemption, while it was estimated that there might be as many as another 20,000 men locally who had neither applied for exemption nor come in to join up. At the Manitoba Agricultural College every student appeared before the tribunal with a form letter from the college saying it was in the public interest to spare them.[11] On November 12 men who had not reported were liable for arrest. Military police and members of the Dominion police began to round up men who had not reported or applied for exemption, arresting over 100 in the first week and sending them to Minto Barracks. The exemption boards in Winnipeg would eventually deny half of the exemption claims that came before them, and 900 of these cases were appealed to the Provincial Court of Appeal. In St. Boniface, on the other hand, a very high percentage of exemptions was granted.

Deep divisions were opening up in society over the conscription question. At the Grand Theatre an anti-conscription rally was disrupted by a band of returned soldiers who broke into the theatre and chased the audience out. Most of the speakers retreated out the stage door, but F.J. Dixon stood his ground and was dragged to the lobby where he was struck in the face. He put up a fight, punching one of his attackers and then wisely retreating back inside the theatre. He was escorted from the building by the police, who locked the doors. The chaotic scene ended when Great War Veterans' Association officials ordered the returned men to line up and march back to the group's headquarters. Dixon announced that he would be holding more meetings and that he continued to believe that "conscription is slavery." The association, for its part, promised to "do all in their power to prevent" such meetings.

By December it was clear that conscription was having very disappointing results in Winnipeg. So many exemption appeals were still making their way through the system that it was decided to move the deadline for the completion of the process forward from December 10 to January 3, 1918. Still, it was planned to send the first contingent of drafted men to England by the end of January.

There was a scandal over conscription in December when the millionaire E.F. Hutchings, owner of Great West Saddlery, was visited by volunteers, including Augustus Nanton and A.J. Crossin, asking for pledges for the current Victory Loan Campaign. On December 5 the *Free Press* reported that one of the canvassers, J.T. Hannah, had quoted Hutchings as saying he would invest $500,000 and promote the campaign among his 500 employees if his son, Harold Gifford Hutchings, and one of his executives were granted exemptions from conscription. The same *Free Press* column reported that the younger Hutchings had offered to fund a coast guard patrol boat, provided he could command it. Harold Hutchings later testified that this offer was made by his father. The minister of justice announced that he would look into this case and prosecute if any law had been broken. Two days later Hutchings announced that he intended to sue all the Winnipeg dailies and denied that he had said what Hannah claimed.

In mid-December, Harold Hutchings's exemption application, which had been denied, came up for appeal before Judge Haggart. For two days witnesses testified about the negative effect on Great West Saddlery if Hutchings was conscripted. Others testified that Harold Hutchings, while he had worked in a number of positions in the company, was not yet an expert in the business and could be replaced. Hutchings's lawyer argued that it would be very difficult for Hutchings to get a fair hearing because he had been tried already in the newspapers, where he had been called "a millionaire's son, a joy-rider and a loafer."

When Harold Hutchings took the witness stand on December 14, he told the judge that he had not applied for an exemption and had in fact wanted to join the armed forces since the beginning of the war. His company had sent the exemption application, not him. He was applauded when he stated, "It is well known to my friends in business and society that I have never refused to go and fight for my country and to die for my country. If the judge decides I am of more use in the trenches than in this business, I'll go right out of the door and you will not see me for dust going to the nearest recruiting office."[12] Judge Haggart obliged.

A further appeal went to the Supreme Court. Although the military said that this was not necessary, Judge Haggart wanted to make sure that Hutchings got a fair hearing because prejudices had been aroused in Winnipeg and the record of the first exemption hearings had been lost. On Boxing Day, Hutchings was informed that he would have to report to the Minto Armoury on January 7, regardless of whether the appeal process was complete. He did go into the army and survived the war to become, amongst other things, a famous yachtsman, sailing the Great Lakes.

Inflexible Determination... / Role of Women... / The IODE fights on

In spite of the discord over conscription, the civilian support for the war effort in Winnipeg held firm. The 1917 Decoration Day parade, which took place on May 13, was the largest ever seen in Winnipeg, with 100,000 people lining the streets. Leading the parade were cars carrying wounded and disabled men, termed the "maimed," dressed in uniform. Behind them marched the new recruits and the Boy Scouts. Sailors from British Navy ships also marched in the parade, as did Lieutenant Ishigura, a local man who had served with the Japanese Red Cross in the Russo-Japanese War and had been awarded the highest decoration of the Japanese Empire.

A few months later, 8000 people crowded the Industrial Bureau auditorium to attend the August 4 ceremony that marked the third anniversary of the war. The front rows of the main floor were reserved for returned soldiers and troops training in the city. Hymns were

sung with great gusto and there were solos of "Abide with Me" and
"Invictus." The bands of the Winnipeg Grenadiers, 251st Battalion,
and the Salvation Army played. Premier Norris moved and General
Ruttan seconded a statement that "Winnipeg records its inflexible
determination to continue until the allies are victorious." Sir James
Aikins, T.C. Norris, and General Ruttan all spoke. Local clergymen
reminded the audience of the high ideals for which they were fighting,
using language that was high-minded and a little unrealistic. Reverend
C.R. Flanders of Broadway Methodist Church said, "in the trenches
there are no blacks or whites, Liberals or Tories, aristocrats or poor—
they are all one standing shoulder to shoulder." The Reverend Salem
Bland called the troops present "Knights of the last and holiest crusade."

One way in which Winnipeggers showed their determination to win
throughout the war was by donating money to the cause. Canadian
insurance companies, banks, and investment firms had already purchased $500 million worth of war bonds by spring 1917 when it was
decided to launch a campaign to sell Victory Bonds to the general
public. Augustus Nanton was asked to organize committees in each of
the Prairie provinces. The Manitoba committee, chaired by Nanton,
included local businessmen like A.L. Crossin, W.H. Gardner, R.T.
Riley, W.J. Christie, and Edward Brown, the provincial treasurer.

For many ordinary people the Victory Loan campaigns were the
first time they had ever heard of government bonds, let alone been
asked to buy them. Once again, as happened so often during the war,
parades played an important propagandistic role as the best means
of getting a message to large numbers of people. In Nanton's words,
the parade that launched the 1917 campaign in September "was the
greatest in Winnipeg's history, about three miles long and viewed, it is
estimated, by one hundred thousand people."

The campaign committees were enormously successful. The three
Manitoba Victory Loan drives, in 1917, 1918, and 1919 raised $32 mil-
lion, $43 million, and $42 million respectively for the war effort. On
a per capita basis, only Ontario sold more bonds. Nanton ran the
campaigns like a general and took a personal interest in every detail.
At one point he learned that a Saskatchewan farmer, on the verge of
paying off his mortgage, had told Nanton's firm that he wanted to

renew and use the money to buy war bonds. Nanton wrote to him personally: "My office will be pleased to renew the loan for you, and I am asking them in your case to do it at a reduced rate of interest ... your example in giving assistance to our country in her time of need and thereby furnishing help to those now defending us at the front is one which might well be followed by all true Britishers."[13] Nanton himself set a good example, although he was reluctant to have details of his donations made public. It was estimated that during the war he gave away close to half his personal fortune to war causes like the Patriotic Fund. In addition to managing Osler, Hammond and Nanton Limited and his other business interests he also worked long volunteer hours for the Patriotic Fund and organizing the Victory Loan campaigns.

Groups like the Red Cross and the IODE had reached a high level of efficiency and, not unlike the Canadian Corps in Europe, had become so professional and skilled that their largely female volunteers were now making a significant contribution to the war effort. This development had begun back in 1915, when it became clear that the war was not going to be brief and volunteer work at home had settled into a disciplined routine. In preparation for a larger Red Cross role in Winnipeg, local president George Galt arranged for board chair C.B. Piper to travel to Toronto to meet with the Canadian national executive committee in April 1915. Piper came back in a positive mood. He had won a concession: Winnipeg would pack its own shipments of hospital supplies that would be sent directly to London instead of being checked and repacked in Toronto. This change brought with it the responsibility of maintaining a strict quality control in Winnipeg so that everything shipped conformed to the Red Cross patterns and standards.

The local Red Cross lost no time putting the plan into action. The top floor of the Keewaydin Building on Portage Avenue East was renovated for use as the Winnipeg depot where hospital supplies would be collected and packed for shipment. The Red Cross invited the St. John Ambulance organization to join them in the space to continue their cooperative work. St. John Ambulance agreed, but stipulated that they wanted their own space, budget, and responsibilities, in keeping with the policy of separate organizations.

City councillor Fred Dixon was one of the most vocal critics of conscription.

The depot slowly took shape with the arrival of donations of coun-
ters, desks, and equipment from the Builders Exchange, Fairbanks
Morse, the Bank of Commerce, Heubach and Finkelstein, and
Manitoba Government Telephones. In September 1915 the space was
ready and the depot was handed over to the Women's Auxiliary. Piper
said that the depot was "essentially women's work and the executive

felt that the women should run it. Theirs will be the credit and they therefore have full responsibility and full authority."[14]

The new Red Cross organization experienced some growing pains. The actual work of producing the supplies was done by dozens of volunteer women's groups working in private homes, church basements, and community halls all over the province. Many of these women had not been kept informed about the creation of the depot and the new standards dictated by the national organization. On August 27 a special information meeting was held at Central Congregational Church on Hargrave Street so that women who had questions could ask them. Fanny Rice, who worked "behind the counter" at the new facility in the Keewaydin Building, explained that they had not been notified because the lists of working groups had been lost during the move. The disgruntled volunteers were promised a monthly meeting at which representatives from the various working groups could ask questions and hear reports.

After these initial problems, the work of the Red Cross depot proceeded smoothly. In the first six months of its existence, 409 large wooden cases of material were shipped directly to England. The cases contained supplies such as bandages, underclothes, hot water bottle covers, hospital gowns, pillows, pyjamas, socks, towels, quilts, and surgical dressings. The dressings were prepared and sterilized by nurses at the Winnipeg General Hospital and packed in sealed metal containers.

Each aspect of the depot's work was handled by a separate committee of volunteers. Raw materials, for example, were purchased centrally by Mrs. Bruce Hill and her group in Winnipeg. In their struggle to get the best prices in an environment of wartime inflation, they sometimes benefitted from insider information. In 1916, for example, a wholesaler tipped them off about an expected price war, and they were able to buy wool for 25 percent below the normal cost. Mrs. J.H. Turnbull and her group cut the cloth using Butterick patterns designated by the Red Cross to ensure uniformity, and sent it to sewing volunteers all over the city and province. Church and IODE groups, sewing circles of Aboriginal women on reserves, the auxiliaries of the various Manitoba and Winnipeg battalions, and local Red Cross branches stitched the items together.

When the garments and dressings returned to the Keewaydin Building, Mrs. K.H. Briggs and her committee checked everything carefully to make sure it met Red Cross standards. The quality of the work done by the sewing volunteers steadily improved and the amount of work that had to be corrected and re-sewn at the depot declined. The depot was able to challenge its expert workforce with special orders for such things as surgeons' gowns and amputation dressings, with a turnaround time of a mere three weeks from receiving the request to shipment.

One constant at the Red Cross depot was that about 600 pairs of woolen socks were shipped every week. Warm woolen socks were always extremely important to infantrymen, but during World War I they became essential. Men forced to stand in freezing water in the trenches for days at a time were always in danger of contracting "trench foot," a swelling and inflammation which, if left untreated, could result in gangrene and eventual amputation. The Canadians were the first troops to successfully combat the problem with daily changes of socks and smearing feet with whale oil.

Mrs. C.E. Hobbs and her group packed the completed items in wooden shipping cases—2200 cases were filled in 1917 alone—and sent them down in the elevator to the shipping room at the rear of the Keewaydin Building. They were taken to the railroad yards to begin their journey to Britain. From Red Cross warehouses they were shipped to "individual hospitals in the London area or to Canadian Red Cross depots in Shornecliffe Camp, Paris or Boulogne, and then finally to hospitals in those locations."[15]

The women managing the Winnipeg depot were, for the most part, the middle-class wives of managers and professional men. Mrs. Hill was married to a doctor, Mrs. Turnbull's husband was in the sash and door business, Mrs. Dawson Elliot and Mrs. R.C. Osborne were both married to Winnipeg business executives. Before the war many of these women volunteered for charities, but much of their time was spent participating in social activities like teas and luncheons. The social columns now reported on very few such social events that were not related to fundraising or sewing for the Red Cross, and devoted a good deal of space to the useful war work being done by women. In place of the pre-war social calendar, there were "Twilight

Knitting Teas" where tea was served while useful work was done. All over the city and rural Manitoba groups of women gathered in homes and churches and community halls to sew bandages and knit socks. Lady Nanton converted the music room in her Roslyn Road home into a workroom in which the women's auxiliary of the 27th City of Winnipeg Battalion sewed and collected "comforts" for the men of that unit. There was a realization among women that the war and the work they were doing to support the Canadian war effort were changing their role in society forever. The wife of lawyer Hugh Phillips later recalled the pre-war years as "days when we had ladies who wore white fox and rode in sleighs covered with fur robes. This way of life went with the war. After that there were no 'ladies.' We were all women, anxious for something to do."[16]

Women were also finding profound changes in the working world, and many were for the first time getting paid employment. In 1916 Mrs. Brotherhood of the Waskada, Manitoba, IODE commented, "We are, I think, realizing more and more the widening economic opportunities this war has afforded to women, for example the banks and technical schools are increasing the numbers of women employees...in fact we have less frills and more knitting and are much the better for it."[17] Later in the year, Mrs. H.P. Plumtre, of Red Cross headquarters in Toronto, said that, "most unexpectedly [the war] has demonstrated the value of women and has been the means of letting down the bars of prejudice against their entry into public life."[18] Some even suggested that the war was making Canadian women more spiritual: "Chief of all our duties comes that of helping forward the spiritual uplift which the war is bringing after so much materialism."[19]

In July 1917 the *Telegram* ran a full-page feature article on the work being done in the Keewaydin Building. The writer commented not only on the work itself but on the change it was making in the role of women in Winnipeg: "The ability of women to engage in great business undertakings is proven by the systematic manner in which supply and demand are gauged. Mrs. Bruce Hill, on whose capable shoulders devolve the responsibility of purchasing agent, who regularly buys 10,000 pounds of wool and 20,000 yards of union flannel not to mention numerous other items." The day-to-day organization and work of volunteer organizations had often fallen to women before the war, but the organizations they managed were now often much larger and more complex. The work done by women volunteers in many different settings helped in the struggle for equality with men and it was often cited as an argument for giving women the vote.

At Canadian military hospitals, wounded soldiers expressed their appreciation for the help offered by Canadian women. Mrs. R.F. McWilliams, the Red Cross publicity chair, quoted a soldier who said the Canadian pyjamas "are worth a lot." Of the Canadian hospitals, he wrote, "it was coming to in a Canadian hospital with Canadian nurses and the boys who had been my trench mates beside me that gave me a new interest in life. It wasn't exactly like home but it was the nearest thing to it that I've seen since I sailed." Nurses also expressed their gratitude. Sophie Hoerner, stationed in a hospital near Etaples in 1915, wrote that "the work of the Red Cross is keeping us going. We couldn't do without that. Its superb work and the boxes are all wonderful. Its our reserve when we run short and we need all and everything they send...the patients getting many comforts that they would have to do without."[20]

As the war progressed, more and more Canadian soldiers became prisoners of war, and one of the only ways their families could keep in touch with them was to send parcels of food and cigarettes. In the spring of 1917 letters from prisoners in Germany reached Winnipeg, in which the men complained that they were not receiving their parcels. Once again, Winnipeggers took action on behalf of their boys. C.B. Piper wrote to the Red Cross headquarters, stating that if the operation in London was not efficient, parcels could be packed in Winnipeg. Robert Rogers, who was in London at the time, spent a morning inspecting the Red Cross prisoner-of-war office and then wrote to reassure the Winnipeg branch that although there had been problems, changes would ensure a regular flow of parcels.

In fact, the prisoner-of-war office underwent a major reorganization in December 1916 when British and Canadian work for the prisoners was unified under a central prisoner-of-war committee. This was done to overcome the many problems that had resulted from lack of communication between the Canadian Ministry of Militia and the Red Cross. One of the changes made at this time was to eliminate the ability of families to send individual parcels to their relatives. Instead, generic parcels were sent to all prisoners on a regular schedule from the International Committee of the Red Cross in Switzerland.

This change was unpopular with some, but Clarence Piper defended the new system. In a story that appeared in Winnipeg newspapers, he outlined the eventualities that could delay parcels and the measures that the London Red Cross had put in place to overcome these delays. He pointed out that as food became scarcer in Germany the likelihood of parcels being stolen increased. The attention paid to the complaints of the prisoners demonstrated the care with which the Red Cross did its work, while it also showed the sensitivity to complaints of an organization that depended heavily on fundraising to pay its bills.

Women were heavily involved in raising funds for the Red Cross beginning in 1915, when over $120,000 was raised in Manitoba. As the war progressed, however, organizations like the Red Cross were finding it more difficult to attract donations. People had less money to give and, of course, there were many who had never donated at all. Like many other organizations dependent upon donations, the Red Cross began to feel that it would be more equitable to finance its work with tax money: not everyone who could afford to do so gave money but everyone paid taxes. Treasurer M.F. Christie encouraged Red Cross members to lobby their local government to provide support for the work of the Red Cross and the Patriotic Fund with tax dollars, at least until "the termination of the war." They were successful. In 1916 taxes were levied for these organizations, and in early 1917 the Red Cross received a grant of $100,000 as its share of the new tax income in Winnipeg.

The Red Cross also developed new ways to raise funds. A committee, headed by real estate developer W.H. Gardner, began to collect salvage items, such as clothes, tires, scrap metal, and magazines, which were then sold. On Christmas Day 1916, Boy Scouts spread out over the city in a driving snowstorm, collecting material and loading it into wagons provided by Manitoba Cartage and Eaton's. It was then taken to the Salvation Army building at 259 Fountain Street for storage. This first salvage drive raised $3500. In the years that followed the project expanded, and during 1917 over 25,000 Winnipeg school children collected scrap paper and carloads of material arrived in the city from rural areas.

The Women's Auxiliary of Winnipeg's 27th Battalion met regularly in the home of Constance Nanton on Roslyn Road to sew and knit for the men of the unit.

In the spring of 1918 the Red Cross ran a large fundraising campaign in Winnipeg that employed the first telephone solicitation in the history of the city. From noon, on Saturday, April 6, to the evening of Monday, April 8, sixty women volunteered in three shifts, calling 21,000 homes to solicit donations. They were equipped with a bank of fifteen phones in the campaign headquarters in the Kennedy Building and all the callers had "professional" headsets provided by Manitoba Government Telephones. The callers, many of whom were employed in downtown banks, had a script and were told not to get involved in answering questions. There were three team captains, Mrs. Bruce Campbell, Miss Florence Windatt and Miss Ruth Hesson. The idea originated with R. Young of the telephone system, and lawyer, real estate developer and mayor of Tuxedo David Finkelstein. In contrast to today, only one person in 1000 responded uncivilly or with curses.

One girl said that when she had finished calling all the Campbells and Camerons in the phone book she felt like she had talked to the whole "battalion of the 79th Cameron Highlanders."

The Women's Auxiliary continued to expand the supply depot, and during 1916 their budget reached $32,000, spent mostly on raw materials. From this, the volunteers produced $87,000 worth of supplies. The women's groups who did the sewing thus donated $55,000 worth of labour, roughly the equivalent of $1.3 million in today's funds. In 1917 the figures were $70,000 for materials, $105,000 worth of supplies, and $35,000 in volunteer hours. The decrease in volunteer hours arose partly from the decision to have the material cut in Winnipeg garment factories, where the work was done for free and with greater efficiency.

In 1917 John Galt, still president of the Manitoba Red Cross, paid tribute to the work of women volunteers. "It is the women to whom Canada must extend thanks," he said, for the excellence of the Red Cross hospitals. He added that, thanks to the excellent hospitals doctors and nurses had available to them, wounded men actually had a better chance of survival than in any previous war. The Red Cross continued its work after the end of the war, making sure there were volunteers and small comforts to make the lives of the men confined to military hospitals more pleasant.

IODE members in Winnipeg also continued to work toward the defeat of Germany in a variety of ways. The war had brought to the attention of the ladies of the Fort Garry chapter and other IODE units the suffering of people in non-British Allied nations. In mid-January 1916, Winnipeg women heard a lecture by a Mr. Rose about conditions in Poland, which had become a battlefield during 1915 and where conditions for the civilian population were terrible. After the talk the Polish anthem was played and one of the IODE members, Mrs. Smith Jones, recited the words of the anthem in English, "with marked effect." A collection was taken, with twenty-eight dollars donated to the Polish Society.

During a special "Serbian Week," 38,000 articles of hospital supplies were collected in Manitoba and shipped to Serbian hospitals. A Belgian Week in June concentrated on collecting canned food, and the Fort Garry chapter set up a collection table in the lobby of the

Boyd Building on Portage Avenue. Mrs. Lightcap and Mrs. Wilson sat at the table in the morning and Mrs. Goldstein and Mrs. McKay took the afternoon shift.

Mrs. Goldstein and a Mrs. Kaplansky were among the first Jewish Winnipeggers to begin the process of integrating into organizations like the IODE. Mrs. Goldstein was the IODE treasurer in 1915 and put on a fundraising event that involved members in operating the National Picture House for two days and securing the income from admissions for the IODE. She was nominated for a position on the 1916 provincial executive but declined to stand because of other commitments.

One important issue during the first months of the war had been the ability of women to object to their husbands or sons volunteering for the army, if they felt that the men were needed at home to support them. Sam Hughes had made it clear that no man whose dependents needed him would be accepted. Indeed, over 300 men were sent home from Valcartier in the weeks leading up to the departure of the first contingent because their wives had sent letters of objection. The IODE national president Mrs. Gooderham joined others in condemning these letters. She addressed an open letter to women who tried to hold their husbands back from the army, reminding them that Canada was not only fighting for the Empire, but because their own country might well be ruled by Germans if the Allied cause failed. She added that "the most compelling call for sacrifice rings out from the graves of those who on the fields of Flanders, at Langemark, and Ypres, and Festubert have blazed a trail of glory with their life blood. Can we make their self surrender of no avail by holding back these men who would take up and complete their splendid task."[21] Within a short time, faced with the difficulty of getting enough volunteers, the government discontinued the right of spouses to object to their husbands' enlistment. The IODE had played a role in making this change.

At times, a specific event would produce a response as the women tried to play a role in helping their sons and husbands survive at the front. In May 1915 Mrs. McKay, a member of the Fort Garry chapter executive, received a letter from her son saying that the men in the trenches had a hard time getting cigarettes. The IODE responded immediately by putting collection boxes in twenty-six city cigar stores to raise funds to buy tobacco for the men. Mrs. McKay and Mrs.

Albert Crossin pulling a cardboard tank in a Victory Bond parade.

Colonel Sam Steele, the wife of the commanding officer of Military District Number 10, collected the money and organized the shipment of cigarettes to Flanders and England. In all, they sent 300 packs of cigarettes, mostly to the Duchess of Connaught Hospital at Cliveden, the main Canadian hospital in England. A month later another 536 packages of cigarettes were sent.

As the provision of tobacco to the soldiers overseas became a major activity throughout Canada, some women's groups began attacking the practice. Members of the Women's Christian Temperance Union strongly believed that tobacco was as harmful for young men as liquor and they opposed the use of Red Cross funds to buy it for the troops. In fact, Mrs. J. Waters, a temperance leader from Hamilton, said that "all who send tobacco to soldiers at the front are participating in a national crime."[22] But the men appreciated the smokes as one of the few things that alleviated the boredom and discomfort of life at the front, and so the shipments continued. The 44th Battalion history made special mention of the cigarettes given out to the men: "The survivors of these days will, perhaps, never forget the cigarettes that are issued free (but not freely): Red Hussars, Allied Flags, 'arf a mo,' Trumpeter; nor the French Briquette lighters bought in the canteen, that, all too often, continue to smoulder after being returned to the pocket. But most of all the smokers enjoy the 'Players' that come, usually, in the parcels from home. Their round tin is ideal for measuring out the morning rum ration."[23]

In October 1916 the Fort Garry IODE listened to a talk by Major J.W. Andrews about life in the trenches. He assured them that the men appreciated receiving the field comforts, especially socks and cigarettes. An army nurse, Miss Hood, confirmed that the men being treated at the Connaught Hospital at Cliveden were happy to receive cigarettes from home.

The IODE was seen by many Canadian women as a place where they could do their duty. In January 1917, when Prime Minister Borden made a plea to the men of Canada to volunteer for the army, the Manitoba chapter of the IODE passed a resolution supporting him. They expressed once again their commitment in this new kind of total war, pledging that they "would leave nothing undone in our service for our Country, believing every man woman and child is called to the colors to sacrifice and service and that victory and peace will come only when all do their duty." By 1917 the total Canadian membership of the order had risen to 40,000, twice what it had been in 1914. In 1916 and 1917, eighty-nine new chapters had been established across the country. During 1917 these members and chapters raised a total of $800,000 for various war charities—an amount roughly equivalent to $20 million today.[24]

The IODE was involved in creating memorials for the dead, in graveyards like the Brooklands Cemetery and elsewhere. On May 10, 1917, the IODE along with other city women's groups began to plan a memorial that would eventually become the Women's Tribute Building at Deer Lodge Hospital. There was a parade of returned soldiers and women carrying the Union Jack through the streets and collecting money for a memorial. They then went to a concert at the Walker Theatre, with Lieutenant Dunwoody, a wounded veteran, as the master of ceremonies. Some of the men sang trench songs, suitably cleaned up for the audience. Manitobans who had been serving in the French Army were there and they came dressed in their French uniforms. The Women's Volunteer Auxiliary were out in their uniforms, and hundreds of widows attended dressed in black. People from the audience, including many of the women who had lost their husbands, walked across the stage one by one to announce how much money they were contributing to the cause. The tragedy and loss produced by the war was given human form as these black-clad women crossed the stage. And the war would create many more widows in the city in the year and a half remaining before the armistice.

1918

For Winnipeg, 1918 would be a year of new challenges, a year when the effects of the war would combine with other factors that shaped the city in the coming years. Anti-foreign and nationalist sentiments would drive a growing distrust of the city's non-British residents and impatience with those who opposed the war. The majority of the population continued to support the war effort as conscripted men and a smaller number of volunteers left for the front. The massive German advance in the spring was followed by the Allied response beginning in August. Canada's "hundred days," the period from August to November when Canadian troops distinguished themselves as some of the toughest and most successful in the British forces, ended with the final collapse of the German Army.

Meanwhile, the wounded came home and the city's military hospitals expanded to accommodate them. In the months after the armistice all the troops returned home bringing with them their memories, their trauma and their pride in the victory. The impact of the return of these men is a story that cannot be told here because it worked itself out over many years.

Just as the city was preparing to celebrate victory, the global influenza epidemic assaulted the city, killing 1300 Winnipeggers and infecting many more. Esyllt Jones in her study of the epidemic, *Influenza 1918*, writes that "many thousands were infected. At the peak of the epidemic in early November 1918, there were nearly 700 new cases reported to medical authorities daily."[1] Jones shows how the disease overwhelmed the health care resources of the city so that many victims died without having been treated. Not that there was any effective treatment in the days before antibiotics. Living conditions, nutrition, and general health played a major role in whether patients survived the infection, so the death rate was much higher among the city's poorest families.

There were also many flu victims among the returning troops. For reasons that are still not completely understood, the influenza killed young healthy individuals in great numbers and took a terrible toll amongst soldiers. Allen Arnett McLeod, who won the Victoria Cross for showing great courage in action as a pilot over the Western Front and returned to Winnipeg on October 1, was met at the station by a large crowd and two military bands. Three streetcars took him and some of the crowd home to Stonewall. A short time later it was reported that he had caught the flu and died.

Conscientious Objectors

Earlier in the year, in January 1918, new groups of 120 draftees were arriving each day at the Minto Armoury. Once there, they rose early, spent the day drilling and taking care of their equipment, and were in bed by 9:30 p.m. After a few weeks of this uneventful routine they would begin to move out on their way to England.

Those few who insisted upon not joining up on the basis of their religious or political beliefs were given a much more difficult time. The *Military Service Act*, which established conscription in 1917, provided that an exemption would be given to "Persons who, from doctrines of their religion, are averse to bearing arms or rendering personal military service, under such conditions as are prescribed." The conditions named only the Quakers, Doukhobors, and Mennonites as being exempt from military service. While groups not specifically mentioned, such as the Seventh Day Adventists and the Plymouth Brethren, an evangelical sect with a long history of objecting to military service, asked that persons claiming to be conscientious objectors be examined on a case-by-case basis, they were not successful in convincing the exemption tribunals. Non-religious, philosophical objections to war

Captain Christopher O'Kelly was one of the men from Winnipeg who won a Victoria Cross at the battle of Passchendaele. He survived the war but died in a boating accident near Red Lake, Ontario, in 1922.

were also not considered. It appears, however, that if a man agreed to join the army but did not want to be involved in killing the enemy he could usually be assigned to non-combatant roles.

William Ivens, minister of the McDougall Methodist Church, spoke out in favour of expanding the conscientious objector category. He said that people objected to serving in the war on the basis not only of religion but also on intellectual grounds or because they were socialists. He argued that all these categories should be recognized in the Act. Expressing opinions like this in the last year of the war was risky, and Ivens was criticized by some members of his congregation and asked to step down from his post. In June 1918 he founded a new Labor Church in Winnipeg and he continued to oppose conscription and the war.

One group that opposed military service in an organized manner was the International Bible Students or Russellites, now generally known as Jehovah's Witnesses. This small sect—they numbered less than 100 in Winnipeg according to the 1916 census—were deeply committed to pacifism and not even willing, as some were, to take on non-combatant roles in the army. In March 1916 the Canadian Russellites had written to their founder Charles T. Russell in Britain, asking for guidance on what to do about military service. Russell wrote an answer that was published in the *Watchtower* magazine, the group's publication. He quoted relevant sections of the *Military Service Act* and gave his followers the wording for an affidavit that they could file with the military, claiming exemption on the basis of their religious beliefs. Neither the affidavits nor the arguments contained in them made any impression upon the exemption tribunals, and the Russellites were told to report for duty.

The experiences of three Russellites from Winnipeg, Robert Clegg, Ralph Naish, and Charles Matheson, became front-page news for a brief period in January 1918. Their story reveals a good deal about the climate of opinion in Winnipeg at the time and the deep divisions conscription was creating. Because there was a military inquiry into their case, the transcript of which survives, we have an unusually detailed record of what happened to them.

Robert Clegg, the main character in the drama, was a thirty-two-year-old clerk, a native of Liverpool. He and Ralph Naish were friends and they and other members of their sect, on the advice of the elder H.E. Cameron, had agreed that they would not respond to their conscription notice, but wait to be arrested. Naish described that moment: "a Military Policeman came down to my house around 11 o'clock and asked me if I was going to report. I showed him the notice I had had from Mr. Chapman, the Conscription Registrar, I said I was a conscientious objector," and would not swear any oaths of allegiance.

Naish and Clegg were arrested and taken to military police headquarters in the Immigration Hall on Higgins Avenue. There they refused to sign their attestation papers and swear an oath of loyalty to the king, the acts which marked the entry of a civilian into the army. Robert Clegg's attestation paper was signed by an officer with the notation, "I certify that this has been read over to Private Clegg, R.L. and he refuses to sign it as a conscientious objector."

The two men arrived at the Minto Armoury at four in the afternoon on Friday January 18. They were separated, and Naish was taken to an orderly room where, he said, "about five officers" questioned him on his beliefs: "Well, I was subjected to some very coarse and very rude remarks, which I didn't retaliate to in any way, from various of the officers."

Naish and his friend met on Friday evening in the dining hall, in the basement of the building. They discussed how they were going to deal with the various problems confronting them, such as whether or not to sign for and take army equipment such as dishes, blankets, or uniforms. They decided not to do so, nor would they eat army food or do any work. They were soon both confined to the guardroom lockup, charged with disobeying an order to join a work detail.

On Tuesday morning they were taken before Major Bolton, their company commander, to receive punishment. Naish was confined to barracks for two days, but Clegg was taken before Colonel Hugh Osler, the commander of the depot. After some questioning he was given the same punishment. At this point soldiers would normally have been returned to their company, but instead the two Russellites were turned over to the provost sergeant and taken back to the guardroom. This departure from normal procedure was not commented on by the inquiry.

In the afternoon they were taken separately from the guardroom by military policemen and walked down to the basement of the armoury to the shower room. The provost sergeant, Gordon Simpson, and other military policemen all testified that they gave the men the usual "regimental bath" that was standard procedure for soldiers before being issued a uniform. Both men refused to undress for their shower, and Simpson said that Clegg had told him that "they will never clothe me," meaning he was going to refuse to put on the uniform. Simpson told the enquiry that "I told him he had better reconsider this thing, as he was going to soldier, and there was no use in him making enemies in the barracks." Simpson held out the possibility of being assigned non-combatant duties: "I also told him we had had similar men to him, Conscientious Objectors who had agreed to put on the uniform and do work around the barracks."

Clegg made it clear to the sergeant that he was not about to take this route and "under no consideration would he do anything...as it would show he was part of the military machine." Naish took the same position. He told the enquiry that he was undressed and put into a shower stall and held there under ice-cold water. After about five minutes the water was turned off and he was asked, "Now will you put on the khaki?" When he said no, he was put back into the stream of cold water. Eventually he collapsed, was propped up against the wall, and sprayed with a fire hose. Then he was taken back to his cell in the guardroom.

Charles Matheson described similar treatment. When he put up a hand to protect himself from the cold water, Simpson made him take it down. He took Matheson out of the shower and asked, "Do you give in now?" When Matheson said no, Simpson replied, "In again," and pushed him back into the stall. Finally he was taken back to the guardroom where he was told he would be taken to the showers every fifteen minutes until he gave in. Matheson did give in and swore his oath the second time he was taken down to the basement. He said, "When I said what I said I didn't say it from my heart at all; it was just fairly wrung out of me...I am kind of nervous, and I guess it upset my nerves."

Robert Clegg also described being undressed by Sergeant Simpson and led to a shower stall. Clegg testified that the water was ice cold and that after about fifteen minutes he was taken out and told to dry himself. He refused to do this, and so Simpson dried him above the waist and had him dressed. Simpson then told two of the military policemen to run him around the basement to warm him up. They held him up during this run. Then they took him back to the guardroom.

After a period of time—different times were given by different witnesses—Clegg was again taken down for another cold shower. Afterwards, he was unable to walk and was dragged all the way back to his cell. He told of seeing an officer in the shower room, wearing the bonnet of a Scots regiment and on the way back to the guardroom the military policemen pulled him up onto his feet in front of an officer. These details suggest that his treatment was known to and approved by officers in the depot, and that the army's claim that the men were simply the victims of hazing by private soldiers was untrue.

Clegg lay on the guardroom floor covered with Naish's overcoat. He was moaning and complaining of cold and seemed to be only semiconscious. Sergeant Simpson and several other military policemen later testified they thought he was just malingering and pretending to be sick. At the time, however, Simpson seems to have been worried enough to go to his superior, the adjutant, Captain W.C.D. Crombie, and say, "if there is something wrong with this man wouldn't it be best to safeguard ourselves and send him to hospital." A medical orderly, Sergeant Gibbons, also told Crombie that Clegg was in pretty bad shape and that "he didn't want to have the responsibility of keeping him in the barracks during the night."

And so Clegg was sent to St. Boniface Hospital in an ambulance. Once there, an army doctor, Lieutenant A.T. Mathers, said Clegg was chilled and exhibiting symptoms of shock. The nurse who checked him said he was very cold and his pulse was quite high, probably because of "nervousness." She gave him brandy and massaged his arms and legs and he began to calm down. He stayed in the hospital for ten days.

On January 23, the day after he was given his cold showers, Clegg signed an affidavit in which he described the treatment to which he had been subjected. The document was prepared for Clegg by Winnipeg lawyer J.E. Davidson, who, with E.J. McMurray, had been retained by the Russellite elder H.E. Cameron to represent the men. McMurray would be one of the lawyers for the leaders of the General Strike in 1919 and would serve as McKenzie King's attorney general in the 1920s.

On January 25 the affidavit appeared in the *Free Press*. Printed beside it was a letter from Private Paul Case, an American volunteer in the Canadian Army, who had witnessed some of the events in the shower rooms. He had sent a letter to the *Free Press* and the *Telegram* on January 23, describing the treatment Clegg and Naish had received and saying that he and other soldiers, "as men, regret that there are those who would tolerate such treatment on human beings when it would be unlawful to mete out such treatment to even a dog."[2] Case also objected to an official statement issued by the military that had said that the conscientious objectors had simply been "man handled" during some harmless hazing by their fellow soldiers and that the authorities at the barracks knew nothing of it. He pointed out that men could not be sent to the guardroom except by the orders of a commissioned officer. These were serious charges and made it very difficult to ignore the matter.

Case was considerably less talkative the next day when he was called to testify at the military inquiry. By that time he had likely been informed of the serious consequences of his letter writing. He refused to answer any questions, beyond admitting that he had sent the letter to the papers. As an American citizen, he had wanted the American consul to be present. The consul stated that Case's status as a soldier in the Canadian Army meant that he could do nothing for him. Case was placed under arrest, and he, too, was held in the armoury's guardroom.

The army tried to downplay the importance of what had happened to Clegg and his co-religionists. The registrar of the *Military Service Act*, E.R. Chapman, said the men were being most unreasonable, and the minister of militia, General Mewburn, informed the prime minister that the case was greatly exaggerated. Sergeant Simpson was charged with "hazing" and his court martial began to hear evidence.

The lawyers E.J. McMurray and J.E. Davidson had Simpson brought before Magistrate Hugh John Macdonald charged with assault causing bodily harm. Macdonald refused to hear the case because he said it was a matter for a military court. His decision was appealed to the Court of King's Bench where, on February 13, the two lawyers appeared before Justice Galt. They argued that Macdonald should be ordered to hear the case because Canada was governed by civil, not military law, as far as criminal charges like assault were concerned. The lawyer for the army, Captain Harry Whitla, said that it was too late to try Simpson in a civil court because his court martial was already underway. He argued that since both men had been in uniform when the alleged assault took place, they were governed by military law.

McMurray said that H.E. Cameron had sworn that Clegg was unlawfully assaulted, and Whitla interrupted, asking, "Who is this Cameron?" McMurray explained that he was an elder in the Bible Students Society. Judge Galt interjected, "Oh, those people whose literature has just been prohibited in Canada." McMurray answered, "Yes Your Lordship, I am ashamed to say so."[3]

When Galt asked if Clegg himself had any complaints, he was told that Clegg had testified at Simpson's court martial that he had not authorized any action and had not requested the arrest of Simpson. Galt then dismissed the appeal and ordered Cameron to pay the costs. Two days later, Simpson's court martial ended with the finding that the charges against Simpson were groundless and that he was not guilty of "hazing." Cameron allowed the matter to drop.

The military authorities had been able to keep the matter of Clegg's treatment from leading to any serious legal action. The fact that Macdonald, Galt, Whitla, and Osler were all members of the Winnipeg elite, well known to each other and sharing similar views about the war, made this task easier.

Not everyone agreed with the handling of the matter. Fred Dixon announced that he was investigating the incident, and Winnipeg member of Parliament Thomas Crerar, the minister of agriculture in the Union government and the future leader of the Progressive Party, brought it to the attention of the minister of militia, General Mewburn. Crerar noted that the case was attracting a good deal of negative attention in the newspapers. Still, Mewburn told the prime minister that, from what he could understand, the case was not of great importance.

Members of the public were upset by the news reports about Clegg's treatment. The Roaring River branch of the Manitoba Grain Growers sent a resolution to General Mewburn, objecting to the treatment the men had received, which the group described as "German frightfulness methods being used in Canada." Mrs. E.C. Tingling wrote to the *Free Press* on January 24, saying that she was concerned and as she was personally acquainted with General Ruttan, the commanding officer of Military District 10, she had gone to his house to talk to him about the matter. He had assured her that it would be fully investigated. Mrs. Tingling apparently wanted to pass this reassuring news on to the paper's readers.

About a month later another court martial found Clegg and several others guilty of refusing to obey an order and sentenced them to two years hard labour in Stony Mountain Penitentiary. One of the men, David Wells, was, for some reason, sent on to the Selkirk Mental Hospital, where he committed suicide shortly after. The other men did not serve their sentences at Stony Mountain. According to army routine orders, they were released and sent to England, under arrest, with a draft of new recruits. This practice was objected to by relatives and friends of the men, and telegrams were sent to Prime Minister Borden, but nothing was done to stop their being sent overseas. After the war, there were charges in a Jehovah's Witness publication, the *Golden Age*, that the men were mistreated while in Seaford Camp in England. It was reported that they were punched and kicked and threatened with execution. This sort of treatment was often experienced by British conscientious objectors at the hands of sergeants trying to get them to become soldiers and obey orders, although it was not so common by this time because the War Office had officially forbidden it in September 1916. Commanding officers were instructed to court martial and punish the objectors by military law and not try to torture them into submission. Nevertheless, the mistreatment continued in the war zones. Fourteen Seventh Day Adventists serving in the British Army in France were imprisoned for refusing to work on the Sabbath. One of these men later described their treatment:

> In the most offensive and blasphemous language we were told that this particular prison was the worst place in France, that they were able to break men's hearts there, and that after a few days we should be glad enough to work seven days a week. As soon as we ceased work, five or six sergeants armed with sticks and revolvers rushed at us and knocked us down in turn with their fists. As each man rose from the ground this treatment was repeated. The attack was renewed with sticks and we were brutally kicked whilst we were on the ground. Two now drew their revolvers, but were prevented from firing by the others. We made no resistance.[4]

The *Free Press* expressed the naive hope that if the Winnipeg Russellites "made good" in the trenches they would earn a pardon for the crimes for which they had been sentenced and "might yet become good soldiers." The sentences of the conscientious objectors were remitted in October of 1918 and they were sent home. Robert Clegg was released from the army in early December 1918.

A crowd gathers at city hall to support the 1918 Salvation Army campaign to fund services for returned soldiers.

Many others were sentenced to two years hard labour at this time. Joseph Murray, for example, went before Magistrate Macdonald on January 25, charged with being a military absentee because he refused to report when he received his notice. He claimed to be a conscientious objector on the grounds of his socialist beliefs. Macdonald discounted his claim because he said he was an atheist and sentenced him to two years in the penitentiary. Another man, David Cook, a farmer and conscientious objector, was also sent to jail for two years for refusing to serve.

Pacifists paid a high price for their beliefs in Winnipeg in the last years of the war. After four years of sacrifice and loss, feelings against anyone who would not support the cause were very strong. J.S. Woodsworth, by then a prominent clergyman and social worker, lost his position with the Methodist Church because of his strict pacifist philosophy and was forced to make his living as a dock hand in British Columbia. Both the Beynon sisters, well-known journalists and political activists, left the city to live in New York. Lillian Thomas, formerly Lillian Beynon, left when her husband, Vernon Thomas, was fired from his job at the *Free Press*. He had been in the press gallery at the legislature when F.J. Dixon made a stirring anti-war speech. Thomas walked out onto the floor of the legislature and shook Dixon's hand, a gesture for which J.W. Dafoe fired him. Lillian's sister, Francis Beynon, soon followed the Thomases, also because her pacifist views were so unpopular in Winnipeg.

Exemptions, Treason, and Anti-Foreign Hysteria ✓

There were many others who did not want to fight. On February 4 the Military Service Council made its first report to Cabinet in Ottawa, revealing that 52,000 men across Canada had claimed exemption and, in many instances, their cases were still pending; 4000 more had simply not reported when called up, while 19,612 had joined the colours. On February 13 the first contingent of 936 drafted men left Winnipeg for the front. At this point in the war the enthusiasm of the volunteers of 1914 was long gone and there was no longer any doubt about conditions at the front or about a soldier's chances of survival. As well, members of visible minority groups and "non British" ethnic groups had no illusions about the racist treatment they were likely to experience from many of their fellow soldiers and superiors in the armed forces.

The local registrar of the *Military Service Act*, J.B. Toole, frustrated by the small numbers of new troops being secured through conscription, began to depart from the procedures outlined in the Act. He sent a questionnaire to all the men in Winnipeg who had been exempted from the service, explaining that he wanted to ensure they were actually deserving of an exemption. A few weeks later, during an interview with the *Telegram*, he complained that "under the voluntary system of enlistment the young man who did not at least try to do his bit for his country was considered a 'slacker,' but now it is considered the proper thing for people to buck the Act by putting up all sorts of excuses to get these people exempted. It is preventing the proper working of the Act. There are 23,000 exempted men in District 10 and a very large proportion of these have no right to be exempted." Toole said that he was angry that many employers helped their workers to get exemptions and he predicted that only around 5 percent of available men would actually go to France.

Winnipeg was second only to Montreal in the percentage of men who had defaulted or not shown up when drafted—19.67 percent, compared to 25.81 percent in Montreal. The Dominion Police were very active arresting draft evaders. One of their favourite tactics was to ride the streetcars, as described by a *Telegram* reporter:

> A young man stepped into the car. Very soon a polite gentleman either sat down beside him or leaned in over him, turned up a coat lapel to disclose his badge of authority and quietly inquired if he had evidence to show why he should not be in khaki. Where evidence was forthcoming nothing untoward happened. The polite gentleman merely hovered about until a new possible victim appeared and then spoke to him. The result was a steady procession from street cars to the Boyd Building where the headquarters of the force are located. There the young men proceeded to make arrangements to produce documentary evidence of their freedom from service, or else they were hurried out to the barracks to await further investigation.[5]

With the beginning of the massive German advance on March 21, alarm spread through the country that the Allies were in danger of losing the war for want of reinforcements. It seemed that the sacrifices of the past four years had been for nothing. In early April, Robert Borden asked Cabinet to approve an Order-in-Council cancelling all exemptions and calling everyone up due to the situation in France. Essentially, the Order-in-Council replaced the system laid down in the Act with universal conscription. Cabinet debated the issue for three days. On April 17 it was announced that all exemptions would be cancelled for men between twenty and twenty-three. The Order-in-Council said that "an immediate and urgent need for reinforcements for the Canadian Expeditionary Force" was the reason. The only exemption now possible was that of having a family member already serving.[6] Many men whose exemptions had been cancelled rushed to enlist in the cavalry, artillery, or the flying corps in the belief that these arms of the military were less deadly than the infantry.

All across the country desperate measures were taken to raise troops. Police raided pool halls looking for eligible men. All men had to carry their conscription papers at all times and men picked up on the street were sometimes taken directly to army camps.[7] Those who did not show up when called were fined $200 and charged the equivalent of army pay for each day they stayed away.

The general atmosphere of worry over the outcome of the war and bitterness because of the price the country had already paid created an unsettled state of mind in Canada. There was increased concern about spies and uneasiness about what was perceived as the growing threat of the left. The "Bolsheviki" had overthrown Britain's ally, Tsar Nicholas, and taken Russia out of the war and, after the collapse of Imperial Germany, there appeared to be a real possibility of soviet style governments in Germany and Hungary. These events, along with growing union activity in Canada, resulted in more attempts on the part of the police to harass and control left-wing activists. Indeed, some scholars have called this the "second front of the war," meaning the campaign waged against labour and left-wing political groups in Canada under the authority of the *War Measures Act*.[8]

The police began to pay closer attention to Winnipeggers suspected of treasonous ideas. This broad category included an assortment of suspected sympathizers with the German cause, left wingers and, conscientious objectors. Once again the tiny Jehovah's Witnesses group came in for completely unwarranted scrutiny. In early April the military police raided the homes of Russellites, searching for prohibited literature, specifically a book called *The Finished Mystery*. The Bible students were erroneously believed to be pro-German—they were suspected of being traitors in Germany too—and their publications, including the *Watchtower*, were banned in the consolidated orders on censorship under the *War Measures Act*.

The police arrested eight Winnipeg Bible students: W.L. Brown, Mrs. A.L. Vanstone, a Mr. Maunders, J.T. Bevan, E. McAllister, A.G. Cameron, C. Sherman, and L.G. Des Brisays. They appeared before Hugh John Macdonald, charged under the *Defence of the Realm Act*. He gave them suspended sentences and warned them that if they were charged again he would impose heavy fines and jail time. He added the bizarre statement that they would have been burned at the stake in Henry VIII's time. Macdonald, an Anglican and a well-respected figure in the city, was expressing the sort of hostility we can assume many people were feeling toward people who were not doing their part to win the war. The Russellites' lawyer, E.J. McMurray commented that the Crown could not ban any religion, but the Crown prosecutor R.B. Graham countered that a religion could indeed be banned, because Parliament could pass any law for the benefit of the country.

Idleness was added to treason as an offence when an anti-loafing Order-in-Council was passed during April. Perhaps one of the silliest of the measures that came out of the overheated atmosphere of 1918, it provided that a magistrate would examine men arrested for loafing and decide whether or not they were usefully employed. This was too much even for the *Telegram* and the paper commented that "the day of heavy and prolonged standing around has passed. The Ancient and Benighted Order of the Sons of Rest has been suppressed by the Legislative Ukase on the grounds that a surfeit of leisure is a national liability."

It was no joke for the men arrested. At the end of April, the first man apprehended in Winnipeg was brought before Magistrate Hugh John Macdonald, who fined him ten dollars. The man was a tailor, Gabriel Solaway from Toronto. He said he had recently arrived in Winnipeg and was looking for a regular job. He could not speak English very well and may not have understood the nature of his crime. By May 1 the police had a list of idle people. Two more men had been arrested, one caught sunning himself on the bank of the Assiniboine and the other walking along the street on McMillan Avenue. Nationwide, 700 idlers had been arrested.

On May 4, with the situation at the front still perilous, it was announced that all nineteen-year-old men would go into the army with no exemptions allowed. Only the medically unfit would be spared, and a month later 43,136 nineteen-year-olds had registered, 2982 of them in Winnipeg.

The level of tension over the war continued to rise and the actions of police and magistrates reflected this. In June, military intelligence began arresting people for seditious remarks. William Ged, a

Netherlander, was arrested in the downtown Bowes Dairy Lunch for saying "that he hoped the Germans win the war." George Schwab of 548 Aberdeen Avenue got into trouble when he told his son not to put on the Canadian uniform when he was drafted but to die like a good German. The son did put on the uniform. Nick Balan of 448 King Street and Nick Kostiniuk of 253 Austin Street were both arrested for saying the Germans would hang every Canadian when they got here. All these dangerous agitators appeared before Hugh John Macdonald.

Ukrainian and other eastern European men, smarting from the treatment they and their compatriots had received during the war, were not now anxious to be drafted. There were many accounts in the papers of the campaign the police waged to conscript them into the army. Fred Jacks, a "Russian Pole" from Whitemouth, was arrested as the leader of a group of men who were determined to avoid military service. The Dominion Police had tracked him down at his mother's house where he confronted them with a rifle and said he would not be taken. The policeman drew his revolver and told him to surrender. Jacks did and was charged.

Dominion and military police, raiding in the Whitemouth area, arrested eight men. They were all "of alien nationality, but most of them are British subjects" and therefore eligible to be drafted. Many of them resisted arrest and would be tried by a military court. The *Telegram* commented sourly that they "will likely receive very heavy jail sentences for resistance; in almost any other country but Canada they would face a firing squad at sunrise in the old approved manner." In mid-September the Dominion Police, searching at Winnipeg Beach for draft evaders, were met by a group of women armed with pitchforks, determined to protect their husbands. The police nevertheless arrested fifteen men.

At this time Magistrate Noble of the Provincial Police Court was levying fines of ten to twenty-five dollars against people who were apprehended without their marriage licence or other documents that proved their exempt status. Noble turned many men over to the military police to be enrolled in the army. About seventy-five men appeared before Noble, charged as draft evaders or as having aided evaders. He fined two men $100 each for the latter offence. His justification was revealing; he said the very steep fine was intended "not

so much to punish these people as to stamp out this beginning of an-
archy in the country; we cannot allow the Bolsheviki to get a foothold
here." Noble seems to have seen himself as being in the front lines of a
struggle against social dissolution.

The defeat of the German forces was becoming more of a certainty
by the fall, and the men of the Canadian Corps were distinguishing
themselves by their bravery and the success of their determined
advance deep into the territory behind German lines. The Hundred
Days of fighting from the beginning of the offensive on August 1 to
the German surrender on November 11 was a glorious success for
Canada's army. On the last day of the war it was the Canadians who
recaptured Mons, the city that had witnessed the first defeat of the
British Army in 1914.

Worry over losing the war gradually subsided as the Allies pushed
the Germans back in France and Belgium. On September 23, Registrar
Toole, who had just returned from a conference in Ottawa, announced
that there would be no new drafts until the new year and that nineteen-year-olds would not be called up until then. For the first time in
four years, the pressure to recruit new men was off. By the time of the
Armistice, the *Military Service Act* had cost $3,661,417 to administer
and had produced 24,132 new Canadian soldiers on French soil and
75,519 men in training in England for a total of 99,651 troops. This
was very close to Borden's original goal of 100,000 additional troops,
and the drafted men had played a role both in gaining the victory and
relieving some of the Canadians who had been in the fighting for a
very long time. If the war had continued, they would have been a crucial element in securing a final victory.

At home, the pursuit of draft evaders became less important, and the
police turned their attention to searching for spies and revolutionaries
who wanted to overthrow the government. On October 3, a massive
raid was conducted by Deputy Police Chief Newton, four Winnipeg
city police, and nine military policemen. They raided fourteen houses
and offices of a wide variety of organizations belonging to "foreigners" and confiscated one and a half tons of paper, which would now
have to be examined and translated to determine if it was seditious
under the *War Measures Act*. Books published in both Ukrainian and
Russian were banned, leading to raids of printing plants, like that of

Rabotokyz Narod in Winnipeg. Police also raided the Liberty Temple and the New Labor Temple at Pritchard and McGregor, bookstores at 798 Main and 822 Main, Baker Press at 394 Selkirk, and the Israelite Press at 811 Main Street. They entered the houses of several people known to be in touch with local Bolshevists. Sarah Knight of Edmonton was arrested because she had addressed a socialist meeting at the Rex Theatre on September 29 and had said things that might be considered seditious under the *War Measures Act*. She and her husband were well-known socialists in Edmonton. During her visit to Winnipeg she had been staying with Mrs. George Armstrong on Jubilee Avenue. In the months ahead a wide variety of leftists and labour activists would experience increased harassment from the Dominion Police and the North West Mounted Police.

There was also a great deal of lingering animosity toward the defeated enemy, personified for many Manitobans by the "Austrians," usually of Ukrainian heritage, who lived in their midst. Harry Terelski, an "Austrian," was fined $500 for making seditious remarks—saying Germany would win the war. Appearing before Magistrate Noble, he greeted the news of his fine by saying, "No jail for me." At that, Noble changed his mind and sent him to jail for a year. Noble lectured Terelski, saying, "You had better hold your tongue as it has gotten you into too much trouble already.... You are intoxicated with liberty since you left military Austria, and if I knew how long the war was going to last I would make the sentence accordingly, as you are a dangerous person at large.... You have been used to the rigidity and autocracy of your own country and think we are easy marks over here."

Noble's comments were typical of the overheated anti-"Austrian" and anti-German feelings that were widespread in the last year of the war and afterward. The attitudes of many people grew out of a combination of bitterness over the losses Canada had suffered at the hands of the German Army and fear of the rise of revolutionary movements that were enjoying success in Russia and would soon appear to be on the verge of success in Germany and Hungary.

One expression of these negative feelings was the Reverend Wellington Bridgman's book, *Breaking Prairie Sod*, which was published in 1920. More than half of Bridgman's work is a memoir of his early years as a Methodist minister on the prairies. His descriptions of the founding of Methodist congregations are full of stories of the homesteaders and other immigrants of the 1880s, of how they worshipped in unfinished buildings in the newly founded towns and then built their little churches. Scenes of people praying with all their hearts, sometimes in a mixture of English and Gaelic and of people pooling their money to help a family that has had a setback are described by Bridgman.

But this undoubtedly accurate praise of the Methodist congregations is marred by his negative attitudes toward other groups—Aboriginal people and those he refers to as "the Hun" and "Austrians." In his view, they can do nothing right. Bridgman gives examples to prove that the courts are almost completely occupied in dealing with cases of murder and assault committed by "foreigners" and "enemy aliens." In a chapter called "The Alien in Western Canada" he gives a sampling of heinous crimes, usually committed while the perpetrator was drunk, and talks about the cost of housing criminals in jail. The alien, writes Bridgman, "thinks evil and does wrong and commits crime because his nature is responsive to it, hence his high criminal record. But to the finer feelings of honour and integrity, there is no response because his moral nature is dead. He concludes that the Austro-Hun never had "moral or religious convictions.... As a race they stayed where they were three hundred years ago." His solution is to send them all back home and to make them pay their passage from the large savings that they usually have. This sort of anti-foreign feeling had always been present in western Canada, but the war and issues such as bilingual schools brought it to the surface. Bridgman and others argued that when Canadian soldiers returned home, they should be rewarded for their war service by being given the farms of "Hun" settlers. It was not uncommon to hear demands that "Huns" and "foreigners" be put off their land, deported, or fired from their jobs so that returning soldiers could take their places. It was part of what was almost a collective insanity at the end of the war.

The Jitney Problem Resolved

In 1918, the Minto Armoury saw the arrival of many new recruits, but also served as the site for interrogating conscientious objectors like Robert Clegg, Ralph Naish, and Charles Matheson.

On the streets of Winnipeg, three years of fierce competition between the drivers of jitneys and the mighty Winnipeg Electric Railway came to an end in 1918. The little black cars had steadily eroded the company's monopoly of public transport and its profits during the war. By the summer of 1916 the cars had become well established with 410 licensed jitneys bringing in $420,000 in five-cent fares. A particularly lucrative jitney route was the one that terminated in Point Douglas at McFarlane Street and neighbouring streets where the city's brothels were located. In September 1916 twenty jitney licences were cancelled because the cars had been noted by police as regular visitors to the area. The owners of these cars hired a lawyer, E.R. Levinson, to sue the city. He argued that they had no choice but to carry passengers where they wanted to go, adding that they had not paid for their cars and would not now be able to earn a living. Their suit was unsuccessful.

Jitneys increased the traffic on downtown city streets during the war years. In 1917 the volume of traffic moved the city to install its first traffic signal at Portage Avenue and Donald Street. It was a "semaphore" signal, consisting of a pole with "stop" and "go" signs at the top. A policeman turned the pole by hand to signal drivers.

Police were concerned about the many accidents involving jitneys. A particularly bad one involved Leopold Spodarek, whose car jumped the curb at Maryland and Notre Dame, killing Anne Friederich. It was found that Spodarek was driving with faulty brakes. Another jitney driver, William Bonnar, crashed into a store window and injured two women.

In September 1916, the street railway claimed that the licensing of the jitneys contravened their agreement with the city, and the following April the company served notice that it would be claiming $1 million in lost revenues. The company announced it would not be able to pay the city its share of profits. Of more concern was their decision to postpone new extensions to their lines, a decision supported by the Public Utilities commissioner.

The street railway appealed directly to Winnipeggers through an advertising campaign in the city papers, arguing that their service could be depended upon, unlike the jitneys. They warned that "unrestricted jitney competition will wear away your present car service to leave you with no new bed rock structure in its place—nothing that will greet the newcomer as a sign of real worth and progress—nothing that will characterize Winnipeg as possessing the greatest of assets— stability."

The labour paper the *Voice* was unimpressed by the company's arguments. The December 15, 1916, issue said, "Jitneys have placed the people in a position to tell the company—you either do the right thing by us or be quiet." The paper said that when jitneys offered better service "the company followed suit." When jitney drivers gave free rides to orphans, the Winnipeg Electric Railway instituted "Gladsome Days for Kiddies." "Competition in light and power proved a saving to the people. Competition in transportation facilities will at least assure the people of a better service," said the *Voice*.

While the *Voice* extolled the benefits of competition, the business community began to ask for more regulation. In May 1917, at the annual meeting of the Board of Trade, the president, A.L. Crossin, called the lack of regulation of the jitney "intolerable." The *Telegram* printed a story in August 1917 saying the jitneys should have to pay the same kind of taxes and fees as the street railway and should be obliged to run on specific routes at scheduled times. In September, city council responded by establishing new regulations for jitneys: licensees would now have to be bonded so that any damage or injury resulting from accidents would be covered and only companies with at least $10,000 in capital who were licensed by the insurance department of the province would be bonded. As well, jitney owners would now have to produce an annual financial statement prepared by a chartered accountant.

Of the 565 licensed jitneys, only 235 took out a bond during the first month after the bylaw was passed. It was believed that many of the others would be forced out of the business by the new regulations. The free-wheeling small-time capitalism of the jitneys was at an end.

The Winnipeg Electric Railway's annual report for 1917 stated that, once again, net income had decreased, this year by $151,000. The report added, "This is a disappointing statement, but so long as the materials required by your electric railway in its operations continue to increase in price and demands for increased rates of wages to employees predicated on higher cost of living have to be met, and the jitney question remains unsettled, no substantial improvement in net income can be expected."

There can be no doubt that the Electric Railway was in serious trouble. It is likely that the company would have gone into receivership in 1917 if the directors themselves had not put up collateral for loans negotiated with New York lenders. The undeniable distress of the company and pressure exerted by its directors now led to a willingness on the part of the city to take action.

On February 5, 1918, the company's new general manager, A.W. McLimont, sent a proposal to city council offering to accede to many of the long-standing demands of the city in return for the abolition of the jitney business. The jitney competition had succeeded in bringing about the company's capitulation, something the city council had never been able to do.

Augustus Nanton, now the president of the Winnipeg Electric Railway, visited a meeting of the Board of Trade council and asked it to support the company's proposal to the city. After some heated discussion, the Board of Trade passed a motion supporting the abolition of the jitney. They qualified their motion slightly by asking for a guarantee from the street railway that the public would not suffer any inconvenience because of the change.

Only Board of Trade councillor Alex Macdonald, a former mayor and wealthy businessman with progressive views, opposed this motion, arguing that the city should not be making any concessions to the street railway. But when he moved an amendment to the council's motion he was unable to get a seconder. City council soon began to draft new bylaws to abolish jitneys and establish a new relationship with the company.

Labour did not support the actions council was taking, and the Winnipeg Trades and Labor Council passed a resolution in April opposing them. During the debate on the bylaws, pro-labour aldermen A.A. Heaps, John Queen, and Arthur Puttee charged that the whole agreement was being railroaded through council as a favour to the railway. They proposed various amendments, all of which were defeated except one stipulating that its employees be paid "at the rate of wages set forth in the Provincial Fair Wage Schedule."

On April 29 the city council passed bylaw 9750, making it unlawful to operate a jitney car or bus on city streets. The Jitney Owners Association attempted to fight the bylaw, but the era of the jitney in Winnipeg came to an end. At the same time council also passed bylaw 9757, which stipulated that the railway would now invest in the repair and remodeling of their cars, operate motor buses on feeder streets like Westminster with the same fares and transfers as street cars, and begin to make the electrolysis repairs immediately. On April 26, as if to remind people how important it was to get the agreement signed, a large water main, damaged by electrolysis, broke at the corner of Graham and Kennedy and the street was flooded.

The company took one of its cars, number 314, out of service and completely rebuilt it in the Fort Rouge car barns. The newly renovated car, equipped with smaller wheels that brought it closer to the ground and new folding steps, was put on display for a week on William Avenue next to the city hall, and 50,000 people came to take a look at it.[9]

In the years after 1918 the Winnipeg Electric Railway continued to upgrade its equipment according to the agreement, but although jitney competition was eliminated, a new threat, the private car, became increasingly common and street railways in Winnipeg and elsewhere never recovered the dominant position they had enjoyed before the First World War.

City Issues

Already in 1916, the city's economy had begun to recover as the war prosperity that was washing over eastern Canada also, to some extent, improved conditions in the west. There was more work and wages began to improve for some, but the cost of living also rose steadily. Even those with good jobs found that they were struggling to feed their families. For working people, the only way out of this squeeze was to organize in order to press for better wages. As a result, union membership in Winnipeg and across Canada increased during the war years.

The high cost of living had been a political issue for years in western Canada, but it became central in the war years when wartime inflation was added to the normal high freight charges to push up prices. On October 30, 1916, Winnipeg city council heard a delegation, including Barbara Newcombe and Mrs. R.F. McWilliams of the local Council of Women, who spoke about the high cost of essentials like milk, meat, flour, and bread, and called for an investigation to see if the high prices were really justified. They also asked for a change to the City Charter so the city could sell coal and wood at fixed prices. In response to these and similar requests, Public Utilities Commissioner P.A. Macdonald opened an inquiry into the high cost of living. The resulting report provided people with solid information to use when asking for changes. R.A. Rigg and Harry Vietch, the vice-president and president of the Trades and Labor Congress, referred to this report when they met with provincial Minister of Public Works Thomas Johnson to discuss the general distress being caused by high prices and the almost universal demands by working people for wage increases.

Feeding their families was difficult for many Winnipeggers and the cost of food was one expense that many people thought should be regulated. At the start of the war only Germany had an effective food control system, although it eventually broke down under the stress of the British blockade. Britain depended upon its Dominions, and especially Canada, for food. As soon as the war began, Canada had sent a huge donation of flour, the first trickle in a massive river of food during the war. For the British, Canadian food production was probably as important to the war effort as the steady supply of Canadian munitions and the Canadian soldiers who went to the front to fight.

In 1917 German submarines did the most damage to the supply convoys sailing from Canada to Britain. With thousands of tons of food being sent to the bottom of the Atlantic, an Order-in-Council was passed setting up the office of the Canadian food controller. W.J. Hannah, the former attorney general of Ontario, was the first controller and was responsible for erecting a system of regulations designed to provide food supplies for Britain and the army while ensuring the population in Canada had enough to eat. He was only partly successful, because Canada opted for voluntary compliance in the case of most rules and initiatives. Prices continued to climb, although not as disastrously as in some countries.

By February 1918 the position of food controller was replaced by a board that governed such things as the rationing of meat, wasting food, and hoarding. The board licensed food dealers and manufacturers and used the threat of pulling licences to ensure compliance. At certain times of crisis they intervened more directly, such as in 1918 when the board "commandeered" millions of pounds of butter to ensure a steady supply for Britain and Canada at a reasonable price.

But the most important commodity supplied by Canada to the Allies was wheat. Bread was a staple food in the allied countries and it was felt that while shortages of most other foods could be tolerated, a scarcity of bread could not. Britain, France, and Italy all depended heavily on imported wheat to feed their populations. Pre-war sources of supply dried up as the Germans blocked access to the Baltic and the Turks closed the Dardenelles, cutting off shipments from Russia, Romania and Bulgaria, western Europe's main suppliers of wheat. In addition, some of France's best grain-growing land was in the hands of the Germans. Canada, the United States and, to a lesser extent, Argentina, Australia, and India became the Allies' main sources for flour and wheat. German submarine warfare and the consequent high ocean freight rates diminished supplies and raised prices.

The Canadian grain trade was very important to the Winnipeg economy. In the three decades before World War I, Winnipeg had established itself as the headquarters of the growing western Canadian grain trade. In 1914 the Winnipeg Grain Exchange was one of the most important trading floors in Canada and the U.S., sometimes surpassing Chicago in the volume of wheat traded. Although many farmers were deeply suspicious of the exchange and its members, the institution provided them, as producers of a commodity for export, with the complex mechanisms needed to sell into foreign markets.

A farmer's only direct contact with the grain trade was at the country elevators, most of which were owned by grain companies or milling companies like Ogilvie's. They brought their wagonloads of grain and were paid the Winnipeg price of the day. In the fall, when there was plenty of grain on the move, the prices went down. This irritant would be removed after the war when the pool movement introduced the two-price system—a farmer received one payment on delivery and another when the total profit from the sale of the pooled crop was divided among pool members. But in 1915 farmers received the price for the day when they came to the elevator, and it was seldom judged to be a fair price. Grain companies were accused, sometimes with reason, of colluding to fix prices. The quality, expressed as a grade, and weight of the grain were factors in deciding the price, and farmers felt that grain buyers often cheated them on weights and grades.

In the years between 1900 and 1914 western grain growers had used their considerable political clout to convince the federal government to erect a regulatory system that protected them as sellers. The *Canada Grain Act* and the Board of Grain Commissioners were the cornerstone of this system. The board, among other things, supervised scales to ensure fair weights from elevator operators and managed a complex grading system that guaranteed farmers a fair price for their grain.

Grain Exchange members were generally not averse to this sort of regulation, creating, as it did, an orderly market and a good reputation for Canadian grain among buyers. The exchange had, however, fought the application of the farmer-owned Grain Growers' Grain Company for exchange membership in 1907. There was much animosity among exchange members toward Grain Growers' leaders, like William

Tens of thousands of people crowded downtown Winnipeg to celebrate Victory Day, November 11, 1918.

Partridge, who were critical of the exchange's operations and accused the exchange of price fixing and gambling with farmers' grain. By World War I, however, the Grain Growers' Company had become an exchange member and, under the astute management of its president, Thomas Crerar, a major player in the industry.

The Grain Exchange was one of the most important economic engines of the Winnipeg economy. The huge office building owned by the exchange members housed not only the trading floor but dozens of firms involved in the industry. Elevator companies, grain exporters, milling companies, shipping firms, insurance companies, and grain inspectors employed by the Board of Grain commissioners all occupied offices within the building's eight stories. The Grain Exchange handled the selling of western crops, and domestic and overseas buyers had representatives on the trading floor to get the supplies they needed. Those who made their living buying and selling grain depended on a per-bushel commission that was very low but could translate into a lot of money because of the enormous volume traded in Winnipeg. Grain companies that owned country elevators and larger terminal elevators at the Lakehead also earned money from storage and handling charges. Many of the city's wealthiest families and close to 50 percent of Winnipeg firms worth more than $1 million were involved in the grain trade.[10] Many other institutions, such as the banks that provided the huge amounts of short-term credit required by the exchange, also profited from the grain trade.

In the fall of 1915 western farmers harvested the largest wheat crop in the history of the region. In response to the demand from the allied nations they had brought an extra five million acres under the plough and yields were high. The grain was also of generally high quality, making 1915 the kind of boom year that everyone involved in the wheat industry always dreamed of. The private trade in Canada and Britain handled the 1915 crop but it was to be the last time this happened.

In the fall of 1916, concern over plans to increase the submarine war announced by the Germans led to the allied governments taking control of wheat buying in order to ensure an adequate supply at a good price. A Royal Commission in Britain established a Wheat Executive to manage this process and they in turn established wheat export companies in the U.S. and Canada.[11] Having a single buyer in the market ended the ability of the Grain Exchange to function in a normal fashion. The local representative of the company, James Stewart, began to buy wheat futures for delivery in spring 1917 and rapidly gained control of the bulk of the 1916 crop. The quality and size of the 1916 crop were both low, and grain elevator companies feared they would not have enough grain of the quality they had promised to deliver when the contracts came due. The price rose rapidly as Canadian grain companies scrambled to buy grain to fulfill the futures contracts.

The crisis was resolved by the Grain Exchange essentially ceasing to operate. A government-appointed Board of Grain Supervisors, including representatives of the Grain Exchange, took over the task of setting prices. At the same time, futures trading was suspended. The resulting losses for the private grain trade were gladly accepted by the Grain Exchange as its contribution to the war effort. The organization's secretary, Robert Magill, spoke of the grain industry putting "their elevators, their organizations and their experience" at the service of the government.[12]

The Winnipeg Board of Trade was less positive. In his annual report for 1917–18, President Alvin Godfrey commented that the Grain Exchange had been "virtually destroyed" by the Board of Grain Supervisors and that some members of the Exchange had lost "their entire business connection." He wanted the government to compensate them for their losses and said that the Exchange was "too big an institution to lose" and that it would be needed again after the war to move the western crop to market.[13]

Grain traders went along with the board, with the understanding that once the war was over, commerce would return to normal. In reality, the system of grain supervisors was succeeded, for two seasons, by a Wheat Board, which would act as the sole purchaser of western wheat. In 1920, the Grain Exchange did again begin to trade in wheat, but western farmers had had a taste of selling to a government board for fixed prices, and they had prospered during the war and received record prices for their grain. They did not want to return to dealing with the private trade alone and would soon embark on the Pool movement as a method of trying to achieve independence from the Grain Exchange and the private elevator companies. Eventually, in the 1930s, the Canadian Wheat Board was established on a permanent basis as the sole purchaser of the western wheat crop, a change that benefitted western farmers. The removal of the west's major crop greatly reduced the volume of trade on the Grain Exchange and ended its importance as a major factor in the Winnipeg economy. All these factors would lead to a long and slow decline in the number of wealthy Winnipeg families involved in the trade as consolidation of companies through mergers and purchase led by the 1950s to two or three large firms dominating the private side of the industry.[14]

Labour Organizing

Wartime inflation continued to cause hardships for Winnipeggers, and strikes continued in the city. Beginning in 1916, and escalating through 1917, 1918, and 1919, Winnipeggers witnessed many strikes over wage increases and the issue of collective bargaining. As we have seen, wage earners were finding it hard to make ends meet because of rising prices. At the same time they were working to establish their unions as their collective voice in the bargaining process.[15] The Teamsters Union achieved some success in establishing itself in two strikes in late 1916 by the drivers at Crescent Creamery and Milton's Bakery. By November 15, the strike at Crescent Creamery was over and the company had recognized the union, although it did not agree to becoming a closed shop. In the case of the bakery, the owner and a Teamsters representative went together to the Labor Board to negotiate a solution.

The year 1917 saw a good deal of labour organizing among the city's workers. In the spring the city firemen were establishing a union, but giving the firemen the right to strike was extremely controversial. City council received resolutions from over twenty-five unions supporting the firemen. Officers of the Fire Brigade complained that some firemen were being intimidated into joining the union. In April, council passed a large number of salary increases, including an additional 2 percent for married workers. The overall average of the increases given by the city was 9.35 percent, but some workers got no increase at all. The lists of names printed in the paper indicated that these raises were normally for clerical and managerial people, names which were uniformly "English."

But the time of selective wage increases was coming to an end. Alderman Henry Pulford called for an outside group to examine wages and hours of work, to ensure that all city employees were being fairly treated. His motion to this effect was defeated. It is significant that Pulford was not one of the council's labour alderman. A longtime councillor and owner of a small business, he supported public ownership of city utilities and was a progressive voice on the council. In the months ahead, Pulford and some of his liberal colleagues would support the labour group on certain key occasions, and allow change to take place.

By May 1917, there were a number of strikes and labour disputes going on in the city. The telephone operators stopped work for a few hours on the morning of May 1, putting on hold a service that was essential to many of the city's businesses and industries—banking, the Grain Exchange, grain handling and shipping—that depended upon contact with the outside world. Attorney General A.B. Hudson conferred with their union representatives, and then the whole provincial Cabinet talked with them before agreeing to the operators' demands. The operators had gathered in the Labor Temple and there they sang songs until 11 a.m. When word came that Hudson would meet with them they cheered and swarmed outside to have their pictures taken. A board of arbitrators was appointed to settle the details.

Meanwhile, the streetcar conductors were also making demands. Lawyer Isaac Pitblado and Trades and Labor Council representative R.A. Rigg were appointed to settle their claims. The city electrical workers, both the generator operators at Pointe du Bois and the City Light and Power staff, were on strike. The city decided to burn only some street lights on Portage, Main, and Assiniboine, and council warned the striking power workers that if they did not go back to work their jobs would be filled. They accepted an arbitrated settlement, and on May 9 they went back to work.

As May 1917 wore on 900 men working in the Grand Trunk Pacific shops in Transcona for the Transcona Shell Company announced that they were going out on strike in sympathy with fifty toolmen and repairmen in the shops who had been on strike for a week. Many other groups—bricklayers, garment workers, and many more—were asking for wage increases from between 7.5 cents to 10 cents an hour.

Aldermen John Queen and Abraham Heaps worked to protect a group that could not go out on strike—the families of soldiers. In a motion to city council, they stated that, because soldiers' pensions and payments to their families were inadequate to "maintain them in a decent standard of living," council should petition the Dominion government to establish a minimum of $100 a month for their support and to make pensions equal regardless of rank. When the motion came to a vote, only the pro-labour aldermen, Heaps, Puttee, Queen, Simpson, and Hume, supported the idea.

Heaps and Queen then made a further motion regarding pensions. They proposed that people should get at least $840 a year and that the children of officers and men should get the same pensions and the separation allowance—part of the payment all soldiers' families

One year after the war had ended, there were still large and enthusiastic Winnipeg crowds for the parades celebrating the formal signing of peace treaties in 1919.

received—should be at least fifty dollars. The whole matter was referred to the pension committee, which recommended that both must be revised upward so people could live and that all payments of this sort should be made by the government and not private charities.

In July 1917, 435 local milk producers announced that, beginning the following day, they would be cutting down on the milk supply. They had been getting twenty cents a gallon, but they had now been asked to take nineteen cents in a new contract. Unwilling to be the ones to solve the food crisis, they were demanding an increase to twenty-three cents per gallon to be phased in over the next three months. The producers also asked to be allowed to deliver milk directly to homes as they had once done. The city responded that it would approve this change only for dairy famers who had cooling and clarifying equipment and very clean premises. The city Health Department was not willing to abandon the regulations they had introduced in recent years to improve the quality of milk and to ensure that it was free of tuberculosis and other diseases. On July 10, a dairy farmer from Lorette, John Tennison, was stopped on his way to the city by strikers wanting him to stop delivering milk. He was then beaten up and given a milk bath, and his milk cans were poured out on the road. He laid charges against the two men he knew, R. Wanderkere and Frank Gottlab, for assault and the provincial police arrested them.

At the end of September, 600 telegraph operators of the Great North West Telegraph Company were out on strike, sixty of them in Winnipeg. Because of the importance of their work both for business and for the government communications, the federal government brought pressure to bear and the strike ended on October 1. That time, the victory was in favour of the operators.

But by the spring of 1918 there had been no improvements in the cost of living and workers struggled to feed their families. The determined actions of the workers and some of the city's aldermen led to historic changes as the City of Winnipeg accepted collective bargaining with the unions of its employees. In April 1918 civic employees had rejected the offer of a war bonus of $104 per worker, demanding instead a general 15 percent increase for everyone. The Trades and Labor Council passed a motion condemning the idea of a war bonus and called upon city council to recognize and bargain with the unions of their employees. By May, 200 city employees were out on strike. Council formed a committee to confer with the strike leaders, and by May 18 an agreement was reached. The report was amended by council with a provision that anyone working for the city must sign a document giving up the right to strike and promising to submit disagreements to arbitration. This amendment passed by a single vote. Those voting against were controllers Cockburn and Puttee, and aldermen Sparling, Queen, Heaps, Hume, Hamlin, and Wiginton. Not all these men were left-wing politicians: Cockburn was a progressive businessman and engineer with a record of backing public utilities like the City Light and Power Company and Alderman Sparling was a successful lawyer. The balance of power on council was beginning to shift as liberal aldermen began to support their labour colleagues, at least where issues of fairness in dealing with employees were concerned.

The next day, the mayor appealed to the Board of Trade annual meeting, saying it was important for all citizens to support the city council in its move to ban strikes. The board duly passed a resolution of support and started setting up a volunteer fire brigade to replace the firemen who were striking. The strike nevertheless continued to spread. With the Fire Department out on strike an arsonist began lighting fires in the city and anonymous letters sent to the press promised there would be more. A house burned on Ashburn Street and volunteer fire fighters managed to prevent the flames from spreading to the neighbouring houses. In early June the McDermot Avenue offices of the *Telegram* newspaper, traditionally the Conservative paper and generally opposed to the strike, were destroyed by fire. An investigation subsequently established that volunteers arrived at the fire in good time but did not get the water flowing quickly enough to stop the blaze. The paper did not publish for several months.

The business community began formulating its response. At a meeting held at the Royal Alexandra Hotel on May 17, businessmen called for strikes to be outlawed for the duration of the war and proposed an amendment to the criminal code making it illegal for firemen to go on strike. Soon after, the Board of Trade appointed a "Committee of 100" that would "coordinate with municipal and provincial authorities during the present strike." With Board president A. Crossin in the chair, the group set up subcommittees for telephones, water, light and power, fire department, police, health, cartage, legislation, and transportation, and a conciliation committee to hear the views of the strikers.

Various appeals were made to the striking workers. The women of the Central Battalion Auxiliaries sent a letter to the striking telephone operators addressing them as "fellow women," and saying, "our men and some of your men are fighting the hun; we cannot summon help if we are sick. In the name of our men and in the name of the cause of womanhood, which our men defend, we appeal to you to return to work."

As the strike continued, there were violent incidents and a good deal of extreme talk in the city. Controller Gray and two other men in a car chased a group of men who had been turning in false alarms to make things difficult for the volunteer firemen. One of the pranksters was beaten up. At a strike meeting at the Columbia Theatre, Harry

Laidlaw said that "this strike is merely the beginning, simply the echo of what will happen when the soldiers come back and find that the democracy they went to fight for is nothing but a pipe dream." At the same meeting labour leader Sam Blumberg said that scabs would have to be fired before the men returned to ensure they had jobs and because "we are going to run this city and we will not consent to having any scab working beside us."

Gideon Robertson, a Conservative senator and minister in Borden's Union government, visited Winnipeg during the strike. He was the former secretary of the Railway Telegraphers Union. He brought a message from a concerned federal Cabinet, afraid that the strike would spread to other cities and damage the war effort. He advised city council to give up their attempts to break the strike and reopen negotiations with the unions.

The conciliation subcommittee of the Committee of 100 received a list of demands from the Strike Committee. The city was asked to negotiate with the various unions at a specified time; there would be no strikes during negotiations, wages would be outlined in a special report to council, and strikers would be guaranteed their old jobs back. There was a long debate in council, and the agreement was finally given unanimous support, although the right to strike for firemen remained contentious. But by mid-June the Board of Control worked out the details of agreements with the Firemen's Association and the Water Works Local Union. The board recommended that council accept and execute these agreements, thus establishing collective bargaining as the method of dealing with city employees' working conditions.

In October, the establishment of collective bargaining was confirmed by city council. On a motion from aldermen Heaps and Queen, the council recommended to the Police Commission that they "recognize and deal with" the new Policemen's Union, "following the policy that employees in the service of the public shall have the right to form unions." This motion passed with a vote of nine to eight. An amendment moved by aldermen Fowler and Pulford, saying "an association or union shall not be affiliated with any other," was defeated, also by a single vote. Collective bargaining was thus established for Winnipeg city employees by the efforts of the pro-labour aldermen and their allies among other council members. This victory of the progressive members of city council in establishing collective bargaining provides a measure of how the city had changed and of how the old elites were not as securely in control as they had been in 1914.

Memorials

The end of the war was near, but in Winnipeg there had been a false alarm. On Friday, November 8, both the *Tribune* and *Free Press* announced that the war was over with huge, front-page headlines. They had jumped the gun. In the days leading up to the armistice, with Austria out of the war and peace being negotiated, everyone felt that the end would come soon, but the exact date was unknown. The *Telegram* had the pleasure of reprinting the front pages of its two rivals in its evening edition under the headline, "The Greatest Newspaper Fraud in History."

When the end did come it was the *Telegram* that got the scoop. On Monday, November 11, at ten minutes to two in the morning, the news came over the Associated Press wire that the war would end at 11 a.m. that day. Forty *Telegram* newsboys were on the streets with an extra "four seconds later, fifteen minutes faster," claimed the paper, than its two rivals. The *Telegram* also called the CPR yards, and at 2:15 in the morning all the steam whistles the railroad could muster started blowing. People woke up to the sound of the whistles and the shouting newsboys and made their way downtown to Portage and Main, to the newspaper offices, to the same streets they had crowded in those long ago days of August 1914.

By 2:30 a.m. the city's main corner was already packed and by 4 a.m. all the downtown streets were more crowded than at any time "in the business hours of the busiest day of the boom days." The people of the city, who had endured so much and waited so long, turned night into day in a crazy, happy celebration of the end of their long night of waiting. People wore paper hats, blew tin trumpets, and "Winnipeg laughed, Winnipeg cheered, Winnipeg wept with those who wept in secret sorrow for the departed, Winnipeg wept in public joy with those whose tears were of gladness and relief. Winnipeg turned itself to every device, every ingenuity for making noise and in producing

noise Winnipeg succeeded."[16] Little boys with pot lids and fire crack-
ers, a man with a trench mortar firing blanks, people driving their cars
up and down blowing their horns all contributed to the joyful din.

Miss Taylor, who had been a stenographer in the Pitblado and
Hoskin law office in 1918 remembered how she was awakened by the
whistles. She decided to go to work as usual, sure that the office would
close. Eaton's, the Hudson's Bay Company, and most other stores did
so and their staff members were out on the streets. But Pitblado and
Hoskin was a serious firm and the excited staff members were made
to stay at their desks until 1 p.m. Miss Taylor could not stay away
from the windows though, and finally "at ten minutes to one, we made
a mad dash for the elevator. What an afternoon and evening we had!
Crikey! It was good to be alive! We shouted and yelled and blew horns
till our cheeks threatened to burst. Tirelessly we went up and down
Portage and Main yelling at our friends and acting generally as though
we'd taken leave of our senses."[17]

The crowds kept coming until by evening on November 11 there
were estimated to be 100,000 people downtown. Most streets were
completely blocked by people of all ages. The flags of the Allies were
everywhere, and the kaiser, who for four years had been the physical
embodiment of German perfidy, was burned in effigy and dragged
behind cars. Impromptu parades complete with pipers and brass
bands moved back and forth in the streets. Miss Taylor remembered
that Eaton's store was decorated and that decorated vehicles paraded
around the streets. "Wood Vallance company had a big truck crowded
with their people and they had a jazz band. Talk about jazz say!" There
was a service in front of the Bank of Montreal accompanied by the
Salvation Army band. After dark there were fireworks and "Portage
Avenue was a scene of wild tumult as the rockets rose high into the sky
and then burst in a shower of beautiful colours."

At 8 p.m. the crowd jammed into the space in front of the *Free Press*
building on Carlton. They were told by Lieutenant Governor Aikins
that this was "our day" and reminded them to remember the dead.
The premier, the mayor, and General Ketchen all spoke. The messages of Lloyd George and the king were read out, and Miss Taylor
remembered that the band began to play "old favourites like Annie
Laurie" and military tunes: "On the outskirts of the crowd couples

were waltzing. Sometimes people joined in the music singing softly." It was not until the early hours of November 12 that people finally went home to bed.

The End of the War

Winnipeg had done her duty. The city's contributions to the war effort had been enormous and they had been given freely. Millions of dollars had been given to the Red Cross, the Patriotic Fund, and other charities; more millions were invested in Victory Bonds; thousands of the city's young men and women had gone to fight and many had come home wounded or shattered psychologically. Many had not come home at all.

The war had changed the city forever. In many important areas, private charity had been replaced by government agencies. The heavy demands of the war had overwhelmed private charities and made the transition necessary. The professionalization of what we would now call social services was one result of this change. Indeed, some of the leaders of the volunteer groups tried to help this along.

As the war ended, the city's labour movement was enjoying a year of triumphs, the greatest of which was the establishment of collective bargaining as the way the wages of many workers would be set. The hardships caused by wartime inflation and the consequent shrinking of the buying power of the worker's wages had created irresistible pressure in this direction.

The war had created a climate in which the reform groups in Manitoba, united in support of the Liberal Party, had been able to triumph and reach their objectives after many unsuccessful years. Prohibition, women's suffrage, and unilingual schools were their three greatest victories, won largely because they had managed to relate these causes with being patriotic Canadians.

EPILOGUE
1923

On May 13, 1923, Winnipeggers gathered on the northwest corner of the legislative building grounds to dedicate the new Winnipeg Soldiers' Relatives war memorial.[1] Five years after the war had ended, the speakers strove to give the deaths of their children some nobility and value. Whatever they may have suffered in private, soldiers' families rarely, if ever, expressed doubt in public about the necessity for the war and the nobility of the sacrifice that was made.

The families who attended the dedication were living in a city much changed from pre-war Winnipeg. The postwar depression hit the city hard because it had not enjoyed the same prosperity during the war that eastern cities had achieved. The hopes that everyone had that the pre-war boom would resume once the fighting stopped were not realized in Winnipeg. All the building blocks of the boom were absent. Investment capital continued to be scarce and the flow of immigrants in the 1920 to 1924 period was only one-third of what it had been in 1913. The growth of other western cities and the boost given to Vancouver by the Panama Canal put an end to Winnipeg's claims of being the western metropolis. The city's dominant position as a wholesale centre was lost and many Winnipeg firms closed their doors in the early 1920s.[2]

With the end of the war ocean freight rates dropped and Australian, Indian, and Argentinian wheat were once more able to compete in the European wheat market. One result was the collapse of Canadian wheat prices from $2.45 a bushel in 1919 to 81 cents in 1921. For Winnipeg, so dependent on prosperity in the agricultural sector, the fall in prices was a disaster. City firms that depended upon the grain trade suffered, as did companies that manufactured rails, bridge components, and cement. If there was very little building going on across the prairies there was little for Winnipeg firms and workers to do.

The leaders who had literally built Winnipeg from a dusty village were disappearing from the stage in these years—Augustus Nanton died in 1925, James Ashdown in 1923, and Douglas Cameron in 1921, to name only three. There seemed to be no one to replace them. Many of the city's leading families had lost sons and in other cases the next generation migrated to other cities like Vancouver.

As the crowd listened to the speeches at the dedication of the monument, they may have felt a sense of loss for their city as well as for their children. They may have been comforted when T.R. Deacon, the president of the Memorial Association, talked about the "might and strength of a righteous cause" and how the young people they were commemorating "shook down from his throne and power the would-be despoiler of the world and ... restored the birthright of the British race and of Humanity to freedom." At least the sacrifices made by their sons and daughters had not been in vain.

This rhetoric of sacrifice often likened the young soldiers to Christ, giving up their lives so that other Canadians would not be threatened by the kaiser and his evil regime. The German emperor was commonly painted as being out to destroy the British traditions of democracy and freedom and replace them with a militaristic "Prussian" system. Whether or not the bereaved relatives really believed these things, these words represented the official line that had been repeated by clergymen, politicians, and community leaders since the early days of the war to explain and justify the terrible losses Canada had suffered.

The reactions of bereaved Canadians to the massive cemeteries and to monuments like the one at Broadway and Osborne in Winnipeg was probably more personal than political by 1923. Sculptor Marguerite Taylor, speaking about her bronze soldier created for the Soildiers'

The Soldiers' Relatives war memorial on the grounds of the Manitoba Legislature.

Relatives monument, said that she intended him to be a happy soldier, celebrating the end of the fighting, "so the bereaved wives and mothers would not be too saddened when they looked at it." He holds his rifle in his left hand with the butt resting on the ground rather than aggressively at the ready, as was the case in so many other war memorials, and he waves his helmet above his head with his right hand. Despite Taylor's desire to comfort her viewers, the figure, precisely because of his happy informality, creates a scene of great poignancy as he seems to wave goodbye to his loved ones.

Originally placed in front of the Canadian Pacific Railway station on Higgins Avenue, this monument, which commemorates railway workers who died in the war, now resides on the grounds of the Deer Lodge Centre. It is one of three copies of the statue, with the others located in Vancouver and Montreal.

An inscription on the memorial states that it was erected with "Loving Hearts" by the families of the city's war dead. On its huge bronze plaques are recorded the names of 1658 Winnipeg men and women. The names, arranged simply in alphabetical order, ignoring rank, do not constitute a complete list of Winnipeggers who died, but only those whose names had been compiled by the association that erected the monument. They did their best to get a complete list, but they had to rely on families reporting names to them. This is a very personal and deeply emotional war memorial, intended, as Judge Robert Dennistoun said in his dedication speech at the May 13 event, not as a memorial "of war, or of patriotism, or of glory, or of victory" but as a "simple tribute of affection, a memorial of love, a testimony to personal loss." He said the monument would be a comfort to their families who had no "green cemeteries to which we could go, no place where we could deposit a few flowers ... for our dear ones were not here. They rest far away across the sea." The new monument would provide them with a place they could visit and honour and care for. In fact, relatives continued to gather there to remember their dead, at least until the 1960s, on Memorial Day in May.

The family monument was only one of several private memorials established after the war. Other notable sites included the statue of the angel and the fallen soldier erected in front of the CPR station for railroad employees, the plaque put up by the Women's Canadian Club at the corner of Portage Avenue and Valour Road to remember the street's three Victoria Cross winners, and the Bank of Montreal monument at Portage and Main. There was some frustration that the government had yet to put up an official monument, and it was only in 1928 that the cenotaph on Memorial Boulevard was dedicated.

The monuments were important because most people who lost someone in the war could not make the trip to visit their graves in the vast cemeteries in Belgium and France. As well, of the 750,000 British and Dominion troops who were killed on the Western Front, fully 300,000 had no known grave. Many were buried under the tons of earth thrown up by shelling, while some simply sank into the filthy mud. They might have been hurriedly buried in mass graves or their battlefield grave might have been obliterated in the fighting. One of the most moving passages in Canon Frederick Scott's memoir of World War I describes his visit to the battlefield during the Battle of the Somme to find his son's body. Miraculously, with the aid of one of his son's comrades, he did actually find it, buried in no man's land near Regina Trench, and was able to give his boy a proper burial.

Immediately after the war, the trench lines of the Western Front were closed to civilians. John Dafoe, in March 1919, when he was attending the Versailles Treaty negotiations, was given special permission to travel through the closed areas with a party of officials, a trip he later detailed in a small book. He described a raw landscape where working parties laboured to clear the detritus of war from the farmer's fields. Canadian soldiers were gathering the bodies of their dead comrades from scattered graves and moving them to large, new cemeteries. Dafoe argued that Canada's "way of glory" should be marked with memorials so their countrymen, "with reverent hearts and shining eyes," could learn about their sacrifice. He wrote that "Canada's participation in the war is a fountain from which succeeding generations should drink deep, learning thereby lessons in valour, sacrifice, patriotism and pride."[3]

In the early 1920s those who could do so began to make trips, often called "pilgrimages," to the battlefield cemeteries and monuments. In May 1922, King George V spent two days doing so in France and Belgium. An illustrated book about the trip was published, with the proceeds from its sale used to subsidize similar trips by ordinary families to visit the graves of their relatives. As the head of state and commander-in-chief to whom British and Dominion soldiers had sworn allegiance, the king had a symbolic personal connection with all the young men lying in the enormous cemeteries. As he walked along the rows of white headstones and examined the various monuments at the battle sites, he was participating in what was to become a sort of religious rite. In visiting the graves of the dead who had sacrificed themselves, people were expected to gain inspiration from that sacrifice.[4]

Alec Waugh's name is on the massive bronze plaques of the Soldiers' Relatives memorial. The monument was quite literally the only memorial that his parent's had in order to remember him—his grave was never found. Waugh was buried where he died, shot by a sniper. Another soldier, Captain Boulton wrote to his father to tell him that "the following morning I went up with his sergeant and corporal and buried him just where he had fallen. We fashioned a cross and burnt his name and unit into it and after reading half a chapter from the Bible we left him."

The Waughs tried to locate their son's grave. Soon after he died they wrote to General Sam Steele to ask for his help in finding out "whether his body was recovered and if so where he is buried." The Waughs told Steele, "we felt that in applying to a dear old friend like

Aerial view of Portage and Main, c. 1928. Life would resume a normal pace in Winnipeg after the upheavals of the war and the unrest of the 1919 General Strike. But by the late 1920s, it was clear that the unrestrained growth of earlier decades would not return to the city.

yourself we will get all the information that is possible and that you will not consider it a trouble."[5] Steele was unable to help him, other than get the Imperial War Graves Commission to make a search, but it was unsuccessful because of the vast number of men who were unaccounted for. But, unlike many parents, the Waughs were able to go to France to continue the search, and as one of the commissioners of the League of Nations administration in the Saar, Richard Waugh had access to the battlefields. Still, his search was unsuccessful. He wrote to a friend in Canada that "I am going again in the spring to make a very careful search. If his grave is ever found I guess I will have to find it myself. This unknown grave is only one of hundreds of thousands."[6]

The Waughs had also been asked by other Winnipeggers to look for the graves of their sons. Richard wrote to one father, "We visited the Ecoivres military cemetery and want to say first of all that it is one of the bonniest of all the many cemeteries visited. I took a picture of the cemetery and will send you one as soon as I get time to develop and print them.... There are many Winnipeg boys there and the flowers are lovely and tastefully laid out. Although it is against the rules I plucked to send to you the enclosed flower from your boy's grave." He added, "we were unable to find the burial place of our own dear boy.... We found the trenches still intact and searched with breaking hearts the shell torn wilderness of weeds, for some evidence of his grave, but without success."

The next year, when he was back in Canada, Waugh received a letter from one of Alec's men, Ed Large, who sent him a map showing where the grave was in 1917. He thanked Large and said he would send the map to Major Goodhand of the War Graves Commission, writing, "even yet our boy's grave may be located." But in reality Waugh seemed to have given up, as he added the melancholy lines: "Naturally we'd like to find it but, after all, it does not matter much. He died and was buried where he did his duty like tens of thousands of other young Canadians whose graves will never be located."

This bleak statement expresses what the war really came to mean to the Winnipeggers who fought it, both at home and in France. For so many, the powerful draw of duty seemed to blot out individual concerns. The war came between the ambitious citizens of the bustling, self-promoting city of 1914 and their "business" of getting rich. It altered their course as they responded to the patriotic appeals of Canadian and British leaders. Far from doing what would have been best for them and their businesses, they made great sacrifices for causes that had profound meaning for them—the survival of the Empire, democratic freedoms, and their own country.

For Alec Waugh and his father there was no doubt that they would both "do their duty" in fighting the war. For Alec, as for many young Winnipeggers, the war was where he came of age. His early letters, written to his parents soon after he volunteered, show us a callow boy, slightly spoiled and demanding. In England and at the front he slowly matured into someone who was more concerned about his men than himself. By living in England he was able to contrast his own character and attitudes with those of the mother country and develop a sense of himself as a Canadian. He wrote, "We Canadians have overrun the towns and villages and practically own the streets. From our barracks to Hythe is a distance of five miles and never a day passes but we pass several detachments coming from the ranges, all with the

arrogant swing of their rifles and the devil may care walk that marks
the Canadian infantry."[7] When a British army doctor commented
on his "absolutely perfect health," he answered, "we make real men
in Canada, even out of some pretty poor material."[8] In his letters he
wrote that he did not like the English towns, which seemed crowded
and confined: "Winnipeg is crude as yet, but I want a street where one
is able to breath, and where a wagon does not need to occupy the walk
while another passes." Later he told his father, "Say Dad, if I hadn't
been in the game I wouldn't have ever wanted to live in Winnipeg. My
one ambition now is to finish up with some German helmets, about a
hundred notches in my gun and a brass band to go home with."[9]

Alec Waugh was in many ways typical of the Anglo-Canadian soldiers from Winnipeg who went to fight in the Great War. His father
was an immigrant from Scotland and his mother was descended from
Robert and Alexander Logan, old Red River pioneers and founders
of the city. He is also an example of what the city lost in the young
men who were killed. His letters demonstrate a developing skill as a
writer that would have pleased his grandfather, a well-regarded newspaper editor. In the end his potential was unrealized and his short life
is summed up in his father's comment that "he died and was buried
where he did his duty."

In the Great War Alec and Anglo-Canadian soldiers like him carried on Winnipeg's military traditions, which had begun in 1885 and
the Boer War. But in this conflict young men from Alec's class also
fought alongside Ukrainians, Jews, Icelanders, and many others from
the city's diverse ethnic groups. In doing so, they helped to begin the
long process toward equality and acceptance.

Winnipeg had done its duty. In people and money the young city
contributed more than most in proportion to its size. In the process
the city came of age. Beginning as a brash and overconfident place,
bragging about its growth and future potential, it ended the war having acquired a new sense of perspective. The old boosterish Winnipeg
had had the wind taken out of its sails and the city would now be
a more cautious and conservative place. The war had brought many
changes to Winnipeg, and as peace returned the city set out on a very
different path than the one that, in 1914, most of its citizens assumed
it would take.

Notes

Introduction

1. R.B. Bellan, "The Development of Winnipeg as a Metropolitan Centre" (PhD thesis, Columbia University, 1958), 245–246.

1914

1. Charles W. Gordon, *Postscript to Adventure: The Autobiography of Ralph Connor* (New York: Farrar and Rinehart, 1938), 203.

2. Archives of Manitoba (AM), MG14 B28 Box 5, Letter from Irene Evans to Sanford Evans, August 31, 1914.

3. Nellie McClung, *Next of Kin* (Toronto: Thomas Allen, 1917), 26.

4. Ibid., 32.

5. *Winnipeg Telegram*, August 4, 1914, 7.

6. *Winnipeg Morning Free Press*, August 5, 1914.

7. Ibid.

8. Robert Allen, *Hometown Horizons: Local Responses to Canada's Great War* (Vancouver: University of British Columbia Press, 2004), 50.

9. Cameron Highlanders of Canada Web site, http://ca.geocities.com/cameronhighlanderscanada/43pg1.htm (accessed July 2008).

10. *Winnipeg Telegram*, August 8, 1914.

11. James W. Walker, "Race and Recruitment in World War I: Enlistment of Visible Minorities in the Canadian Expeditionary Force," *Canadian Historical Review* 70, 1 (1989): 1–26, offers a good overview of the experience of visible minorities in the Canadian army.

12. James Farney and Bohdan S. Kordan, "The Predicament of Belonging: The Status of Enemy Aliens in Canada, 1914," *Journal of Canadian Studies* 39, 1 (2005): 78.

13. *Canadian Finance*, May 5, 1915.

14. *Winnipeg Telegram*, August 10, 1914.

15. M.B. Biskupski, "Canada and the Creation of a Polish Army, 1914–1918," *Polish Review* 44, 3 (1999): 339–80.

16. Stella Hryniuk, "The Bishop Budka Controversy: A New Perspective," *Canadian Slavonic Papers* 23, 2 (1981): 154–65.

17. Edgar Russenholt, *Six Thousand Canadian Men* (Winnipeg: Montfort Press, 1932), 174.

18. Professor V.J. Kaye was the first to research this question and his findings were reported in "Ukrainian Canadians in Canada's Wars," *Materials for Ukrainian Canadian History, Volume 1* (Toronto: Ukrainian Studies Research Foundation, 1983).

19. Joseph Wilder, *Read All About It* (Winnipeg: Peguis Publishers, 1978), 94–5.

20. Duncan Campbell Scott, "The Canadian Indians in the Great World War," in *Canada in the Great World War*, vol. 3 (Toronto: United Publishers, 1919), 305.

21. Ibid.

22. *Canadian Annual Review*, 1916, 685.

23. *Winnipeg Telegram*, October 11, 1917.

24. Robin Brownlie, "Work Hard and be Grateful: Native Soldier Settlers in Ontario after the First World War," in *On the Case*, ed. Franca Iacovetta (Toronto: University of Toronto Press, 1998), 181–203.

25. Debates of the House of Commons, Ottawa, March 13, 1900.

26. Sanford Evans, *The Canadian Contingents and Canadian Imperialism* (Toronto: The Publishers' Syndicate, 1901), 68.

27. Debates of the House of Commons, Ottawa, August 22, 1914, 95.

28. R. Matthew Bray, "Fighting as an Ally: the English-Canadian Patriotic Response to the Great War," *Canadian Historical Review* 61, 2 (1980): 145.

29. *Winnipeg Telegram*, August 3, 1914.

30. J.L. Granatstein and J. Mackay Hitsman, *Broken Promises: A History of Conscription in Canada* (Toronto: Oxford University Press, 1977), 35.

31. S.H. Williams, Stand to Your Horses (Winnipeg, the author, 1961), 44.

32. AM, P3348, letter of December 19, 1915

33. Philip Morris, *The Canadian Patriotic Fund: A Record of its Activities from 1914 to 1919* (N.p., 1920), 107.

34. Ibid.

35. R.G. MacBeth, *Sir Augustus Nanton, a Biography* (Toronto: Macmillan, 1921), 46.

36. Sarah C. Glassford, "Marching as to War: The Canadian Red Cross Society, 1885–1939" (PhD Thesis, York University, 2007), 119.

37. McClung, *Next of Kin*, 43.

38. AM, MG10 B29, Canadian Red Cross Society, Executive Committee Minutes, April 14, 1915.

39. Glassford, "Marching as to War," 110.

40. *Winnipeg Free Press*, May 3, 1915, 4.

41. *British Journal of Nursing*, August 21, 1915, 161.

42. *Canadian Annual Review*, 1914, 337.

43. *Canadian Annual Review*, 1915, 332.

44. *IODE Souvenir*, Winnipeg, 1916, 5.

45. AM, P2498, letter of November 17, 1914.

46. *Canadian Annual Review*, 1914, 232.

47. AM, P2498, IODE Executive Meeting Minutes.

48. For the best discussion of Winnipeg's election laws, see A.F.J. Artibise, *Winnipeg: A Social History of Urban Growth, 1874–1914* (Montreal: McGill-Queen's University Press, 1975), 38–42.

49. Winnipeg City Council Minutes, 1914, letter no. 10254.

50. Ibid., letter no. 10283.

51. Ibid., letter no. 10289.

52. Roz Usiskin, editor and translator, *A Lifetime of Letters: The Wolodarsky Family, The Period of Separation 1913–1922* (Winnipeg: The editor, 1995).

53. R.T. Riley, *Memoirs* (Winnipeg: The author, 1950), 88.

54. Winnipeg City Council Minutes, September 21, 1914.

55. Bellan, "Development of Winnipeg," 263.

56. AM, MG10A2, Board of Trade Annual Report, May 11, 1915.

57. *Winnipeg Telegram*, January 26, 1915.

58. *Canadian Annual Review*, 1914, 596.

59. Peter Melnycky, "A Political History of the Ukrainian Community in Manitoba, 1899–1922" (MA thesis, University of Manitoba, 1979), 124.

60. Ibid., 127.

61. *Canadian Annual Review*, 1913, 537.

62. *Canadian Annual Review*, 1910, 490.

63. Alexander Gregor, *The Development of Education in Manitoba* (Dubuque, IA: Kendall Hunt, 1984), 81.

64. J.E. Rea, "My Main Line is the Kiddies," in *Identities: the Impact of Ethnicity in Canadian Society*, ed. W. Isajiw (Toronto: Peter Martin, 1977), 3.

65. Melnycky, "Political History," 143.

66.   Ibid., 169.

67.   *Canadian Annual Review*, 1914, 599.

1915

1.   *Winnipeg Telegram*, February 17, 1915.

2.   *Winnipeg Free Press*, April 29, 1915.

3.   http://www.sciencemuseum.org.uk/broughttolife/people/johnscotthaldane.aspx (accessed March 8, 2009).

4.   Tim Cook, *At the Sharp End* (Viking Canada, 2008), 142.

5.   Roy St. George Stubbs, *Men in Khaki: Four Manitoba Regiments* (Toronto, Ryerson Press, 1940), 43.

6.   J.L. Granatstein, *Canada's Army* (Toronto: University of Toronto Press, 2002), 67.

7.   *Winnipeg Free Press*, May 12, 1915.

8.   http://www.mts.net/~rwpgrif/Museum/MusMain.html (accessed July 16, 2008).

9.   Francis Marion Beynon, *Aleta Dey* (Virago Press, 1988), 203–205.

10.   Williams, *Stand to your Horses*, 53.

11.   *Winnipeg Telegram*, May 10, 1915.

12.   *Winnipeg Free Press*, April 30, 1915.

13.   *Canadian Annual Review*, 1918, 376.

14.   AM, P3348, letter of August 30, 1915.

15.   Susan Mann, ed., *The War Diary of Clare Gass, 1915–18* (Montreal: McGill-Queen's University Press, 2000), 39.

16.   Ibid., 30.

17.   Ibid., 147.

18.   AM, MG10 A2 Box 38.

19.   J.M. Bliss, "The Methodist Church and World War I," *Canadian Historical Review* 49, 3 (1968): 203.

20.   I.H.M. Miller, *Our Glory and Our Grief: Torontonians and the Great War* (Toronto: University of Toronto Press, 2002), 114.

21.   R. Matthew Bray, "The Canadian Patriotic Response to the Great War" (PhD diss., York University, 1978), 150.

22.   R. Matthew Bray, "Fighting as an Ally: The English Canadian Patriotic Response to the Great War," *Canadian Historical Review* 61, 2 (1980): 141–68 traces the development of public opinion on this issue.

23.   Bray, "Canadian Patriotic Response."

24.   Granatstein and Hitsman, *Broken Promises*, 36.

25.   *Winnipeg Free Press*, January 7, 1916.

26.   Robert Rutherdale, *Hometown Horizons: Local Responses to Canada's Great War* (Vancouver: University of British Columbia Press, 2004), 81, and Miller, *Our Glory and Our Grief*, 82.

27.   Granatstein, *Canada's Army*, 77.

28.   *Winnipeg Telegram*, July 22, 1915.

29.   AM, letter of January 5, 1917, Drewery Family Scrap Book, 1913–1918.

30.   Stubbs, *Men in Khaki*, 26.

31.   AM, MG10 A2, Board of Trade Annual Report, 1915–16.

32.   Lord Derby, the British minister of war, was an opponent of conscription and he had put the system of categories in place to encourage men to agree, of their own free will, to being called up if necessary, with the understanding that married men would be called upon last. Only two months before, in December 1915, conscription had replaced Derby's scheme in the United Kingdom.

33. Granatstein and Hitsman, *Broken Promises*, 38.

34. Bray, "Fighting as an Ally," 156.

35. Military History Society of Manitoba, Camp Hughes Web site, http://mhsmb.taniwha.ca/hughes/hughes.html (accessed June 2008).

36. J. Robinson, *Life and Times of Jimmy Robinson* (Winnipeg: The author, 1973), 8–9.

37. AM, P3348, letter of June 1915.

38. AM, P3348, letter of July 3, 1915.

39. Williams, *Stand to your Horses*, 54.

40. Ibid., 17.

41. Robinson, *Life and Times*, 11.

42. O.C.S. Wallace, *From Montreal to Vimy Ridge and Beyond: Correspondence of Lieutenant Clifford Wells* (Toronto: McLelland, Goodchild and Stewart, 1917), 165.

43. Ibid., 167.

44. All quotes from Alec Waugh's letters from AM, P3348.

45. Bruce Tascona, *From the Forks to Flanders Fields: The Story of the 27th City of Winnipeg Battalion 1914–1919* (self-published, 1995).

46. AM, P3348, letter of January 30, 1916.

47. George Godwin, *Why Stay We Here?* (Victoria: Godwin Books, 2002), 40–41.

48. R.B. Fleming, ed., *The Wartime Letters of Leslie and Cecil Frost*, 1915–1919 (Waterloo: Wilfrid Laurier University Press, 2007), letter of November 2, 1915.

49. N.M. Christie, ed., *Letters of Agar Adamson* 1914–1919 (Ottawa: CEF Books, 1997), 125.

50. Wallace, *From Montreal to Vimy Ridge*, 152.

51. AM, P2362, letter of July 31, 1916.

52. *Canadian Annual Review*, 1918, 360.

53. Ruben Bellan, *Winnipeg's First Century, An Economic History* (Winnipeg: Queenston House, 1978), 135.

54. *Canadian Finance*, February 3, 1915.

55. City of Winnipeg Archives, Council Minutes, letter no. 10737, 1915.

56. This issue is discussed in Marion L. McKay, "Saints and Sanitarians: The Role of Women's Voluntary Agencies in the Development of Winnipeg's Public Health System, 1882–1945" (PhD thesis, University of Manitoba, 2005).

57. AM, MG10 A2 Box 38, Industrial Bureau Executive Minutes.

58. *Canadian Finance*, April 21, 1915, 273 and 281.

59. Bellan, *Winnipeg's First Century*, 136.

60. Dominion of Canada, Sessional Papers, 1918, Volume 1, Part 3, Auditor General's Report Part ZZ War Appropriation Act Details of Expenditure.

61. Bellan, "Development of Winnipeg," 265.

62. C.S. Prodan, "The Building of the Winnipeg Aqueduct," *Manitoba Pageant* 24, 2 (1979).

63. Bellan, *Winnipeg's First Century*, 135–6.

64. In 1912 McKenzie had been unsuccessful in having a rail line built along the river through the site of Elm Park. In retaliation he had moved part of the Canadian Northern freight yards to Portage la Prairie.

65. John E. Baker, *Winnipeg's Electric Transit* (Toronto: Railfare, 1982), 56.

66. F.W. Doolittle, "The Economics of Jitney Operation," *Journal of Political Economy* 23, 7 (1915): 663–95.

67. Norman Ward, *The Public Purse: A Study in Canadian Democracy* (Toronto: University of Toronto Press, 1962), is the classic source on this topic.

68. J.G. Bourinot, *How Canada is Governed* (Toronto: Copp Clark, 1918), 83.

69. Ibid., 83.

70. Alpheus Todd, *Parliamentary Government in the British Colonies* (Boston: Little Brown and Co., 1880), 431.

71. Ibid., 572.

72. Report of the Royal Commission Appointed to Investigate the Charges Made in the Statement of C.P. Fullerton (Winnipeg: King's Printer, 1915), 17.

73. *Canadian Finance*, August 18, 1915.

1916

1. *Winnipeg Telegram*, November 22, 1915.

2. AM, P4594, letter of December 1916.

3. *Winnipeg Free Press*, Evening Bulletin, February 12, 1916, 1.

4. Granatstein, *Canada's Army*, 87.

5. Quoted at http://www.ww1battlefields.co.uk/index.html (accessed November 10, 2008).

6. Stubbs, *Men in Khaki*, 42.

7. Ibid., 44.

8. J.D. Sinclair, ed., *The Queen's Own Cameron Highlanders of Canada, 25th Anniversary Souvenir* (Winnipeg, 1935), 74.

9. Ibid.

10. Russenholt, *Six Thousand Canadian Men*, 61.

11. Godwin, *Why Stay We Here?*, 71.

12. Gordon, *Postscript to Adventure*, 267.

13. Robinson, *Life and Times*, 21–22.

14. J. Hughes-Wilson, *Blindfold and Alone: British Military Executions in the Great War* (London: Cassell, 2001), 257–58.

15. Desmond Morton, "The Supreme Penalty: Canadian Deaths by Firing Squad in the First World War," *Queen's Quarterly* 79 (1972): 346.

16. Andrew Godefroy, *For Freedom and Honour?* (Ottawa: CEF Books, 1998), 24–25.

17. Ibid.

18. *Canadian Annual Review*, 1916, 635.

19. J.E. Rae, "My Main Line is the Kiddies, Make Them Good Christians and Good Canadians," in *Identities: the Impact of Ethnicity on Canadian Society*, ed. Vaclav Isajiw (Toronto: Peter Martin, 1977), 3–11.

20. *Winnipeg Free Press*, January 24, 1916.

21. Melnycky, "Political History," 179.

22. *Winnipeg Free Press*, February 5, 1916.

23. *Canadian Annual Review*, 1916, 657.

24. *Winnipeg Free Press*, January 12, 1916.

25. Although Ukrainian was becoming the name favoured by Ukrainians themselves, Ruthenian, a term used in the Austro-Hungarian Empire to signify ethnic Ukrainians, was still used during the Great War in Canada.

26. *Winnipeg Free Press*, January 13, 1916.

27. *Canadian Annual Review*, 1916, 645.

28. Ibid., 671.

29. Ibid., 674.

30. Ibid.

31. Melnycky, "Political History," 174.

32. J.J. Bergen, "A Historical Study of Education in the Municipality of Rhineland" (MEd thesis, University of Manitoba, 1959), 73.

33. Ibid.
34. Melnycky, "Political History," 154.
35. *Winnipeg Free Press*, February 2, 1916.

1917

1. Wallace, *From Montreal to Vimy Ridge*, 232.
2. *IODE Souvenir*, Winnipeg, 1916, 7.
3. *IODE Manitoba Souvenir*, 1916, 55.
4. Desmond Morton and Glenn Wright, *Winning the Second Battle: Canadian Veterans and the Return to Civilian Life, 1915–1930* (Toronto: University of Toronto Press, 1987), 20.
5. *Canadian Annual Review*, 1917, 425.
6. Ibid., 729.
7. Ibid.
8. Ibid.
9. Granatstein and Hitsman, *Broken Promises*, 64.
10. Ibid., 52.
11. Ibid., 85.
12. *Winnipeg Free Press*, December 17, 1917.
13. R.G. MacBeth, *Sir Augustus Nanton: A Biography* (Toronto: Macmillan, 1931), 51.
14. Canadian Red Cross Society, Red Cross Annual Report, 1915, 14. PAM, MG 10 B29.
15. Glassford, "Marching as to War," 191.
16. Lillian Gibbons, *Stories Houses Tell* (Winnipeg: Hyperion Press, 1978), 122.
17. *IODE Souvenir*, 1916, 45–6.
18. *Canadian Annual Review*, 1917, 430.
19. *IODE Souvenir*, 1916, 6.
20. Glassford, "Marching as to War," 195.
21. *Canadian Annual Review*, 1915, 332.
22. Ibid., 337.
23. Russenholt, *Six Thousand Canadian Men*, 66 and 67.
24. *Canadian Annual Review*, 1917, 425.

1918

1. Esyllt Jones, *Influenza 1918* (Toronto: University of Toronto Press, 2007), 13.
2. *Winnipeg Free Press*, January 26, 1918.
3. At about this time the publications of many groups deemed to be sympathetic to the enemy were banned.
4. Graham, *Conscription and Conscience*, 152.
5. *Winnipeg Telegram*, March 25, 1918.
6. Granatstein and Hitsman, *Broken Promises*, 91.
7. Miller, *Our Glory and Our Grief*, 163.
8. Gregory Kealey, "State Repression of Labour and the Left in Canada, 1914–20: The Impact of the First World War," *Canadian Historical Review* 73, 3 (1992): 281–314.
9. John E. Baker, *Winnipeg's Electric Transit* (Toronto: Railfare, 1983), 58.
10. *The Mercantile Agency Reference Book (and Key) Containing Ratings of Merchants, Manufacturers, and Traders generally throughout the Dominion of Canada* (Montreal: R.G. Dun, 1923).
11. See Mitchell Sharp, "Allied Wheat Buying in Relationship to Canadian Wheat Policy, 1914–1918," *Canadian Journal of Economics and Political Science* 6, 3 (1940): 372–389.
12. Allan Levine, *The Exchange* (Winnipeg: Peguis Publishers, 1987), 97.

13. AM, MG10 A2, *Board of Trade Annual Reports, 1917–1918.*

14. Charles W. Anderson, *Grain* (Winnipeg: Watson and Dwyer, 1991), 144–154.

15. Joseph Harry Sutcliffe, "Economic Background of the Winnipeg General Strike: Wages and Working Conditions" (MA thesis, University of Manitoba, 1972), has a good account of the spiraling cost of living during the last years of the war.

16. *Winnipeg Telegram*, November 12, 1918.

17. W. Fraser, "Armistice Day in Winnipeg, 1918," *Manitoba History* 3 (1982): 29–30.

Epilogue
1. Marilyn Baker, "To Honour and Remember: the Next of Kin Monument," *Manitoba History* 2 (1981), gives the background to the construction of the monument.

2. Bellan, *Winnipeg's First Century*, 153–162.

3. John W. Dafoe, *Over the Canadian Battlefields: Notes of a Little Journey in France, in March 1919* (Toronto: T. Allen, 1919), 26.

4. *The King's Pilrimage* (London: Hodder and Stoughton, 1922).

5. AM, P4595, letter from R.D. Waugh, December 14, 1917.

6. AM, P4595, letter of R.D. Waugh, November 23, 1920.

7. AM, P3348, letter of A. Waugh, October 27, 1915.

8. AM P3348, letter of A. Waugh, October 14, 1915.

9. Ibid.

Index

A Note on the Type

This book has been set in Cochin, with display
type in Bernhard Modern Engraved.

Charles Malin cut Cochin in 1912 for the Paris
foundry Deberny & Peignot, based on the design
of Georges Peignot. This font is named after the
French engraver Charles Nicolas Cochin (1715-
1790), although its style had little to do with that
of the copper artist's. It displays a curious mix of
style elements and could be placed as a part of
the typographical Neo-Renaissance movement.
Cochin was especially popular at the beginning
of the 20th century.

Bernhard Modern Engraved was designed in
1937, although its designer, Lucian Bernhard,
created his first popular font, Bernhard Antiqua,
in 1912.